WAL-MART

A History of Sam Walton's Retail Phenomenon

Twayne's Evolution of Modern Business Series

Series Editors

Edwin J. Perkins
University of Southern California

Kenneth Lipartito
University of Houston

Other Titles

WAL-MART

A History of Sam Walton's Retail Phenomenon

Sandra S. Vance
Roy V. Scott

TWAYNE PUBLISHERS
An Imprint of Simon & Schuster Macmillan
New York

Prentice Hall International
London · Mexico City · New Delhi · Singapore · Sydney · Toronto

Wal-Mart: A History of Sam Walton's Retail Phenomenon
Sandra S. Vance and Roy V. Scott

Published by Twayne Publishers
An imprint of Simon & Schuster Macmillan
1633 Broadway
New York, NY 10019

Library of Congress Cataloging-in-Publication Data
Vance, Sandra Stringer, 1946–
    Wal-Mart: a history of Sam Walton's retail phenomenon by Sandra S. Vance and Roy V. Scott.
        p.   cm. — (Twayne's evolution of modern business series ; no. 11)
    Includes bibliographical references and index.
    ISBN 0-8057-9832-3 (cloth). — ISBN 0-8057-9833-1 (pbk.)
    1. Wal-Mart (Firm)—History 2. Discount stores (Retail trade)—United States—History. 3. Walton, Sam, 1918–1992. I. Scott, Roy Vernon, 1927–   .
II. Title. III. Series.
HF5429.215.U6V36   1994
381'.149'0973—dc20   94-14575
                                                                            CIP
The paper used in this publication meets the minimum requirements of American National Standard for Information Sciences—Permanence of Paper for Printed Library Materials. ANSI Z3948-1984. ∞ ™

10 9 8 7 6 5 4 3 2   (hc)
10 9 8 7 6 5   (pb)

Printed in the United States of America

For
Emily, Larry, and Beecie

SSV

CONTENTS

TABLES

ILLUSTRATIONS

PREFACE

WHEN *FORTUNE* MAGAZINE declared in June 1993 that the $23.5 billion belonging to Sam Walton's widow, Helen, and their four children was the second largest fortune in the world (surpassed only by the Sultan of Brunei's $37 billion), the pronouncement made national news. This is but a recent example of the increasing attention and publicity that Wal-Mart Stores, Inc., the source of this staggering wealth, has received in the past few years. In 1990 we undertook our research out of a wish to answer the rising demand for information regarding Sam Walton's remarkable firm with a scholarly account of Wal-Mart's growth and development from its inception in 1962 until its founder's death in 1992.

Business historians are well aware of the value of corporate records in their research and of the need to make use of such records when feasible. For this project, however, it was not possible to utilize the internal records of the company, since Wal-Mart, which is highly guarded concerning its business affairs, has not made such information available to scholars and is not likely to do so in the near future. We were compelled, therefore, to construct our narrative from documents published by the company and from trade journals, newspapers, and other sources.

During the course of our research we incurred many obligations, and it is appropriate that we acknowledge the efforts of those individuals who aided us in this enterprise. While we were not permitted to examine corporate records, we were nevertheless warmly received when we toured Wal-Mart's general headquarters in Bentonville, Arkansas, and we are indebted to Thomas N. Smith, former vice president for operations, and Don Shinkle, executive vice president for corporate affairs, for the courtesy they extended to us and for their assistance in securing information vital to this endeavor. We are grateful to the editors of the *Journal of Southern History* and *Essays in Economic and Business History*, who permitted us to draw from our articles that appeared, respectively, in the May

1992 issue and the 1992 and 1993 editions of those publications. We must recognize the assistance of Steven Wheeler of the New York Stock Exchange, Helen Davis of the Delaware Department of State, and Virginia Nabinett and April Keyes of the U.S. Securities and Exchange Commission, all of whom went out of their way to provide us with the documents we needed. Professor Ronald Savitt of the School of Business Administration at the University of Vermont and Professor John Ozment of the Department of Marketing and Transportation at the University of Arkansas offered insights that otherwise might well have escaped our attention. We also appreciate the contributions made by Professor Kenneth J. Lipartito of the University of Houston.

Librarians and archivists are indispensable to the work of historians, and we were fortunate to enlist the services of several able professionals who assisted us in numerous ways. We are indebted to the fine staff of the George M. McLendon Library, Hinds Community College, in Raymond, Mississippi, especially Norma Wall, director; Gayle Keefe, interlibrary loan librarian; Nancy Tenhet, reference librarian; Janice Nail, periodicals librarian; Alice Margolis, public services librarian; and Judy Myrick, central technical processing librarian. Among those at the Mitchell Memorial Library, Mississippi State University, whose support was outstanding are Frances N. Coleman, associate director; Thomas P. Williams, former reference librarian; and Martha B. Irby, manager of the interlibrary loan office. Librarians at the universities of Arkansas, Missouri, and Illinois; at Millsaps College and the Eudora Welty Public Library in Jackson, Mississippi; and at the Chicago Public Library were most helpful. Emily Clark of the Chicago Historical Society and Ara Kaye and Elizabeth Bailey of the State Historical Society of Missouri engaged in research for us, and Lynn Eldred of the Bentonville Public Library permitted us to borrow microfilm of the local newspaper.

Sandra S. Vance wishes to thank President Clyde Muse of Hinds Community College for his support of this undertaking and Vice President of the Raymond Campus Michael J. Rabalais, Academic Dean J. David Durham, and Social Sciences Department Chair Lura Scales, all of whom extended aid in various ways. She also is grateful to departmental secretary Brenda Morgan for her efforts, to departmental colleagues for their encouragement, and to Ann Laster and Professor William Durrett for their help.

Roy V. Scott desires to express his gratitude to Professor John R. Darling, former provost and vice president for academic affairs at Mississippi State University, whose contributions he deems worthy of special note. He also wishes to thank the Mississippi State University Office of Research, headed by Professor Ralph E. Powe, which provided some financial assistance at a crucial juncture; the Department of History for its support; departmental secretary Peggy Bonner for her efforts; and his student assistant, Sandra Melissa (Watson) Barnes, for her labors.

This book is a volume in Twayne Publishers' Evolution of Modern Business Series, and we wish to convey our appreciation to the editor of that series, Professor Edwin J. Perkins of the University of Southern California, and to senior editor Carol Chin of Twayne Publishers for their excellent work on the manuscript.

1

Beginnings and Ben Franklin

FOR A BOY GROWING up in small rural towns during the Great Depression, hard work and thrift were a way of life. Many of the character traits that would serve Samuel Moore Walton, the founder of Wal-Mart Stores, Inc., so well during his business career—his amazing industriousness, his legendary frugality, and, above all, his burning ambition to succeed—probably were forged during a childhood that was shaped by economic struggle.

Sam Walton was born on 29 March 1918 to Thomas Gibson and Nancy Lee Walton, a young farm couple living near Kingfisher, Oklahoma. To provide for his growing family, which included a second son, James L. (Bud) Walton, who was born in December 1921, Thomas Walton decided to leave his unprosperous farm to go back to working as a farm loan appraiser. In 1923, in pursuit of that goal, Thomas Walton and his family left Oklahoma and subsequently lived in several different towns in Missouri. They first moved to Springfield, where Sam Walton started school; later they lived in Marshall and then in Shelbina, where Walton entered the eighth grade and became the youngest boy in the state's history at that time to become an Eagle Scout. In 1933 the family moved to Columbia, the site of the University of Missouri and two colleges for women. Columbia had a population of about 30,000, counting the students, and was the largest community between St. Louis to the east and Kansas City to the west.

Because of the depressed conditions in agriculture during the 1920s and the 1930s, times were hard in the rural Midwest, and Sam Walton, like other boys of that era, was expected to get an education and at the same time to contribute to the family's meager income. Walton's work included milking the family cow, bottling and delivering the surplus milk, and delivering newspapers. In his autobiography Walton would reveal that from these boyhood endeavors he learned "how much hard work it took to get your hands on a dollar, and that when you did it was worth something. One thing my mother and dad shared completely was their approach to money: they just didn't spend it."[1]

At Hickman High School in Columbia, Walton participated in numerous activities. His love of competition found a natural outlet in athletics. He played basketball and was quarterback of the school's football team, which won the state championship in 1935. Although he was not a superior student, he applied himself in his studies and made the honor roll. Endowed with remarkable energy and leadership abilities, he was a member of several clubs and was vice president of his junior class; in his senior year he was president of the student body and selected as the school's "most versatile boy."[2]

Following his graduation from high school, Walton enrolled at the University of Missouri. To meet his college expenses, he waited on tables in exchange for meals, served as a lifeguard at the school's swimming pool, and delivered newspapers. During his college years other significant traits in Walton's character became more pronounced, especially his ability to work with others, which was reflected in his gregarious enthusiasm for participating in campus organizations. He was an officer in his fraternity, a member of the student senate and the national honor society, an ROTC officer, and president of a Sunday School class attended by many of the college students in the area. Joining in such activities gained him a listing in *Who's Who in American Colleges and Universities* and earned him the respect of his fellow students. His fraternity newspaper referred to him as a "hustler" and praised him for his work on campus and in his church, while his classmates elected him the permanent president of the class of 1940.[3]

Walton graduated from the University of Missouri in 1940 with a degree in economics. He had considered attending the Wharton School at the University of Pennsylvania but realized that he did not have the money to do so. Deciding instead to get a job, he interviewed with representatives of the retail firms J. C. Penney and Sears, Roebuck and Company, both of which had come to the University of Missouri to recruit employees. He received job offers from both companies and chose to go to work for Penney's. Walton's career in retailing was born three days after graduation, on 3 June 1940, when he reported to the Penney's store in Des Moines, Iowa, to begin work as a management trainee at a salary of $75 a month. Walton was a good salesman, although he did not excel in the record keeping that was a part of his job, primarily because he "couldn't stand to leave a new customer waiting while I fiddled with paperwork on a sale I'd already made." Walton found Penney's a good firm to work for, and he was especially impressed with his store manager, Duncan Majors, who had trained more Penney's store managers than anyone else in the organization. Working for Majors, Walton learned about the long hours that retailing entailed, but he found the experience exhilarating and identified Majors as the motivating force that first "got me excited about retail." Walton also recalled the day that James Cash Penney himself came by the store for a visit. Among other things, "he taught me how to tie a package with very little twine and very little paper and still make it look nice," recalled Walton.

Early in 1942 Walton resigned from Penney's. World War II had begun, and while Walton was waiting to be inducted into the military service, he took a job in a Du Pont munitions plant near Tulsa, Oklahoma. In Claremore, a small town near Tulsa, Walton met Helen Robson in April 1942. The daughter of L. S. Robson, a prosperous banker and rancher, she had been the valedictorian of her class at Claremore High School, had attended Christian College for Women in Columbia, Missouri, and had graduated from the University of Oklahoma at Norman with a degree in business. The couple married on 14 February 1943, and they had four children: Samuel Robson (Rob), born in 1944; John Thomas, born in 1946; James Carr (Jim), born in 1948; and Alice, born in 1949.

During the war Walton served in the U.S. Army intelligence corps in the continental United States, supervising security at aircraft plants and prisoner of war camps. He ultimately earned the rank of captain. As he anticipated leaving military service, Walton resolved to go into business for himself, and he decided he wanted to own a department store. Following his discharge from the army in 1945, Walton went to St. Louis, where he and a former college roommate planned to purchase a Federated department store, one of the Butler Brothers franchises.[4]

Established in 1877, Butler Brothers was a Chicago wholesale company that sold products to small general-merchandise and variety stores. The firm purchased its merchandise in large quantities from manufacturers throughout the country and then distributed it from warehouses in Baltimore, Chicago, Dallas, Minneapolis, New York, St. Louis, and San Francisco. From its inception through the first two decades of the twentieth century, Butler Brothers' business had flourished. During the 1920s, however, the firm had found its business threatened by two developments. Following World War I, inflation had caused retail prices to rise, and some variety-store merchandise no longer could be purchased for merely a nickel or a dime. This change had caused some customers to desert variety stores and start shopping instead at department stores. Far more threatening to Butler Brothers, however, was the rapid increase in the strength of variety-store chains. The F. W. Woolworth Company, for example, the nation's leading variety-store operation, had increased the number of its outlets from 684 in 1913 to 1,111 in 1920 and 1,890 in 1930. Other variety-store chains also had grown dramatically. The S. S. Kresge Company had increased in size from only 100 units in 1913 to 188 in 1920 and 678 a decade later, and the W. T. Grant Company had gone from 22 stores in 1915 to 38 in 1920 and 348 in 1930. Because these developments damaged the small, independent retailers with whom Butler Brothers did business, the firm's net profits had fallen from $3.4 million in 1925 to $2.2 million in 1928 and $1.4 million in 1929. In an effort to thwart the chains' encroachments on its commercial activities, in 1927 Butler Brothers established a business franchising operation by affiliating itself with independent general-merchandise and variety stores such as those it had served for decades.[5]

In business franchising, a franchisor licenses a number of outlets, or franchisees, to make a product, offer a service, or engage in a business developed by the franchisor. The franchisees use such resources as the franchisor's trade name, trademarks, or methods of doing business, in exchange for which they pay fees or royalties to the franchisor. The franchisee benefits from being associated with a large company but retains many of the characteristics of an independent firm, while the franchisor enjoys rapid growth at a limited cost, since the franchisees provide most of the capital.

The practice of franchising originated during the nineteenth century, and four types have evolved. First was the manufacturer-retailer arrangement, in which a manufacturer solicits retailers to handle the sale and servicing of the manufacturer's products. Examples include the major oil companies and their associated gasoline stations, and automobile manufacturers, whose franchised dealers sell a stipulated make of car and to some extent operate their businesses in compliance with the manufacturer's wishes. A second type of franchising involves a manufacturer and one or more wholesalers. The soft drink industry relies on this arrangement. A third kind of franchising is the service sponsor–retailer arrangement, in which a service provided by a franchisor is performed by a retailer. Examples are motel chains, such as Holiday Inn, and fast-food chains, such as McDonalds. The fourth category of franchising is the wholesaler-retailer system, of which there are two forms, cooperative and voluntary. In the cooperative form, retailers band together to acquire or establish a wholesaler to supply them with goods. An example is Certified Grocers, headquartered in Los Angeles. In the voluntary form, independent retailers voluntarily enter into a franchise arrangement initiated by a wholesaler. Butler Brothers originated voluntary franchising in the general-merchandise and variety-store fields. Other firms that practice different forms of voluntary franchising are the Walgreen Company, the Western Auto Supply Company, the Ace Hardware Corporation, and Super Valu Stores.[6]

The Butler Brothers franchise operation consisted of two chains, Federated department stores, which were small or "junior" department stores, and the Ben Franklin variety stores. In the franchising arrangement, the members of the chains and Butler Brothers were united in a contractual relationship designed to benefit both parties. As the franchisor, Butler Brothers was ensured a market for its merchandise, since the members of the chains were required to place the "larger part of their orders" with Butler Brothers. As a franchisee of Butler Brothers, the independent merchant was promised a "professional merchandising and promotional service, comparable in quality with that which his chain competitors receive from their headquarters."[7]

While Walton was enthusiastic about the prospect of going into business in St. Louis, Helen Walton was not. She told him that she did not wish to live in a big city but preferred instead to live in a town of no more than 10,000 people. She also did not like the idea of a business partnership and wanted Walton be the sole proprietor of his company. Because of his respect for his wife's wishes and judgment, Walton told Butler Brothers that he would consider only a business that was located in a small town. In response, the firm informed Walton that the owner of a Ben Franklin variety store in Newport, Arkansas, desired to sell the business.

In the fall of 1945, with $20,000 borrowed from his father-in-law and $5,000 saved from his military pay, Walton purchased the store, and he and his family moved to Newport, a town of about 5,000 people located approximately 80 miles northeast of Little Rock. Newport is located on the White River and enjoyed regular railroad service. Railroad shipping, cotton, pecans, a shoe factory, a metal mill, and some other industries formed the basis of its economy.[8]

As a franchisee of Butler Brothers, Walton agreed to pay a fee based on sales volume and to purchase the bulk of his store's merchandise from the wholesaler. In return, Butler Brothers assisted Walton and its other franchise merchants in various aspects of store management. The firm sought to ensure that Ben Franklin stores were properly stocked at all times by offering the retailers a broad range of goods at lower prices than they could obtain individually. It extended guidance to them by means of operating manuals and monthly newsletters, and provided a staff of retailing specialists at its Chicago headquarters to help with such storekeeping chores as reordering, pricing, and displaying merchandise, as well as with advertising and store construction or remodeling. A corps of supervisors and service men in the field provided additional assistance in implementing the company's programs. Many of these services were paid for by merchants' fees. This supervision was intended to ensure that any Ben Franklin outlet resembled other stores in the chain both inside and out. Butler Brothers emphasized that it had no financial interest in the stores that were members of the Ben Franklin chain. On the contrary, its assistance was designed to equip a franchise merchant to compete with the outlets of Woolworth's, Kresge's, and the other chains, while allowing him to retain the full advantages of independent business ownership.[9]

In most respects the store that Walton purchased, which was 5,000 square feet in size and had an annual sales volume of $72,000, was typical of the variety stores that were members of the Ben Franklin chain during the post–World War II years. The stores tended to be located in country towns, and they usually were smaller than Woolworth's, Kresge's, Grant's, and other chains' outlets. They generally generated an annual volume of about $75,000. Like other variety stores, which were popularly known as five and tens or dime stores, the standard Ben Franklin outlet carried a wide assortment of convenience goods at prices that ranged from a few pennies to a dollar or more. The inventory included both nationally advertised merchandise and Butler Brothers' private brands. Among the latter were Nancy Lee lingerie, Ben Franklin men's underwear, DuBarry hosiery, Majestic notions, Snow Bird cleaning supplies, Juliette cosmetics, All Purpose paints, and Pennant sporting goods. Such merchandise was displayed on counters along the walls and on several sets of double counters that ran lengthwise in the store. The store clerks were women, and they earned meager salaries. Clerks were stationed at the counters to wait on customers, promote sales, collect money using cash registers located at the counters, and wrap purchases.[10]

Due to the nature of its inventory, location was vitally important to the success of a variety store. Since variety goods generally were inexpensive, customers would not go out of their way to find a store, and, once there, they tended to buy on impulse. For these reasons, a store needed to be easily accessible to the largest number of people. Downtown corner locations were preferred, because two streams of pedestrians would converge there. Walton's location was ideal: his store was situated on a corner that was considered the best retail site in Newport.[11]

Walton's variety store also benefited from business practices that were characteristic of country towns. In the typical rural community there were four or five grocery stores but often no more than one or two hardware, drug, general-merchandise, appliance, or variety stores. Consequently, those enterprises enjoyed something of a local monopoly. This situation was the result of several factors. First, the business properties along the main street usually were owned by members of the local business community, who exercised general if somewhat informal control over the types of new businesses that were allowed to open. Second, there was a widespread sentiment among local merchants that prices should be kept uniform. For most items, prices charged by local businesses tended to be higher than in cities, where more competition existed. For national-brand goods, however, merchants would deviate little from the manufacturers' suggested retail prices, partly because they all understood that if their prices were too high customers would seek the goods elsewhere. Major purchases, such as automobiles and large household appliances, were more competitively priced because their greater cost would make a higher price more obvious. Overt collusion and price control among local merchants were rare. A final factor that tended to limit competition in small towns was the shopping habits of farmers and other small-town customers, who generally preferred to shop locally and thereby avoid relatively long trips to distant cities.[12]

The inventory in Walton's store was made up of goods in common use in and around the home. It consisted of such items as aluminum and cast-iron cooking utensils, tableware of various kinds, Turkish bath towels, Kleenex tissues, candy, cosmetics, apparel (especially for women and children), and greeting cards. The store also featured small hardware items, various kinds of buckets (including 14-quart dairy pails), and galvanized wash tubs, a necessity in many rural homes of the 1940s. In addition, the store stocked a variety of toys, such as tricycles with red metal frames and rubber tires.

Like the other merchants in Newport, Walton closed his store at 5:00 Monday through Friday and at 9:00 on Saturday. He and another merchant in town elected to remain open every night until 9:00 during the week preceding Christmas. Walton advertised regularly in the local newspaper, and he ran special sales promotions, in which he reduced prices on specified items, during holiday seasons such as Christmas and Easter. "Trade Days" were another promotional event that Walton staged monthly during the summer. During the summer of 1949, for example, Walton informed readers of the local newspaper that he was offering clothes pins at 9 cents a dozen; Cannon bath towels at 49 cents each, a 20-cent reduction in the regular price; men's red and blue bandannas at 15 cents each, down sharply from the usual 39 cents; and fruit and oyster bowls at 5 cents each.[13]

In his first business venture Walton revealed astute retailing skills and a willingness to use unorthodox sales techniques. Under its previous owner, the store had done only half as much business as a competing variety store across the street that was affiliated with the Sterling chain. Walton welcomed the competition and soon came to admire the business ability of the other store's manager. He made frequent visits to the Sterling store to observe his competitor's methods of marketing and pricing. At the same time, he set for himself the goal of surpassing that store's sales volume, which he would do.

When Walton opened the business in September 1945 he had no experience in running a variety store, and he found Butler Brothers' training program and operating procedures helpful. He would recall years later that he considered the firm's accounting system, for example, so satisfactory that he would carry it forward into his Wal-Mart operation. He soon chafed, however, under Butler Brothers' strict merchandising stipulations, which required him to purchase 80 percent of his goods from the Chicago wholesaler through its warehouse in St. Louis. He began to experiment with Butler Brothers' merchandising guidelines by buying some goods directly from manufacturers and wholesalers, and he found that he could purchase them more cheaply than he could buy the same types of goods from Butler Brothers.

Then Walton hit upon another innovation. He decided to sell the goods at a lower price. When he purchased ladies' panties, for example, from Butler Brothers, he paid $2.50 for a dozen and sold them at three pairs for $1.00, but he found that by buying directly from wholesalers he could purchase a similar product for $2.00 a dozen and sell it at four pairs for $1.00. He discovered that by lowering his price per item he could sell a greater quantity of goods, thereby increasing his sales volume and profits. To his dismay, however, he found himself limited by his commitment to Butler Brothers in the amount of inventory he could merchandise in this manner. Without realizing it at the time, Walton had begun to experiment with discount merchandising, and he found the experience very much to his liking.

As a result of his personality traits and business skills, which later would be instrumental to the success of Wal-Mart, Walton soon became a civic and business leader in Newport. He demonstrated a genuine affection for people and made friends easily. He assumed a prominent role in the town's civic life, serving in the Rotary Club and as president of the chamber of commerce, and he also got involved in the activities of the local Presbyterian church. In his business, his overwhelming desire to succeed, his determination to beat his competition, his boundless capacity for hard work, and his willingness to experiment with new retailing methods made his store astonishingly successful. Its sales volume climbed to $105,000 after the first year. After five years it was generating $250,000 in sales and $30,000 to $40,000 a year in profits, making it the leading Ben Franklin store in sales and profits in its six-state region. Unfortunately, Walton's retailing success was also his undoing. He had only a short-term lease on the building, without a renewal clause, and when he tried to renew the lease, his landlord refused. Impressed with the store's new earning power, the owner of the location wanted it for his son. Years later Walton called his inability to renew the lease "the low point of my business life." He chose not to relocate the business; instead, he agreed to sell it to his landlord for a profit of more than $50,000. The new owner took possession of the store in January 1951.[14]

Convinced that he could recreate his Newport success in another town, Walton began looking for a variety store to purchase. He and his wife desired to remain in northwest Arkansas because the region was near his wife's family in Oklahoma and afforded excellent quail hunting, one of Walton's lifelong enthusiasms. After attempting unsuccessfully to buy a store in another town in the area, Walton found Harrison's variety store in Bentonville, Arkansas. Because the store was one he could afford to buy and because he believed that Bentonville was a "good place to raise a family and with a quality of life that we would enjoy," Walton purchased the store in May 1950.[15]

Bentonville is situated in the heart of the Ozarks, a 60,000-square-mile region of heavily wooded mountains, hills, and plateaus that includes portions of Missouri, Arkansas, Kansas, and Oklahoma. Founded in 1837, Bentonville was the seat of Benton County, and both were named for Thomas Hart Benton, the famous senator from Missouri in the early nineteenth century who had supported statehood for Arkansas. At the time of Walton's arrival, Bentonville, with a population of only about 3,000, was rural and remote. Because the nearby town of Rogers, located six miles to the east, was on the main railroad line and enjoyed some industry, it overshadowed Bentonville. During the 1930s and 1940s Bentonville had been mainly a trading and supply center for surrounding farms; during the early 1950s poultry was becoming an economic mainstay.[16]

Located in the middle of a block on the town square, the old variety store that Walton purchased was small and dimly lit, and it lacked a stockroom and even a back door. In part because of competition from two other variety stores in town, its sales volume had been only a scant $32,000 a year under its previous owner. None of these liabilities deterred Walton, who went to work immediately to remodel and improve the store. With the help of his father-in-law, he had secured a long-term lease on the building next door, and he began by tearing down the dividing wall between the two properties, which allowed him to double the store's frontage to 50 feet and its total size to 4,000 square feet. He installed fluorescent lights and new shelves and counters and redesigned the windows. He kept, however, the ramshackle 8-by-8 foot office in the back of the store. Located in a loft, it was accessible only by a ladder. Its furnishings consisted of a piece of plywood laid across a file cabinet and two rows of shelves, which Walton used for a desk, and the bottom of a wooden crate nailed to the wall, to which Walton attached wooden pegs, where he hung his invoices and other business documents. There was only one chair; anyone who called on Walton had to sit on an apple crate.

The Bentonville store was named Walton's 5 & 10, although, like the store in Newport, it was a member of the Butler Brothers' Ben Franklin chain. To celebrate the store's new appearance, Walton staged his first sales promotion, a "remodeling sale," in July 1950, followed by a grand opening the following March. Walton had spent $55,000 to purchase and refurbish the store, a sum that consumed his profits from the sale of the Newport store and took his finances, in his words, "down to zero again." He also suffered the temporary inconvenience of having to commute between the Newport and Bentonville stores for the remainder of 1950 to keep both businesses running. Nevertheless, Walton's new venture was a resounding success.[17]

As he had in Newport, Walton advertised regularly in the local newspaper, giving sales promotions special attention. As part of a community-wide sale staged by Bentonville merchants in 1952, for example, Walton advertised ladies' purses for $1.98 and $2.98 and half-slips for $1.00 instead of the usual $1.37. Plastic tablecloths were 50 cents; kitchen wastebaskets sold for 79 cents; men's work socks were four pairs for $1.00; children's short-sleeve shirts were two for $1.00; and three pounds of chocolates cost $1.00. With the purchase of any fishbowl came one free goldfish. The following year Walton's 5 & 10 staged a three-day sale and, as a special attraction, held a drawing for a deluxe bicycle valued at $54.95. School supplies were featured: a three-piece pen and pencil set sold for 98 cents, a box of 24 Crayola crayons was 25 cents, school bags in brightly colored rayon were offered at $1.59, and lunch buckets with vacuum bottles were $1.98.[18]

After moving to Bentonville in January 1951, Walton and his wife became active participants in the affairs of the town. Walton, for example, served as president of both the Rotary Club and the chamber of commerce. He also was elected to the city council and served on the hospital board. In 1954 Walton was instrumental in launching a Little League baseball program in Bentonville, serving as a member of a finance committee that raised money to support the league and obtain the necessary equipment. The Rotary and Kiwanis clubs and more than 30 businesses, including Walton's, were sponsors. Walton's store also was one of the sponsors of the town's high school football team. Both Walton and his wife were involved in the activities of the PTA and the local Presbyterian church, where Walton served as a Sunday school teacher and an elder of the church. Like their father before them, the Walton boys had paper routes to earn spending money, and all of the children worked in the family business.[19]

With his store in Bentonville thriving, Walton expanded by opening a second store in Fayetteville. Located some 20 miles south of Bentonville, Fayetteville was a county seat and the home of the University of Arkansas. The new store, which was 2,800 square feet in size and employed four women as clerks, was located on the town square in a building recently vacated by a Kroger grocery store. The grand opening of the store was held on 30 October 1952. Also named Walton's 5 & 10, this store was not a Ben Franklin franchise. Walton's second store would also be successful, enjoying sales of $90,000 its first year in operation.

Even at this early stage in his career, Walton realized that one of the leading pitfalls in retail expansion was competent management. He knew that to succeed, his second store would require an able manager. So, he said, "I did something I would do for the rest of my run in the retail business without any shame or embarrassment whatsoever: nose around other people's stores searching for good talent." Walton hired Willard Walker, the manager of a TG&Y variety store in Tulsa. He attracted Walker by offering him a percentage of the store's profits. Walton generally visited the Fayetteville store once a week to inspect it, and once a month he examined the store's books and compiled a profit-and-loss statement.

Ever alert for new ways of doing business, Walton had read about a novel retailing concept known as self-service. Under this innovation, the cash registers that were located at counters throughout a variety store were replaced by checkout registers located in the front of a store, where customers paid for all of their goods at one time. When he had learned that self-service had been implemented in two Ben Franklin stores in

Pipestone and Worthington, Minnesota, Walton traveled by bus to visit the stores. Impressed by the idea, Walton had decided to open his new store with self-service, making his Fayetteville unit one of only a few self-service variety stores in the nation.[20]

Walton was pleased with the successful implementation of self-service in the Fayetteville store. Speaking before the Bentonville Rotary Club in the spring of 1953, Walton described self-service as one of the most important developments in the variety-store business and indicated that, according to various studies, sales per customer were much higher in self-service stores than in conventional ones. Based on his confidence in the new retailing concept, Walton remodeled his Bentonville store and reopened it with self-service on 20 August 1953. In the local newspaper Walton announced that the new self-service format provided an additional 300 linear feet of counter space for the display of "hundreds of new items" and proclaimed that the variety store now featured "all the most modern fixtures and equipment designed for the ease, convenience, and pleasure of everyone's shopping." In an effort to explain the new operation to his patrons, he assured them that prices were plainly marked; that clerks were "ready and willing" to help them; that "light weight shopping baskets in which to gather your choices as you go from counter to counter" were available; and that a cashier at the checkout counter would "unload your basket and record your purchase as you leave." In the same article Walton also stressed his relationship with Butler Brothers' Ben Franklin variety stores. He emphasized that although his store was locally owned and operated, it was affiliated with "more than 2,000 other Ben Franklin and independent variety stores in every state in the Union plus Alaska and Hawaii" and benefited from Butler Brothers' merchandising and promotional assistance, which enabled it to incorporate the latest trends in variety-store operation.[21]

In large measure Walton followed Butler Brothers' guidelines in managing his stores, but during these years his own business style also began to emerge. Walton insisted that his stores be well stocked with a wide assortment of staple goods. In addition, he placed great emphasis on special promotional merchandise, which he put on tables and racks at the ends of aisles, one of the key display areas in a variety store. He stressed that his stores must be clean and well lighted and that they must generate a profit over time. He demanded that the staff be loyal, and he ensured the allegiance of his key personnel, his store managers, by allowing them a percentage of their store's profits. Walton continued to stock both of his stores with a combination of merchandise purchased from a new Butler Brothers' warehouse in Kansas City, which was located 200 miles north of Bentonville, and acquired on his frequent buying trips to neighboring Tennessee, where he would fill his car and a homemade trailer with goods bought directly from various wholesalers whom he had come to know.[22]

On a trip to the Butler Brothers warehouse in Kansas City, Walton learned that a shopping center was being built in the nearby suburb of Ruskin Heights. Among the tenants to be housed in the 100,000-square-foot center were an A&P supermarket, a Crown drugstore, and a Ben Franklin variety store. Anxious to own that Ben Franklin store and realizing that he needed an investment partner, Sam Walton contacted his brother Bud. Before World War II, Bud also had served as a management trainee for Penney's, and he had worked for Sam for a time as the assistant manager of Sam's Newport variety store. Since 1946 Bud had been operating his own Ben Franklin store in Versailles, Missouri, a town with a population of approximately 2,000. Sam asked Bud if he wanted to "gamble" on the business venture in Ruskin Heights. Bud indicated that he did, whereupon the brothers, in Sam's words, "borrowed all the money we could and went into that Ben Franklin fifty-fifty." The Ruskin Heights store opened in 1954 and was very successful, generating a sales volume of $250,000 and a profit of $30,000 during its first year in operation and $350,000 in sales the following year. Such success gave Sam Walton confidence in the potential for establishing a chain of variety stores, but he allowed himself to become temporarily sidetracked from pursuing this goal by his yearning to become one of Arkansas's premier shopping-center developers.[23]

Walton was so impressed with the concept of suburban shopping centers that he decided to begin building them in Arkansas. Although woefully undercapitalized, he purchased an option on a potential site in Little Rock. He certainly could not afford to develop the property alone, and he found that the newness of the idea made it difficult to interest other investors, all of which forced him to relinquish his option on the land. Although in the end he had invested approximately two years of his time and $25,000, he did not view the shopping-center venture as a total loss, since it gave him valuable real estate expertise that would aid him in selecting and developing sites for future stores.

On abandoning his idea of becoming a shopping-center developer, Walton "went back to concentrating on the retail business," which for him meant opening additional variety stores. Walton's impetus for expansion came not only from the success of his existing units but also from "thin air." By 1957 he decided that he was spending entirely too much time driving between his different store locations. He believed that flying would be the solution to his problem. Realizing what a reckless driver Sam Walton was on the ground, Bud, who had been a pilot on an aircraft carrier in the Pacific during World War II, sought to discourage the idea, but despite his brother's misgivings, Walton purchased his first of several airplanes, and flying replaced driving as Walton's preferred method of business travel. Piloting his own airplane allowed Walton the mobility he needed to oversee multiple stores in an efficient manner. As a result, in relatively quick succession Walton opened variety stores—several of them Ben Franklin franchises—in such places as Little Rock, Springdale, and Siloam Springs, Arkansas, as well as Neodesha and Coffeyville, Kansas, located, respectively, about 60 miles west and 20 miles south of Kansas City.[24]

The variety stores were organized as separate partnerships between Walton and his brother, along with other family members, such as Walton's father and brothers-in-law. In addition Walton allowed store managers to share in the ownership of the expanding chain. Beginning with Willard Walker, his first store manager, Walton offered his managers the opportunity to become limited partners if they would invest in the store they were to oversee and then invest a maximum of $1,000 in new outlets as they were opened. Walton's willingness to allow his managers to become partners helped to ensure that the units in his chain would enjoy competent oversight. One of Walton's best managers, for example, was Robert L. (Bob) Bogle, who in 1955 became the manager of the Bentonville store. Explaining his decision to sign on with Walton, Bogle said, "The thing that fascinated me more than the salary was the opportunity to buy an interest in the other stores as we put them in."[25]

As Walton expanded the business, he began to experiment with larger variety stores, which he named Walton's Family Centers. The first Family Center store opened in 1962 in St. Robert, Missouri, a town with a population of 1,500. The original store, which was 13,000 square feet in size, had to be increased to 20,000 square feet in less than a year, and its annual sales volume of $2 million made it the nation's second largest Ben Franklin store in terms of sales. The St. Robert outlet demonstrated that a store in a small town could attract a large number of customers from considerable distances and generate a substantial volume of business if it offered a wide assortment of goods at reasonable prices. Based on the success of the St. Robert store, Walton opened a second, 13,000-square-foot Family Center in Berryville, Arkansas, a town with a population of 2,000, and a third such outlet in Bentonville. By 1962 Walton and his brother owned and operated 16 variety stores in Arkansas, Missouri, and Kansas, making theirs the largest independent variety-store chain in the nation.[26]

Many of the strategies and practices that would form the basis of Walton's later success with Wal-Mart were forged during the Ben Franklin era. Walton's strategy of using small-town locations would be an undeniable outgrowth of the variety-store years, as would less obvious yet imminently relevant personal qualities: his enthusiasm for expanding his business interests; his willingness to experiment with new and different business techniques; his eagerness to investigate at every opportunity the operations of worthy competitors, such as Woolworth, Kress, Newberry, TG&Y, and Sterling variety outlets, and to copy their successful business practices; and his willingness to allow his employees, at least at the management level, to share in the profits of their own labor and in the company as a whole—a simple process with the Ben Franklin managers, and yet a practice that would form the basis of personnel policy at Wal-Mart, engendering great loyalty among employees and becoming one of the defining characteristics of the firm.

Walton's variety stores prospered not only as a result of his hard work and business acumen, but also because variety-store chains were a significant retailing concept in the United States during the late 1940s and the 1950s, especially in small towns. The popularity of variety stores during this period was reflected in the success of Butler Brothers' business endeavors. Its Ben Franklin chain, for example, increased in number from 1,277 in 1947 to 2,371 in 1956. To supply its growing Ben Franklin operation, the firm acquired the warehouse in Kansas City, where Walton did business, and also one in Memphis. In addition, in 1957 it purchased the TG&Y Stores Company of Oklahoma City, a firm that owned 153 variety stores located mainly in the Southwest.[27] During those same years, however, a different type of retailing had been emerging, and as it grew, it represented an increasingly formidable threat to small-town variety stores such as those owned by Sam Walton.

2

The Evolution of Retailing and the Appearance of Discount Merchandising

WHEN SAM WALTON elected in 1945 to go into retailing, he was entering an industry that had undergone constant change since the late nineteenth century. New retail institutions had arisen to supply the needs of a growing and modernizing nation, while older ones, unable to compete, had faded from the scene. The new kinds of outlets prevailed because they provided customers with greater convenience and a wider variety of goods that were better in quality and usually lower in price.

Prior to the Civil War, there were three dominant forms of retail trade in the United States: the itinerant peddler, the general store, and the specialty store. Peddlers first appeared in colonial America, and as settlement moved westward, they followed the customers into the frontier regions. On the frontier, "Yankee peddlers," so called because many of them came from New England, supplied customers with goods that they could not provide for themselves. Initially peddlers carried goods on their backs or in their saddlebags; they shifted to wagons as roads improved. Since the settlers usually possessed little cash, trade was largely by barter, with the peddlers taking the bartered items eastward to a town where they could be exchanged for another stock of goods. As the nation's population increased, peddlers began to disappear and a second type of retail institution emerged: the general store. Such stores handled a varied assortment of goods, ranging from pins and needles to plows and harnesses, and including textiles (for clothing), groceries, hardware, salt and sugar, spices, and other commodities. Business was often based on barter, with the storekeeper taking in exchange for his goods farmers' produce, which he either sold locally or shipped to an urban market. The stores offered credit to favored customers, and almost every transaction involved haggling with the merchant, since no uniform system of pricing existed.

As villages became towns and cities, general stores were overshadowed by stores that specialized in a particular product or service. These specialty stores prevailed over general stores because they offered a greater selection of their specific type of product and, usually, lower prices, since the merchant was able to buy merchandise in larger quantities. Among the leading specialty operations were dry-goods stores, hardware and farm-implement outlets, butcher shops, and grocery stores. By the middle of the nineteenth century, larger towns also had shops specializing in apparel for men, women, and children; drugs; jewelry; and furniture. General stores and specialty shops continued to exist for the duration of the nineteenth century and into the twentieth century, but after the Civil War their importance declined.[1]

During the late nineteenth century the nation experienced far-reaching economic changes that would lead to the emergence of new retail institutions. A national railroad system now tied all parts of the nation together, and such industrialists as John D. Rockefeller, Andrew Carnegie, and their peers revolutionized the American economy. Mass production was the result, and mass production, aided by the railroad and telegraph systems, made possible mass distribution. As markets grew, new kinds of retail businesses appeared that were able to overwhelm the old specialty and general stores, partly because they were able to bypass the wholesaling stage of the distribution process and deal directly with the manufacturers and the processors of goods. This new mass merchandising took three distinct forms: the department store, the chain store, and the mail-order house.[2]

The first great innovation in retailing after the Civil War was the department store. The rise of this giant establishment can be attributed to a variety of factors, among them: the increase in population and wealth in the cities; technological innovations, such as the electric street car; electric elevators and escalators, which facilitated shopping in the large stores; and glass-front shelving, which enhanced merchandise display.

Department stores sold a broad variety of merchandise under one roof. Because their selection of goods was at least as varied as the specialty stores' and their prices were usually lower, they often supplanted specialty stores in the cities and towns where they were established. Department stores offered the added advantage of convenience, since city dwellers no longer were compelled to do their shopping in a number of different outlets.

Department stores adopted policies that were revolutionary at the time. Almost all of them, for example, set fixed prices, since their size required them to employ clerks whose limited expertise made price negotiation impractical. In their efforts to lure shoppers from specialty shops and other competitors, department stores also became substantial advertisers. In addition, department stores offered a variety of services that had previously been unknown. They were willing to accept the return of merchandise, and, because they catered primarily to women, many of them instituted delivery service and offered charge accounts to favored customers. Some of the larger stores also boasted shopping environments that were elegant and luxurious.

The age of the department store began in earnest during the 1860s and 1870s. The two leaders in the field were R. H. Macy and John Wanamaker, who launched in New York City and Philadelphia, respectively, the retail establishments that carried their names. Wanamaker and Macy established mass-merchandising standards that others followed. Among the early department stores founded in the nation's leading cities were Bloomingdale's, Abraham & Straus, and B. Altman in New York City; Carson Pirie Scott and Company, Marshall Field, and The Fair in Chicago; J. L. Hudson in Detroit; F. & R. Lazarus in Columbus, Ohio; and I. Magnin in San Francisco. Shortly after the turn of the century, Rich's opened in Atlanta and Nieman-Marcus opened in Dallas. Department stores also were established in smaller cities and towns across the nation as soon as those markets would support them.[3]

Chain stores, the second mass-merchandising innovation of the late nineteenth century, appeared a few years after department stores. They were able to attract business and prosper because they in effect combined wholesale and retail operations under the same management. This allowed them to eliminate middlemen and buy in quantity. Their resulting ability consistently to undersell independent merchants, who complained bitterly of unfair competition and monopolistic practices, was a distinguishing characteristic.

Chains initially were successful in groceries and dry goods, later in other lines. The Great Atlantic and Pacific Tea Company (A&P) is generally considered to have been the first true chain store. Its predecessor, the Great Atlantic Tea Company, was founded in 1859, when George H. Hartford and a partner discovered that they could import tea directly from the Far East and, by eliminating several middlemen, sell it to consumers in New York City at lower than prevailing prices. Hartford subsequently opened other stores in New York City, Boston, Philadelphia, and Chicago; at the same time he expanded his inventory to include groceries. By 1880 there were 95 A&P stores, and the chain stretched from Boston to Milwaukee. A&P's great competitor, the Kroger company, originated in 1882. Other chains soon emerged in drugs, shoes, and, in 1909, automobile supplies.[4]

Chains were quite important in dry goods, where a type of retail institution evolved that was known as the "junior department store." Belk Brothers established the first chain of junior department stores in 1888, but the most successful was the J. C. Penney Company, Inc. James Cash Penney established his first outlet, a Golden Rule store, in Kemmerer, Wyoming, in 1902. In 1913 Penney's Golden Rule stores were incorporated as the J. C. Penney Company, Inc., and by 1917 he had 71 stores and sales of $3.6 million. Rapid growth came during and after World War I: the number of stores rose to 475 in 1923, and by the middle of the next decade the chain grew to more than 1,400 stores. Another important junior department store chain was the W. T. Grant Company, which was established in 1906 in Pennsylvania. Like standard department stores, Grant's and Penney's outlets carried a broad assortment of merchandise, but their emphasis was on soft goods, which typically had lower prices.

Another distinctive type of chain was the variety store. Conceiving of the idea of selling merchandise for no more than 5 (and, later, 10) cents, Frank W. Woolworth, after failing in business in Utica, New York, established what would become the leading variety-store chain in the country when he opened a 5-and-10-cent store in Lancaster, Pennsylvania, in 1879. There were 7 Woolworth's stores by 1886 and 59 by 1900, when they generated sales of $5 million. In 1912 the firm was incorporated as F. W. Woolworth Company. In that same year it merged with five competing chains and became a publicly owned entity consisting of 596 stores with total sales of $50 million. Woolworth's stores offered a wide assortment of items, including housewares and hardware, toys, inexpensive jewelry, candy, stationery, notions, dry goods, and apparel, all priced at a dime or less. Merchandise was displayed on counters so that customers could examine the items they wished to purchase, an arrangement that permitted the employment of low-paid clerks, whose primary duties were to wrap purchases and make change.[5]

Other variety-store chains came later, some of which were the S. H. Kress Company, founded in 1896 when Samuel H. Kress established his first store in Memphis, Tennessee, thereby introducing variety stores in the South; the S. S. Kresge Company, which was established in 1897 when S. S. Kresge joined with J. G. McCrory in opening a variety store in Memphis, and, later, in Detroit, where the chain would be headquartered; G. C. Murphy, which opened its first store in 1906 in Pennsylvania; Neisner Brothers, Inc., which opened its first store in 1911 in Rochester, New York; the J. J. Newberry Company, which was formed in 1911 in Stroudsburg, Pennsylvania; and McLellan Stores, which was launched in 1916.[6]

The third major innovation in retailing in the late nineteenth century was the mail-order house. In this form of retailing, customers were contacted by means of catalogs, and they ordered and received goods by mail. The pioneer in the field was Aaron Montgomery Ward, who in 1872 founded his eponymous company in Chicago and mailed his first catalog, a single sheet of paper listing 163 items. Ward explained to his customers how his firm could sell goods at prices well below those of local merchants. According to Ward, the firm purchased merchandise directly from manufacturers, which eliminated the need for jobbers and wholesalers; it bought and sold its products for cash, which avoided interest payments and bad debts; and it operated economically by avoiding such expenses as salesmen's commissions. In 1875 Ward introduced the policy, "Satisfaction guaranteed or your money back." By 1900 Montgomery Ward was a $10 million business, and by 1904 the firm's catalog had 500 pages and was furnished free to customers. Known to millions of rural and small-town Americans as the "wish book," the catalog offered everything from swaddling clothes to tombstones.[7]

Ward's leading competitor was Sears, Roebuck and Company. In 1886 Richard W. Sears, the firm's founder, was working as a railway agent in Minnesota when he purchased a shipment of watches being returned to the manufacturer and marketed them himself. He established the R. W. Sears Watch Company six months later. Soon thereafter he relocated to Chicago, where he recruited Alvah C. Roebuck, an Indiana watchmaker, as a partner. Sears sold the watch business in 1889 and two years later formed a mail-order firm that adopted the name Sears, Roebuck and Company in 1893. In 1896 the company published its first general catalog, which advertised a broad assortment of goods ranging from apparel and housewares to sewing machines, buggies, and farm equipment. In 1900 the firm generated $11 million in sales and surpassed Montgomery Ward to become the leading mail-order business in the country.[8]

A third mail-order house was Spiegel, Inc., of Chicago, which distributed its first catalog in 1904. Unlike Ward's and Sears, which accepted only cash in payment for goods, Spiegel extended credit to its customers. Espousing the slogan, "We trust the people—everywhere," the company in some instances allowed customers to purchase goods with a down payment of only 15 percent, with the balance to be paid over several months.[9] Although denounced by local merchants, mail-order firms were successful. Among the reasons for their success: their money-back guarantees of unconditional customer satisfaction; the growth of advertising in daily newspapers and farm periodicals, which stimulated sales; poor roads in the countryside, which discouraged shopping in town; innovations in the postal service, such as rural free delivery of the mail in the 1890s and, later, a parcel post law; and the ability of mail-order houses to offer customers a wider variety of merchandise at lower prices than could be found in local stores.[10]

The patterns of retailing that developed in the late nineteenth century continued virtually unchanged until the mid-1920s, when Sears and Ward's initiated another major retailing innovation with their decision to open retail outlets. In 1925 Sears established 8 retail stores, and in 1926 Ward's opened 10 stores. This move by the mail-order houses was influenced in part by such factors as the depression in agriculture, which damaged the purchasing power of farmers; the greater mobility of rural shoppers, due to the increasing use of the automobile and the expansion of improved roads; rising competition from retail chains such as Penney's; and the increasing shift of the nation's population from rural areas to the cities. Both firms rapidly expanded their number of retail outlets. By 1928 Ward's operated 244 retail stores, and by 1930 Sears had 324.

Because their range of merchandise was extensive, the retail outlets of Sears and Montgomery Ward were department stores in everything but name. In soft goods, the stores were competitive with such junior department store chains as Penney's and Grant's. Unlike those firms, however, the outlets of Sears and Ward's also carried a substantial assortment of hard goods, including large household appliances, lawn mowers and other yard and garden supplies, and furniture.[11]

In 1930 the next major retailing innovation, the grocery supermarket, was launched when Michael Cullen opened his first store in Jamaica, New York. By 1935 Cullen operated 15 units. The success of the supermarket was based on such factors as the innovation of self-service, instituted in 1916 in the Piggly Wiggly food stores in Memphis, Tennessee, by Clarence Saunders, the company's founder; the invention of the shopping cart by Ellis D. Turnham; and the economic hardships associated with the Great Depression. Cullen's supermarkets and others that appeared during the 1930s were comprehensive grocery stores that were generally located in low-cost facilities that were easily accessible by automobile. They operated on a strict cash-and-carry basis, used self-service exclusively to slash labor costs, were open during evening hours, and engaged in promotional advertising. Most important, because their size and modest overhead expenses allowed them to operate on a low margin (the difference between net sales and the cost of merchandise sold, also known as markup), they were able to sell brand-name goods at prices significantly below those charged by small, independent groceries and the national grocery chains.

Customers flocked to the new stores with such enthusiasm that the major grocery chains, such as A&P and Kroger, found that to compete they had to establish similar outlets and adopt the methods of the new supermarkets. They closed many of their small clerk-service stores and replaced them with fewer—but much larger—stores, which were located on major thoroughfares for the convenience of automobile drivers. There were, for example, 17,000 A&P stores in 1929 and only 4,475 in 1963. As the 1930s progressed, the supermarket chains had to make additional changes, such as offering better-quality merchandise, relying more heavily on advertising, and adding lines of goods not traditionally carried in grocery stores. The small, independent grocers generally were unable to grow to supermarket size; they lingered on in their old locations, many eventually disappearing.

The supermarket chains expanded their product lines to include merchandise that had traditionally been sold in drugstores, such as paper products, household items, nonprescription drugs, and health and beauty products. Drugstores, in turn, were forced to alter their merchandise mix to include many lines normally carried by variety stores. During this era drugstores also became bigger, adopted self-service, and, as they expanded their product lines, engaged in comparatively less prescription-drug business.[12]

During the interwar period the variety-store chains found that they, too, had to modify their business practices. Not only were they affected during the 1930s by the rise of the supermarket chains and the changing nature of drugstores, but they also had increasingly ceased to be genuine 5-and-10-cent stores. The inflation associated with World War I had begun this change, and the trend continued during the 1920s and the 1930s. In response to these factors, variety stores expanded their merchandise mix to include both new lines and more expensive items, they reduced the number of sales clerks they employed, and they moved hesitantly toward self-service. By the late 1930s some variety stores were beginning to look like junior department stores. Overall, however, variety-store prices remained comparatively low, which accounted for their remarkable resilience during the economically distressed 1930s.[13]

World War II created conditions that significantly affected American retailing. Some war-related factors disrupted the retail business. Military service, for example, and the high wages offered by war-related industries reduced the availability of labor and compelled retailers to function with fewer employees; hours of operation had to be extended to permit evening shopping; many goods were in short supply; and there was a threat of serious inflation, which was prevented only by the operations of the Office of Price Administration. On the other hand, some factors associated with the war benefited retailers. Full employment increased the purchasing power of American consumers; a high demand for goods caused merchandise to move so rapidly that there was little need for promotional sales; markdowns were rare; and the gross margins of most retailers rose. Department stores, in particular, benefited during the war, thanks to an increased desire on the part of consumers for quality goods.[14]

Following World War II retailing experienced such dramatic growth that the period from 1948 to 1962 has been characterized as a "retailing revolution." One factor that contributed to the rapid expansion of retailing during these years was technological innovation, which produced a greater availability of consumer goods. A second important element was the growth in the size and purchasing power of the middle class. This growth stemmed from such factors as a more equitable distribution of wealth, caused in part by new tax policies; higher wages, in part a result of the negotiating strength of organized labor; a better-educated workforce; and an increase in the number of two-income families. As the income level of American consumers changed, so did their buying habits. Unlike earlier generations, these new consumers were less willing to postpone the purchase of durable goods such as housing, household furnishings and appliances, and automobiles. Instead, they were prepared to go into debt to obtain them, an inclination strengthened by governmental fiscal and monetary policies that resulted in the rapid increase of consumer credit.[15]

These developments created a new mass market for goods that was highly competitive and that compelled retail institutions to modify their operations. Department stores established regional chains, launched branches and then complete stores in the suburbs, and participated in the creation of huge shopping centers on the edges of cities. The leading mail-order houses continued their shift toward department-store merchandise and joined the rush to establish outlets in the suburban shopping centers. In addition, they endeavored to make their stores more attractive by broadening their merchandise lines and devoting more attention to upscale fashion. Variety stores responded to the heightened competition by upgrading some of their merchandise, largely abandoning the old price maximums, and adding big-ticket items, such as lawn mowers, electric fans and toasters, and patio furniture. Major variety chains also began to move to suburban shopping centers and close unprofitable units in old downtown locations.[16]

The most important retailing development of the post–World War II era was the rapid expansion of a new form of retailing, discount merchandising. The leading magazine for the discount industry, *Discount Merchandiser*, defines a modern discount store as a departmentalized retail establishment that makes use of many self-service techniques to sell hard goods, such as refrigerators and television sets; health and beauty aids; apparel and other soft goods; and other general merchandise, all at uniquely low margins. The concept of discounting was born during the 1930s with the grocery supermarkets and their low margins, inexpensive locations, long hours of operation, and brash advertising. By the early 1940s a sizable number of outlets, called discount houses, sold nationally advertised hard goods—electrical appliances, watches, cameras, luggage, and jewelry—at prices sharply below those offered by conventional retailers. The typical discount houses were small, almost secret outlets located inconspicuously in office buildings in New York and other large cities. They catered to a limited clientele and took orders from samples or a catalog. They relied on word-of-mouth advertising, and they often established business relationships with employees of a large concern or with groups such as municipal employees, teachers, or members of labor unions. These discounters were able to undersell conventional retailers because they obtained their merchandise directly from manufacturers and kept their expenses low. Most of the early firms were managed by their owners; sales were for cash only; inventories were kept small; no delivery service was provided; guarantees were given by the manufacturers of the merchandise; and there were few returns because the stores sold little clothing.[17]

It was following World War II that discount merchandising experienced a surge in popularity, as concern over rising prices caused consumers to seek bargains. A multitude of discount operations began to spring up in major cities throughout the nation. Like the discount houses that preceded them, the postwar discounters specialized in brand-name hard goods such as household appliances, cameras, luggage, sporting goods, and jewelry.[18] During the 1950s discounting emerged from the fringe of American retailing and entered the mainstream. In 1954, for example, the National Association of Discount Merchants was established, and by the early 1960s the industry would have its own trade journals. The rapid growth of discounting during the fifties was caused by several factors. One element was the increased supply of consumer products relative to demand. During the late 1940s the demand for goods had been so great that a seller's market had existed, making price competition weak and at times practically nonexistent. After the Korean conflict ended in 1953, however, production began to match or exceed demand, creating a buyer's market. Manufacturers found that in this buyer's market discounters represented a more effective means of getting products to consumers because their willingness to accept lower margins enabled them to move large quantities of goods more rapidly than conventional retailers, who required higher markups.

Changes in the attitudes of American consumers also contributed to the rise of discount merchandising. Decades of national advertising had developed consumer confidence in manufacturers' brands, so shoppers found that they no longer needed the guarantees offered by conventional retail outlets. Price resistance was also a part of their changed attitudes. Although real incomes rose during the early 1950s, consumers resisted the higher prices brought about by inflation and eagerly embraced the discount stores, where lower markups restrained price—at least in the short run. At the same time, rising incomes created purchasing power in groups of consumers who in the past had not patronized the nation's more sophisticated retail establishments. These shoppers were unacquainted with the services that department stores and specialty shops offered, and they did not want to pay extra for them. In truth, they felt more comfortable in the informal atmosphere of the discount stores.[19]

Certain policies in conventional retailing also stimulated the growth of discount merchandising. Retailers were determined to maintain their traditional margins, for example, which for some had risen dramatically in past decades. According to one calculation, while the gross margin of variety stores had increased from 31 percent in 1899 to 36 percent in 1947, the margin enjoyed by department stores, which had been 22.2 percent in 1889, had reached 35.6 percent in 1947 and 38.8 percent by 1953. Such margins stood in stark contrast to the early discounters' estimated 15 percent markup. Department stores, moreover, often decided not to put "bargain basements" in the new branches they opened in the suburbs. As a result, their former bargain shoppers, who had been responsible for 20 to 30 percent of their sales, now were living and shopping in the suburbs and finding their bargains in the discount stores.[20]

Resale price maintenance further facilitated the growth of discount merchandising. Also known as "fair trade," resale price maintenance is a vertical price restraint in which the manufacturer or supplier of a product sets the minimum retail price that may be charged for that product. Fair-trade laws initially were passed by states during the 1930s to help small retailers combat the increasingly vigorous competition of the chain stores. California enacted the first fair-trade law in 1931. It stated that for products that carried manufacturers' brand names, the manufacturers could establish the retail prices, and thereby legalized price-fixing agreements between producers and retailers. A key provision contained in most fair-trade laws was a so-called nonsigner clause, which stipulated that all merchants in a state were bound by the terms of a resale price maintenance agreement if only one merchant signed such a contract. In 1937 the status of the fair-trade laws was strengthened by the Miller-Tydings Act, which exempted vertical price fixing, including resale price maintenance, from federal antitrust laws. By 1941, 45 states had a fair-trade law with a nonsigner clause. The Miller-Tydings Act stood unchanged until 1951, when the Supreme Court diluted its force by declaring that the nonsigner clause was not included in the law. With the McGuire Act of 1952, Congress moved to protect the nonsigner provision from legal challenges by specifically legalizing it. In the years that followed, however, nonsigner clauses were inexorably voided or repealed in many states. By 1967 only 16 states still had a fair-trade law with a nonsigner clause intact. In the mid-1970s, when Congress enacted legislation that ended resale price maintenance, that number had shrunk to 13.[21]

Even during its legal heyday, fair trade rarely worked well. The states generally did not have the machinery to enforce the laws, so responsibility for enforcement fell primarily to the manufacturers, who often found the task difficult. If a manufacturer took legal action against a price-cutter, the action had to be continuous and vigorous, and it had to be applied consistently. Such action was likely to be expensive, and there was no guarantee of success. Manufacturers could also seek to enforce fair trade by refusing to sell to firms that engaged in price-cutting, a policy known as the Colgate doctrine. Their efforts, however, had to be unilateral, since to unite with other manufacturers would have been a violation of the federal antitrust laws. Moreover, retailers of all types found numerous ways to circumvent the fair-trade laws. If they were selling appliances, for example, they might give unusually large trade-in allowances, and some retailers avoided the problem altogether by selling mainly private brands.

Ironically, the fair-trade laws in practice encouraged discounting, while at the same time the growth of discounting weakened the laws.

Fair-trade prices as established by manufacturers included margins high enough to satisfy most retailers who would handle the goods. These margins afforded aggressive retailers the opportunity to build traffic by cutting prices—the essence of discount merchandising. The fair-trade laws thus constituted something of an umbrella under which discounting grew. As discount stores enlarged their share of the market, it became increasingly difficult to enforce the fair-trade laws, for when manufacturers found themselves functioning in a buyer's market and discovered that the discount merchants were capable of moving large quantities of goods, they had little incentive to push for the enforcement of laws that would only reduce their own volume of business.

The early discounters vigorously denounced the fair-trade laws and their proponents. Stephen Masters, a discounter himself and a leading industry spokesman, argued that the fair-trade laws did little except protect the "inefficient retailer" from competition, since that retailer had "no incentive to . . . cut his costs when he is covered by the fair trade blanket." Masters maintained that the "public sees little justification for paying full list [price] on a growing number of overpriced, overmarginized . . . lines" and asserted that discounters simply were giving "customers the substantial savings that are brought about by efficient, economical selling costs."[22]

Three of the nation's leading discount firms during the 1950s—all of which had originated as hard-goods operations and expanded their merchandise lines to resemble department stores—were Masters, Inc.; Vornado, Inc.; and E. J. Korvette. Masters, Inc., had been established in New York City in 1937 by Stephen Masters and his brother Phillip. At the outset it was a typical New York City discount operation. Located in a "hole-in-the-wall" store, the brothers sold radios and appliances and gradually built their clientele through word of mouth and direct advertising. The little store prospered, its line of merchandise gradually broadened, and, according to some accounts, it numbered Franklin D. Roosevelt among its customers. In 1958 the company had eight stores and was still privately held, but it was preparing to offer stock to the public and to expand. A few years later, however, the firm encountered financial problems. In 1963 it filed for bankruptcy, and Stephen Masters, who was by then one of the most articulate advocates of discount merchandising, resigned as president. The company recovered from its financial difficulties, and in 1966 it operated seven stores for an annual sales volume of $51 million.[23]

Vornado, Inc., originated in 1944, when Herbert and Sidney Hubschman, who operated a diner in Harrison, New Jersey, began to sell radios and appliances as a sideline. Their prices were markedly below manufacturers' list prices, and satisfied customers began to refer to the brothers as the "two guys from Harrison," thereby giving the business its first name. In 1947 the brothers built a cinder-block structure next to their diner. Because the appliance industry was expanding rapidly and the market was not yet saturated, their business flourished, and in the late 1940s the Hubschmans opened several similar outlets. The brothers added housewares to their inventory in the early 1950s, and by the middle of the decade the outlets were beginning to resemble department stores. In 1959 the firm merged with a fan and air-conditioning manufacturer and became Vornado, Inc. In 1966 there were 25 Vornado stores in Maryland, New Jersey, New York, Pennsylvania, and Virginia, and the firm generated an annual sales volume of $258 million.[24]

E. J. Korvette was founded when Eugene Ferkauf, the son of a New York luggage merchant, opened a store in a second-story loft in New York City in 1948. The 1,000-square-foot outlet handled only luggage at the outset, but Ferkauf soon broadened its inventory to include small appliances, fountain pens, and cameras. This merchandise was sold for about one-third less than the prices of conventional merchants. For the larger products, the store was only a showroom where orders were taken, and the items themselves were shipped to customers from a warehouse. Customers had to display a membership card to shop at the store, but to generate traffic Ferkauf reportedly gave two cards to every customer who entered the store.

In 1951 Ferkauf moved his store to the street level and opened a second outlet in White Plains, New York. Two years later the firm had 5 stores in New York City and its suburbs, and they were beginning to look more like department stores, as the merchandise lines were expanded to include apparel and household goods. The company sold stock to the public in 1956, and by the end of the decade it had 12 stores in Connecticut, New Jersey, New York, and Pennsylvania. Korvette created a great deal of discussion in retailing circles when, in 1962, it opened a posh discount store on New York's Fifth Avenue.[25]

The company handled only those goods that moved rapidly and required a minimum of shelf space. Inventory turned from 9 to 12 times a year, compared with the 4 or 5 turns considered normal for department stores. Goods were displayed on tables and shelves and were plainly marked with the manufacturers' suggested retail prices and Korvette's discount prices. The stores provided no delivery, they charged for alterations, and in the early days they permitted no credit purchases. Wages, rent, advertising, and other overhead expenses amounted to about 15 percent of sales, sharply lower than the 33 percent common among conventional retailers. Margins on merchandise ranged from 5 to 30 percent. Since the stores were largely self-service, personnel expenses amounted to approximately 8 percent of sales, as compared with the 18 percent paid by many department stores. Sales clerks earned about $88 for a 48-hour, six-day workweek, which was substantially more than the $1-an-hour minimum wage that prevailed in 1956.

By 1966 E. J. Korvette was to all appearances a successful firm. From its base in New York City, the chain of discount department stores had spread into Pennsylvania and then to Detroit, Chicago, and St. Louis. In all, the company operated 42 discount department stores, some of which were affiliated with a grocery store and formed a complex called Korvette City. As the chain grew, Ferkauf's management of the firm became increasingly inefficient; as a result the company lacked the administrative and managerial structure necessary to control and direct it. In addition, the firm had lost much of its discount character when it improved the quality of its merchandise and raised its profit margin to 33 percent in 1965. In 1966 Korvette merged with Spartans Industries, Inc., and in 1968 Ferkauf retired from the business that he had built.[26]

As discount merchandising grew during the 1950s, other types of discount operations began to evolve, and one of those was the mill store. So named because they were located in buildings that formerly had housed textile mills, mill stores featured apparel rather than hard goods. A pioneer in this type of discounting was Martin Chase, who founded Ann and Hope of Cumberland, Rhode Island. In 1953 Chase and his son Irwin opened a retail outlet in the Ann and Hope mill in Cumberland. Initially established to dispose of surplus goods at reduced prices, the venture was so successful that it subsequently grew into a discount chain with stores throughout New England. At the same time, the firm's inventory was expanded to include a broader range of merchandise. This modification, combined with such features as self-service, a central checkout process, and a liberal return policy, has caused some to regard Ann and Hope as the prototype of the modern discount department store.[27]

Another type of discount operation was the "closed-door" store, which required customers to display a membership card before they could enter. Such outlets had been established in the 1930s, mainly as cooperatives or to avoid the fair-trade laws. They disappeared in the 1940s, only to reappear in the 1950s. California was the scene of their revival, but by 1960 a survey by the National Retail Merchants' Association found that closed-door discounters were in 28 states. They were doing some $259 million in business, and they were united by their own trade association, the National Association of Consumer Organizations.

The closed-door discounters had characteristics that set them apart from other discounters. They charged nominal fees for membership, and, in the formative stage at least, most of them sought to attract specific groups as customers, such as labor-union members, teachers, and government employees. The appeal of such stores, few of which were true cooperatives, was their aura of exclusiveness. Merchandise was essentially the same as was found in department stores, with added emphasis on large appliances, automobile supplies and accessories, and other hard goods. Advertising was primarily by direct mail to members, and promotional sales were rare, since the closed-door discounters took the position that they offered savings of 15 to 20 percent every day. Some of the leaders among closed-door discounters were GEM International, Fedco, Fed-Mart, and Union stores. By the mid-1960s, several closed-door stores had dropped the membership-card requirement while others had gone out of business.[28]

In the early days of discounting, many discount stores operated some, and in several cases most, of their departments through leases to other merchants. Leasing departments in such areas as shoes, health and beauty aids, and pharmaceuticals offered certain advantages to both parties. For the store operator, the use of leased departments minimized risk and capital requirements and brought into the store expertise that the store owner lacked. For the lessee, the arrangement placed him in a huge store where customer traffic, volume of business, and the rapid turnover of merchandise certainly were greater than they would have been in a separate outlet. As time passed, however, a trend developed in the discount industry toward less use of leased departments.[29]

Evidence that discounting was maturing during the early 1960s was demonstrated by the entrance into the field of two of the variety-chain giants, Kresge and Woolworth. In 1955 Kresge had 673 variety stores in 26 midwestern and eastern states and a total sales volume of $354 million, but its senior executives knew that the company faced an uncertain future. Like all variety stores, Kresge suffered from such problems as small unit sales; steadily rising operating costs; the shift of the buying public away from decaying downtown areas, where the firm either owned property or was committed to leases for as long as 99 years; and the encroachment of supermarkets, drugstores, and the new discount stores on traditional variety-store business. Kresge responded to some of these problems by adding higher-priced merchandise, converting to self-service, opening new stores in the suburbs, and experimenting with credit sales. These innovations helped to maintain or increase volume, but at substantial cost. A new strategy was required.

In 1957 the company directed Harry B. Cunningham, an experienced executive with the firm, to make a thorough study of Kresge's options, with a specific emphasis on discounting. Cunningham spent two years at the task. Discount merchants, he found, used many of the principles formulated years earlier by Kresge and the other variety-store chains, but with important differences: the discounters had much larger stores, a broader range of merchandise, and lower margins, which were the result of their focus on the return on total investment rather than on a percentage of profit on sales and which were made possible by self-service, low-cost buildings, a high volume of sales per square foot, and the rapid turnover of inventory.

Cunningham became Kresge's chief executive officer in 1959, and he set in motion a restructuring of the company based in large part on his findings. The primary focus of the company for the next few years was a modernized and enlarged version of the variety store, and the firm operated 750 of these units by the end of 1963. In 1961 the firm also established the Jupiter chain of combination variety and discount outlets. The Jupiter stores replaced marginal Kresge stores that were burdened with long leases. They had a smaller staff than the former Kresge outlets, carried a narrower inventory, and stocked only rapidly selling merchandise that sold at substantially reduced prices.

Kresge's long-term future, however, rested on Harry Cunningham's new discount venture, K mart stores. In establishing the discount chain, Cunningham's goal was to provide consumers with quality merchandise at prices that were consistently lower than those of other retail outlets. While Sears and other major retail operations stressed private-brand merchandise, K mart emphasized nationally advertised, brand-name products and carried private brands only on a limited basis, mainly for products that either had no readily recognized national brand or were unavailable to discount operations. The first K mart opened in Garden City, Michigan, a Detroit suburb, on 1 March 1962; by the end of the following year there were 53 units in the chain. K mart stores contained about 100,000 square feet of space and usually were located along major thoroughfares in small shopping centers in which they were the major enterprise. Kresge leased the buildings in which K marts were located, generally for 20 years with renewal options. Kresge's K marts served both medium-size and large cities. In the latter, company policy was to surround a city by placing several K marts in the nearby suburbs. Management considered this location strategy an innovation, since several of the early discounters had scattered their stores over a wide geographical area.

By the late 1960s the layout of K mart stores was standardized. Stores were wider than they were deep, and a central aisle, or "midway," about 15 feet wide extended from the front entrance to the back of the store. Promotional and seasonal merchandise was displayed on tables there. Lessees provided the expertise that Kresge lacked in some departments. All K mart stores had a central checkout area, but departments handling higher-priced items, such as cameras and jewelry, had their own cash registers. In contrast to the Kresge stores, which sometimes handled irregular merchandise (flawed or damaged goods), K mart sold only first-quality products, and much of the inventory consisted of brand names such as Polaroid, Kodak, Elgin, Zenith, Black & Decker, and General Electric. Customer satisfaction was guaranteed, and all goods could be returned for a refund or an exchange. Such practices made K mart notably successful. By the late 1960s, Kresge was the nation's largest discounter, both in terms of number of stores and sales volume. The firm had evolved from a variety-store chain into a discount-merchandise chain with a variety-store division.[30]

Woolworth's decision to go into discounting was even more of a break with the past. Prior to World War II, Woolworth was the nation's leading variety-store chain. During the 1930s, however, the company experienced rising competition from supermarkets and drugstores, as these operations expanded their merchandise lines to include variety-store goods. Beginning in the 1950s, discount stores posed an even greater threat, since their inventories included the entire spectrum of variety-store merchandise. Woolworth responded to the pressure placed on its business by discounters first by seeking to improve its variety stores. By 1961 the company had converted to self-service in about two-thirds of its 2,100 units, it had begun a major move to suburban shopping centers, and it had closed many of its small downtown stores.

Woolworth's major innovation was the launching of its chain of Woolco stores. The first Woolco opened in Columbus, Ohio, on 6 June 1962. The company studied operating results carefully and expanded its Woolco operation gradually. There were 27 stores by the end of 1965 and 92 by 1968. Woolco stores sold department-store merchandise as well as tires, batteries, and other automobile accessories, all at discount prices. At the outset, because of Woolworth's limited experience with home furnishings, men's apparel, and automobile supplies, those departments were operated by lessees. The stores also featured Red Grill restaurants, pharmacies, and automobile service centers. Store policies included installment plans, revolving credit, and lay-away service. All of the early Woolco stores were located in or adjacent to shopping centers. Management's goal was to situate the stores so that they would dominate these shopping centers. Most of the early stores were huge, ranging from 115,000 to 180,000 square feet, and were located on a single level with wide aisles for shopping convenience.[31]

In 1962 the Dayton Corporation, a regional department-store chain headquartered in Minneapolis, established a chain of discount outlets called Target Stores, Inc. The firm opened four Target stores in 1962, three in the suburban area of Minneapolis–St. Paul and one in Duluth, a smaller city about 125 miles northeast of Minneapolis. Target was an upscale discount chain that specialized in relatively high-quality, higher-price merchandise, almost two-thirds of which was hard goods, including furniture and household appliances. The quality level and merchandise mix were designed to appeal to a more affluent suburban clientele.

All of the Target stores in the Minneapolis–St. Paul area were free-standing structures located adjacent to shopping centers. At the outset, Target's strategy for growth was to develop fully in the Twin Cities area and then to go into smaller cities in Minnesota, Wisconsin, and the Dakotas, but the early profitability of the outlets in Minneapolis–St. Paul as compared with the mediocre performance of the Duluth store caused management to alter this strategy and concentrate on major metropolitan areas. In 1969 Target's parent company became the Dayton Hudson Corporation when the Dayton Corporation merged with the J. L. Hudson Company, a regional department-store chain headquartered in Detroit.[32]

Among the major chains that experimented in a limited way with discount merchandising was J. C. Penney. It went into discounting in 1964, opening on the same day three Treasure Island stores in Milwaukee. The firm subsequently opened another outlet in that city and three in the greater-Atlanta area. These stores were giants that measured 180,000 square feet, and they included supermarkets. These new discount outlets emphasized brand-name products, in contrast to the private brands stocked in Penney's standard stores.[33]

Some chains rejected discounting but operated stores that were similar to discount outlets, the primary differences being less emphasis on price and greater emphasis on quality, especially in soft goods. J. J. Newberry moved strongly in that direction in the early 1960s with its Britt's department stores. While the W. T. Grant Company maintained that it had no interest in discounting, its newer stores resembled discount outlets and emphasized private-brand merchandise, which the firm claimed was of high quality.[34]

In the main, early discounters limited their attention to city and suburban markets, a strategy that reflected their concern with generating a high sales volume and a rapid turnover of stock. According to the census figures of 1960, however, nearly 40 percent of America's population still lived on farms and in small towns and cities of fewer than 25,000 people. As a consequence, some retailers began to view rural America as a promising market for discount merchandising. One of the discounters who recognized the opportunities in the hinterlands was Gamble-Skogmo, a midwestern retail company headquartered in Minneapolis. The firm originated in 1925 when two partners opened an automobile-parts store in St. Cloud, Minnesota. They added hardware to their merchandise lines and sold franchises to other small-town businessmen, and by the end of 1927 the partners had 25 stores in operation. Thirty-seven years later, Gamble-Skogmo had 2,000 franchised stores and 500 company-owned outlets throughout the Midwest.

After studying discounting in detail, Gamble-Skogmo opened its first Tempo Discount Center in 1964 in Willmar, Minnesota. In contrast to the conventional Gamble-Skogmo stores, which ran about 7,500 square feet in size and carried mainly hard goods, the first Tempo store had 22,000 square feet and handled a full assortment of both hard and soft goods. The stores featured self-service, installment credit, and brand-name appliances. Management discovered that there was a distinct advantage to constructing stores of 20,000 to 40,000 square feet in country towns. "If you're first, you're apt to be alone," said a company executive. "Most towns we're in won't take two stores of that size."[35]

Another retailer similarly concluded that there were significant opportunities in small towns because there usually was little competition except from an "outmoded three- or four-story downtown department store." Such logic aroused a few other firms' interest in small towns, among them Woolworth and Fed-Mart. Woolworth opened a few Woolco stores in small cities of 25,000 to 75,000 people. Woolco stores in such communities were smaller, perhaps 70,000 to 80,000 square feet, but they carried a full line of department-store merchandise. In the mid-1960s Fed-Mart, headquartered in San Diego, established outlets of about 15,000 square feet in towns with populations of 12,000 to 35,000.[36]

From the outset, the arrival of discount chains in country towns generated controversy. Local merchants, especially, resisted the competition of the chains. One local druggist, for example, complained, "I can't compete with the way those guys [discounters] operate." Another objection frequently raised was that discounters harmed communities by taking money out of the town. Supporters of new discount stores, who usually included a large number of local residents, held a different view. They maintained that a discount store benefited a local economy by offering consumers lower prices, by boosting employment, and by generating more business within a community, which, in turn, increased tax revenues.[37]

Full-service retailers frequently asserted that the discount merchandising industry could offer lower prices because it sold inferior goods. This charge was false in the case of hard goods, since discount stores handled the same nationally advertised brands as other retailers. With soft goods, however, the accusation had some validity. There was great variation from store to store, but in the early 1960s the discount industry as a whole had difficulty obtaining brand-name soft goods. Although many leading discount stores had stopped selling factory seconds or other distressed goods by this time, the soft goods found in discount stores generally were lower in quality and narrower in selection than department-store merchandise. Apparel, for example, tended to be sturdy and long-wearing but lacking in style.[38]

By the early 1960s the discount industry included many inexperienced and undercapitalized operators who had expanded rapidly with almost no cash reserves and few assets, bought goods on extended credit terms, borrowed from secondary financial institutions at excessively high rates of interest, and engaged in other practices that indicated serious financial weakness. One of the most unstable aspects of the discount industry was real estate promotion, because in order to develop shopping centers, real estate developers had established thinly financed discount operations made up entirely of lease departments. In 1961, for example, a survey of 200 discounters by Dun and Bradstreet revealed that 25 percent had debts that averaged three and a half times their net worth. The intensive competition that characterized discounting during this period led to a wave of business failures in 1962 and 1963. Due to their instability, the marginal operators were the leading casualties of this retrenchment, although some famous names also were eliminated. In 1962, according to Dun and Bradstreet, 146 discounters failed, with total liabilities of $74 million, and 158 discounters disappeared in 1963, with liabilities that amounted to almost $60 million. In 1964 there were only 94 bankruptcies, with a combined liability of $21.8 million, as the shakeout eased. By 1965 the discount industry was healthy once again.[39]

Despite the failure of many poorly managed or financed firms, the discount industry continued to expand in the mid-1960s. Total sales by the discount industry increased from $2 billion in 1960 to $15 billion in 1966. The increase in sales was due not only to the expansion in the number of stores but also to the rise in sales in existing stores. In 1966, for example, same-store sales were 4 percent higher than in 1965. Table 2-1 indicates the nation's leading discount firms in terms of sales volume by the mid-1960s.

Discount merchandising still included many small entrepreneurs in 1966, but their importance was declining as the industry was becoming

TABLE 2-1. The Ten Leading Discount Firms in 1965

COMPANY	NO. OF STORES	SALES (MILLIONS)
E. J. Korvette	40	$594
S. S. Kresge (K mart, Jupiter)	233	490
Interstate	63	372
Gibson Products	209	334
Zayre	80	276
GEM International	33	260
Vornado	25	258
Arlan's Department Stores	56	209
S. Klein Department Stores	10	196
J. M. Fields (Food Fair)	54	173

Source: *Discount Merchandiser* 6 (June 1966): 63.

increasingly dominated by the larger chains. Of the 895 firms that controlled the 3,503 stores in operation in that year, 469 operated only one store. More than 75 percent of the stores, moreover, were operated by firms that had no more than three outlets, but they accounted for only 28 percent of the discount industry's total sales volume in 1966. At the other end of the scale, 8 firms had 50 or more stores, accounting for a total of 704. The largest operator was Kresge, which had 273 K mart and Jupiter stores. Table 2-2 charts the growth of the discount industry during this period.

Table 2-2. Growth of the Discount Industry, 1960–1966

YEAR	NO. STORES AT YEAR-END	NET INCREASE	AVG. SIZE (SQ. FT.)	AVG. SALES PER STORE
1960	1,329	—	38,400	$1,480,000
1961	1,814	485	47,300	1,930,000
1962	2,363	549	53,200	2,920,000
1963	2,730	367	56,900	3,410,000
1964	2,951	221	58,800	3,643,000
1965	3,216	265	63,539	4,089,000
1966	3,503	287	64,585	4,285,211

Source: Milton P. Brown, William Applebaum, and Walter J. Salmon, *Strategy Problems of Mass Retailers and Wholesalers* (Homewood, Ill.: Richard D. Irwin, 1970), 741.

By the mid-1960s discounting was most firmly established in the Middle Atlantic and East North Central states, which had 43 percent of all the discount stores in the country. These stores accounted for a comparable share of all discount business. Discounting was least important in the East South Central and Mountain regions, which together had only about 10 percent of the nation's discount outlets. In the West South Central region—Arkansas, Louisiana, Texas, and Oklahoma—discounting fared little better, with about 9 percent of all discount stores located there and only 7 percent of discount sales. Of the 311 discount outlets in that region in 1966, 180 were in Texas, and 31 were in Arkansas.

Discounting was more important in some lines of goods than others. Discount stores were the nation's leading outlet for toys and children's and infant's apparel; they were the second most important retailers of sporting goods, automobile accessories, garden products, housewares, and domestics, and the third largest sellers of drugs and toiletries, jewelry and watches, women's wear, furniture, floor coverings, and shoes. Discount-store sales to the average family in 1966 amounted to $256, two-fifths of which went for clothing. Household needs accounted for about 10 percent of all discount-store purchases by the average family, and toys and sporting goods made up about 5 percent each.

Studies indicated that by 1966 discount stores were attracting a high percentage of the nation's shoppers. For nine cities, the average was 62 percent. More than three-fifths of all discount-store customers came from households that had an income between $5,000 and $10,000. The percentage of discount store customers who were college-educated was comparable to that of the general-merchandise chains, such as Sears, but less than that of the conventional department stores.[40]

Discount merchandising was but the last in a series of retailing innovations that had evolved in America since the late nineteenth century. First had come the department store and then, in order, the mail-order house, the chain store, the supermarket, and the discount store. All of these institutions were large-scale operations that rested on the development of mass markets capable of sustaining them. Department stores first appeared in the great eastern cities, where large concentrations of people made them feasible; mail-order houses grew in part because the railroads and commercial agriculture had come to rural America; the chain stores and supermarkets served markets created in part by the automobile; and, finally, the growth of discount merchandising was based on the expansion of the nation's consumer market in the years following World War II.[41]

By the early 1960s discount merchandising had become an integral and dynamic segment of the nation's retail industry. As such, discounting had begun to have a significant impact on existing retail institutions.

Like other merchants before him who had been forced to adapt when their businesses had been threatened by new forms of retailing, Sam Walton would be compelled to come to terms with this latest innovation in the history of American retailing.

3

The Birth of Wal-Mart

WHILE HE WAS building his chain of variety stores, Sam Walton had kept abreast of the latest developments in the retail industry. He was aware of the growing influence of discount merchandising, and he foresaw its potentially negative impact on his business. "I could see that the variety store was gradually dying because there were giant supermarkets and then discounters coming into the picture," he recalled years later.[1]

The threat that discounting posed to Walton's variety stores, combined with his innate fascination with innovative retailing ideas, spurred Walton to undertake a thorough investigation of discount merchandising. From 1960 to 1962 Walton examined several of the major discount operations in the country. He began in the Northeast with a visit to the mill store Ann and Hope, where he talked with Martin and Irwin Chase. On subsequent trips to the region he investigated other discount operations, such as E. J. Korvette, Two Guys from Harrison, Spartan's, Zayre, Giant Stores, Mammoth Mart, and Arlan's. Walton also called on closed-door discounters on the West Coast, where he was particularly impressed by the discounting expertise of Sol Price, the founder of Fed-Mart. According to one of the discounters whom he met, Walton presented himself as a "little country boy from Arkansas" and then proceeded to glean as much information about discount merchandising as he possibly could. During these visits Walton observed that discounting could be a lucrative enterprise if one had the requisite modest overhead expenses, low retail prices, and efficient distribution.[2]

Walton's fear that discount merchandising soon would encroach on his area of trade became a reality when Gibson Products Company entered northwest Arkansas by establishing outlets in Fort Smith and later in Fayetteville, a move that placed the discount operation in direct competition with one of Walton's variety stores. Headquartered at Seagoville, Texas, some 20 miles south of Dallas, Gibson Products was the parent company of Gibson's Discount Center retail outlets. The company had been founded by Herbert R. Gibson, Sr., a native of Berryville, Arkansas, who in 1932 had opened a wholesale business in Little Rock. In 1935 he had left Little Rock for Dallas, where he became a wholesale distributor of health and beauty aids. By 1958 he was operating 34 wholesale houses in 10 states, but by that time he had become convinced that the wholesale business had little future. As a consequence, in that same year he had begun to convert his wholesale houses into discount retail outlets, starting with his operation in Abilene, Texas.

In addition to operating his own discount outlets, Gibson began to grant franchises to independent merchants who in his judgment possessed the proper experience and adequate financial resources to ensure success. Gibson Products Company collected from its franchisees a monthly fee. In return, Gibson franchisees received the use of the Gibson's name as well as the company's assistance in a variety of areas, such as store management, site selection, merchandising, and advertising. The parent company also produced store fixtures, which it sold to its franchisees. Most important, the franchisees were able to benefit from the volume discounts received by their parent company because it bought merchandise in large quantities from manufacturers. The shipment of goods directly from manufacturers to the larger franchisees in the chain enabled those merchants to enjoy an even greater savings on the cost of their merchandise.

Herbert R. Gibson defined his company as a "country operation," and many of his stores were located in small cities of 20,000 to 50,000 in population. Gibson's customers were mainly middle- and lower-class shoppers who required serviceable merchandise at an economical price. The firm's outlets, such as the one in Fayetteville, were austere operations that conformed to the company's operating credo: "Buy it low, stack it high, sell it cheap." Gibson's stores handled mainly hard goods, such as sporting goods, small appliances, jewelry, and automotive and lawn-care supplies. Those kinds of products, which amounted to some 75 percent of all sales, generally carried brand names that were regionally or nationally advertised. Apparel departments emphasized staple goods, devoted little or no attention to style, and sold a lot of irregulars. During the late 1960s some Gibson's stores carried dry groceries, and a few experimented with fresh meat and produce as well as frozen foods and dairy products.

During the 1960s the chain grew dramatically. In 1964, for example, there were 138 Gibson's Discount Centers, with total sales of $190 million; only four years later those numbers had climbed to 434 stores and $1 billion. Of the total number of stores, 30 were owned by the Gibson family, and the others were franchise operations. Some franchisees had single stores, but there were 58 multi-unit companies among the Gibson franchisees during that period. The size of the stores varied greatly, from 5,000 to 90,000 square feet. Franchisees paid monthly fees of $200 for stores up to 28,000 square feet and $250 for larger stores.

By 1971 the firm was the second largest discounter in the country, with 583 stores located in 34 states in the South and Midwest. Fifty-three were owned by the Gibson family and 530 were franchise operations, the fees from which earned the Gibsons some $1.2 million in that year alone. The chain continued to grow during the 1970s until it reached a maximum of 684 units in 1978. In that same year, however, Gibson Products began to decline rapidly as some multistore franchisees, such as the 74-unit Pamida, Inc., of Omaha, Nebraska, the largest Gibson licensee, began to withdraw from the chain.[3]

During his years in small-town retailing Walton had come to know well the shopping habits of the consumers in his market area. In Berryville, Arkansas, for example, residents had to travel to the neighboring towns of Fayetteville or Harrison to do routine shopping and even farther, to the cities of Little Rock or Springfield, Missouri, to make major purchases. Based on the success of his variety stores and, in particular, his Family Centers, Walton believed that in small towns such as Berryville a large store that offered a wide selection of merchandise at low prices would appeal to shoppers. "If we offered prices as good or better than stores in cities that were four hours away by car, people would shop at home," Walton recalled thinking.

In fact, Walton was becoming increasingly convinced that for operators of large stores, small towns were an untapped market that offered certain unique advantages. First, existing competition was limited. Major retail chains such as Sears and J. C. Penney were ignoring their outlets in country towns, preferring instead to concentrate their efforts in their new giant stores in shopping centers near major cities, and local merchants would not be able to compete with a large store in price or selection. Second, if a store were large enough to dominate business in a town and its surrounding area, other retailers would be discouraged from entering the market.[4]

Such logic convinced Walton that discounting could succeed in northwest Arkansas, and he resolved to open a discount operation somewhere in the area. With his new venture Walton desired to remain a franchisee of what had been Butler Brothers and was now part of City Products Corporation so that he could rely on its merchandising and distribution systems to stock his discount operation. Walton believed that such an arrangement would enable him to make a smooth transition into discounting, but he realized that it would necessitate a drastic change in business priorities for the Ben Franklin stores' new parent company.[5]

In December 1959 Butler Brothers had sold its entire retail operation, including the Ben Franklin and TG&Y variety-store chains, to City Products Corporation, an Ohio company, for $53 million and the assumption of certain liabilities. The acquisition was completed in February 1960. City Products had gotten started in the 1890s as the Independent Ice Company. It had changed its name to the City Ice and Fuel Company in 1921 and had become City Products Company in 1949. At the time that it acquired Butler Brothers' retail chains, City Products manufactured and distributed industrial and railroad ice in several East Coast cities, operated a coal and fuel business, and owned dairy-products operations in several states and an oil refinery in Texas. The company also owned breweries in Cleveland, New Orleans, and Granite City, Illinois. In 1959 City Products possessed substantial money from the sale of some of its assets. The firm desired to spend its cash holdings in a business acquisition and selected Butler Brothers because of its confidence in the company's growth potential and management quality.

After the sale of its retail operation to City Products, Butler Brothers became the B. T. L. Corporation. The firm possessed some $35 million in cash, and its leadership wanted to return to retailing. It did so by purchasing from the H. L. Green Company 72 percent of United Stores, a firm that controlled McCrory-McLellan Stores, a chain of 451 variety stores in 36 states. In March 1960 McCrory-McLellan joined with the B. T. L. Company and United Stores to form the McCrory Corporation.

Following its acquisition of Butler Brothers' retail operation, City Products inaugurated a program designed to strengthen and expand what was known as the Butler Brothers division, which in 1959 consisted of 269 company-owned and 2,432 franchised variety stores located in all 50 states and the District of Columbia, and 7 department stores. With the Ben Franklin stores, for example, the firm launched a merchandising and promotional program designed to enhance the overall operation of the chain.[6]

Early in 1962 Walton went to Chicago to meet with the executives of the Butler Brothers division of City Products Corporation. He told the executives that he believed a full-scale discount operation could succeed in small towns where Ben Franklin variety stores were located just as they did in urban markets. He indicated that he intended to open such a store in Arkansas and requested that Butler Brothers franchise the venture. He then explained to the startled executives that for his plan to succeed, Butler Brothers would be compelled to reduce the standard margin of 20 to 25 percent on the merchandise it sold to its franchisees to approximately 12.5 percent on the goods it sold to him. Because Butler Brothers' priority at the time was the improvement of its variety-store chains, Walton's proposal of a radical retail departure, combined with his requirement that the company cut its margins virtually in half, was more than the executives could bear. "They blew up!" Walton later revealed. "They just couldn't see the philosophy."[7]

Walton next decided to attempt to affiliate himself with Gibson Products Company either by becoming a franchisee and operating under the Gibson banner or by entering into a merchandising agreement that would allow him to purchase his goods through Gibson's volume-buying program. He traveled to Gibson's headquarters, where he was peremptorily rebuffed by Herbert Gibson, Sr., who viewed Walton as a bush-league variety-store merchant who possessed neither the finances nor the experience necessary to succeed in the Gibson chain.[8]

Twice rebuffed in his efforts to affiliate himself with an existing business, Walton realized that opening a discount store would entail assembling, on his own, a comprehensive organization for buying and receiving merchandise, as well as for selling it. He no doubt found the magnitude of such an undertaking daunting, but he reasoned that he had to forge ahead because, he said, I "really had only two choices left: stay in the variety store business, which I knew was going to be hit hard by the discounting wave of the future; or open a discount store."

Walton decided on the latter course of action and set about finding a suitable location. After studying potential sites, he and his chief banker, James H. Jones of the Republic National Bank of Dallas, selected Rogers, Arkansas. Walton long had been impressed with the business climate of Rogers but had been unable to open a Ben Franklin variety store there because the franchise was owned by someone else. Walton approached the local Ben Franklin merchant and urged him to become a partner in building the new discount store, but he declined. The retailer's reaction was typical, for skeptics abounded regarding Walton's discounting venture. As Walton recounted in his autobiography, "Nobody wanted to gamble on that first Wal-Mart." Since he could not find a significant investor, Walton was compelled to finance the store himself, which plunged him deeply into debt. "We pledged houses and property, everything we had," he recalled. "But in those days we were always borrowed to the hilt." He put up 95 percent of the money needed to launch the enterprise; his brother Bud, who was chary of the idea, invested 3 percent; and the store's manager, Don Whitaker, whom Walton had hired from a TG&Y in Abilene, Texas, invested the remaining 2 percent.[9]

The store opened on 2 July 1962, in a 16,000-square-foot building constructed for Walton by a local real estate agent. Spelled out in huge letters across the front of Walton's new enterprise was the name Wal-Mart Discount City, an amalgam of Walton's name and the word *mart*, a place where goods are sold. Bob Bogle, the first manager of Walton's Bentonville variety store, had suggested the name to Walton, who liked it because of its similarity to Sol Price's Fed-Mart, an operation he greatly admired. On either side of the logo were slogans that would become two of the guiding principles of the firm: "We sell for less" and "Satisfaction guaranteed."[10]

Inside the store, merchandise was grouped into 22 departments: jewelry; drugs; books; hobbies; hair care; toys; curtains and accessories; paint and equipment; sewing needs; automobile supplies; sporting goods; clothing for boys, girls, ladies, and men; infant needs; piece goods; housewares; shoes; small appliances; gifts; and home furnishings. Except for a few racks for soft goods, tables were the store's main fixtures. There were three checkout stands, one of which was the "express" lane for shoppers with fewer than five items. At the outset, the store's staff numbered 25, and clerks were paid 50 to 60 cents an hour, substantially below the minimum wage.

To promote the opening of the store, newspaper advertisements announced that the discount operation represented a new phase in the "ever-changing field of retailing" that had swept the country in recent years. In one advertisement Don Whitaker stated that Wal-Mart would "offer everyday low prices in all departments," which he maintained represented savings of up to 50 percent on brand-name merchandise. He explained that Wal-Mart was able to offer consumers these discount prices as a result of buying in bulk and because "We have been able to cut out the middleman. Most of our goods are purchased directly from the manufacturer, allowing us to pass on our savings to the consumer."[11]

The advertisements called attention to the store's grand-opening sale, which was to be held from 2 July through 7 July, and compared Wal-Mart's prices with manufacturers' suggested retail prices. For example, a Sunbeam automatic coffeemaker, $19.95 in conventional outlets, was advertised at $13.47, a 32 percent reduction in price; a Sunbeam iron, regularly $17.95, was priced at $11.88, a savings of 34 percent; a Polaroid camera, regularly priced at $100.00, was advertised at $74.37, a 26 percent reduction in price; and a lawn mower, usually $59.95, was $37.77, a savings of 37 percent. Promised savings on drugs were 20 percent or more, and prices of dresses, coats, suits, sportswear, blouses, and lingerie were from one-third to one-half off. Prices remained at about the same level even after the grand-opening sale ended. A General Electric portable mixer, for example, sold for $9.86, 51 percent below list price; Geritol tonic, regularly priced at $1.19, was 97 cents; and a Wilson fielder's glove, $10.80 elsewhere, was $5.97.[12]

Like other discount operations of that era, the Rogers store placed great emphasis on health and beauty aids. Using the merchandise as a promotional device known as a "loss-leader," Walton and other discounters would price health and beauty aids at a "loss," or lower than the standard discount markup, to draw customers to their stores, and then stack the products high to attract the attention of shoppers.

In the newspaper advertisements, customers had been assured that every item in the store was backed by the manufacturer's guarantee. They also had been promised "first-quality merchandise. There's [sic] no seconds or factory rejects in the store—our policy forbids it." In reality, however, the quality of much of the store's merchandise was poor, largely because Walton had to buy goods from whoever was willing to sell to him. Some major manufacturers refused outright to do business with Walton because he was a discounter, while others would "dictate how much they would sell us and at what price," he recalled. "We were the victims of a good bit of arrogance from a lot of vendors in those days. They didn't need us, and they acted that way." Walton did manage to purchase some goods directly from the manufacturers, such as paper products, but he had to buy many other products from wholesalers. He had no established network of suppliers when he began, but he was able to procure enough merchandise from a distributor in Springfield, Missouri, to get his store open.[13]

The store was successful from the outset; the grand opening alone attracted "tens of thousands" of customers, according to Walton. Sales the first year were $700,000. Two years after the store opened, Walton enlarged it by 4,000 square feet; after additional expansions in 1968 and 1969, the store contained 35,000 square feet of space. During these years, the store's sales volume increased about 30 percent annually. In 1974 the store was relocated across the street in a new 60,000-square-foot building, and it generated $5.4 million in sales volume.[14]

The year 1962 represented a watershed in the evolution of discount merchandising in America. In addition to Wal-Mart, three other important discount chains, K mart, Woolco, and Target, were launched. It also marked the beginning of a two-year period of industry retrenchment during which many arrivistes failed, along with a few long-standing firms. Walton was personally acquainted with several of the discounters who had enjoyed initial success only to see their companies falter, and he noted the tendency on the part of some to spend money and time in the pursuit of a lavish lifestyle to the detriment of their business:

> "Most of these early guys were very egotistical people who loved to drive
> big Cadillacs and fly around in their jets and vacation on their yachts, and

some of them lived in houses like I'd never seen before. . . . Man, they were living high. And they could afford to back then because this discounting thing was working so well. Customers just flocked to their stores, and these fellows were covered up in cash. Most of them could still be around today if they had followed some basic principles about running good stores. . . . Maybe it wasn't the Cadillacs and the yachts, maybe they just decided it wasn't worth it. But whatever it was, they just didn't stay close enough to their business . . . .[15]

Clearly, Walton was determined to profit from their example. He had no intention of allowing profligate spending or neglect to place his business in jeopardy.

Despite the upheaval in the discount industry as a whole, the success of Walton's enterprise in Rogers encouraged him to open another Wal-Mart, and in August 1964 he opened his second unit in Harrison, Arkansas, a town with a population of approximately 6,000, located some 80 miles east of Rogers. Walton located his store in a vacant building on a site that previously had been used as a cattle-auction yard. The outlet had no amenities. It was only 12,000 square feet in size, with an eight-foot ceiling and a concrete floor. Its fixtures were wooden planks that had been taken from a bankrupt variety store. It even lacked rest rooms.

For the grand opening of the Harrison store, Walton revealed a flair for promotional exploits designed to appeal to rural shoppers that later would become an integral part of Wal-Mart's homespun advertising style. On that fateful day in Harrison, however, Walton's plans went awry. Wal-Mart's future president and chief executive officer, David D. Glass, who at the time was affiliated with a drugstore chain in Missouri, attended the grand opening of the store and described the debacle: "Sam had brought a couple of trucks of watermelons in and stacked them on the sidewalk. He had a donkey ride out in the parking lot. It was about 115 degrees, and the watermelons began to pop, and the donkey began to do what donkeys do, and it all mixed together and ran all over the parking lot. And when you went inside the store, the mess just continued, having been tracked in all over the floor. He was a nice fellow, but I wrote him off. It was just terrible."[16]

Everything did seem to go wrong for Walton at the grand opening of the Harrison store—everything but business, that is. The facility may have been unsightly, but customers flocked to the store because of prices that were 20 percent below those of competitors. The success of the Harrison store would have a significant impact on Walton's fledgling discount enterprise. It would supply a portion of the funds for several other stores and would serve as a training ground for many future managers and other executives, causing one company officer later to note, "There wouldn't be a Wal-Mart Company today if this store [in Harrison] had failed."[17]

Later in 1964 Walton opened a 35,000-square-foot store in Springdale, a town also near Rogers. This large store soon became the leader of the three in sales volume. At this point, Walton was convinced that his concept of discounting in small towns was a sound one, but he feared that other discount chains might come to the same conclusion and begin to enter the smaller communities in his market area, towns that could sustain only one large discount operation. He therefore resolved to establish Wal-Marts as rapidly as earnings and credit would permit. He opened 1 store in 1965, 2 stores a year in 1966 and 1967, and 5 a year in 1968 and 1969, for a total of 18 Wal-Marts by the end of the decade. Eleven of the stores were in Arkansas; the others were in Missouri and Oklahoma, which the firm entered in 1968 (see Table 3-1).[18]

Walton's expansion of Wal-Mart corresponded with the continued growth of the discount industry overall during the late 1960s. By the end of the decade, discount merchandising occupied a significant place in American retailing. During the 1960s the sales of the discount industry caught up with and exceeded those of department stores, rising from

TABLE 3-1. Early Wal-Mart Stores

LOCATION	YEAR OPENED	SIZE IN 1969 (SQ. FT.)
Rogers, Ark.	1962	35,000
Harrison, Ark.	1964	26,000
Springdale, Ark.	1964	35,000
Siloam Springs, Ark.	1965	32,500
Conway, Ark.	1966	22,000
Fayetteville, Ark.	1966	32,000
North Little Rock, Ark.	1967	44,000
Morrilton, Ark.	1967	11,000
Sikeston, Mo.	1968	25,000
Tahlequah, Okla.	1968	25,000
Mountain Home, Ark.	1968	18,000
Claremore, Okla.	1968	31,500
Carthage, Mo.	1968	30,000
Lebanon, Mo.	1969	30,300
West Plains, Mo.	1969	31,200
Van Buren, Ark.	1969	27,500
Neosho, Mo.	1969	30,000
Newport, Ark.	1969	30,000

Source: Wal-Mart Stores, Inc., Preliminary Prospectus, filed with the U.S. Securities and Exchange Commission 30 March 1970, 8.

$15 billion in 1966 to $22.2 billion in 1970. There were 4,635 discount outlets nationwide at the end of 1969, and they were operated by 917 different companies, roughly half of which had only one store. The great bulk of the discount business was in the hands of firms that had 10 or more stores, and there were 62 firms with sales of $50 million or more.[19]

During his early years as a discounter, out of necessity Walton's operation of Wal-Mart was haphazard. He used no modern market surveys, for example, to aid him in selecting desirable communities for his stores; he merely went to a prospective town and counted the number of automobiles on the main street or the public square. Walton moved from his variety-store office to three small rooms located over a lawyer's office and the barbershop on the square in Bentonville, and from these cramped quarters he and a small staff ran the firm. Even with several stores in operation, the company continued to lack an established network of sources for goods and was compelled to buy whatever was available. As a consequence, the nature and assortment of Wal-Mart's merchandise remained inferior, although the firm gradually managed to improve the quality of its goods as large manufacturers became increasingly willing to do business with it.

Because construction costs and rent had to be kept to a minimum, Walton continued to house several of his early stores in primitive facilities. Wal-Mart number eight, for example, in Morrilton, Arkansas, was located in an abandoned Coca-Cola bottling plant. When it opened, the store had pipes sticking out of the floor and no air-conditioning. Although window fans provided some modicum of cool air, in the summer the temperature inside the facility became so hot that chocolate candy could not be stocked because it would melt. Walton also economized on fixtures in the early Wal-Marts, which meant that merchandise display often was crude at best. The Morrilton store, for example, was furnished with old fixtures from a failed Gibson's; shelves were attached to the walls with wire, and clothes were hung in layers on conduit pipes all the way to the ceiling. During this era essential equipment also was in short supply. At the grand openings of some of the early stores, for example, clerks had to use cigar boxes for cash registers.

Despite such shortcomings, Wal-Mart succeeded from the outset, primarily because of Walton's focus on low prices. While he was willing to forgo some of the embellishments of retailing, Walton would not compromise on his commitment to offer customers prices lower than those of his competitors, whose stores he and his managers visited incessantly. His formula for achieving this goal was to sell his goods for a markup that never exceeded 30 percent. Clarence Leis, the second manager of the first Wal-Mart, described Walton's method for keeping his prices low:

"Merchandise would come in and we would just lay it down on the floor and get out the invoice. Sam wouldn't let us hedge on a price at all. Say the list price was $1.98, but we had only paid 50 cents. Initially, I would say, 'Well, it's originally $1.98, so why don't we sell it for $1.25?' And he'd say, 'No. We paid 50 cents for it. Mark it up 30 percent, and that's it. No matter what you pay for it, if we get a great deal, pass it on to the customer.'"

By the end of the decade Walton had made significant improvements in the operation of his growing firm, using K mart as a model for many of the changes. In addition to the repeated enlargements of the Rogers store, in 1969 he relocated and enlarged the store in Siloam Springs and enlarged the store in Claremore. By this time all of the stores, except one that was scheduled to be relocated, were air-conditioned and contained modern equipment and fixtures. Up until 1969 the company had obtained most of its store fixtures under five-year lease-purchase agreements; thereafter, it purchased them outright. The newer stores even had carpeting in the clothing areas.[20]

Walton's 18 Wal-Mart Discount City stores ranged in size from approximately 18,000 to 44,000 square feet (one unit had only 11,000 square feet), and in each approximately 85 to 90 percent of the building area was devoted to selling space. With the exception of the North Little Rock store, the units were located in small communities of 5,000 to 25,000 people. These towns were smaller than the communities in which most major discount chains were located. The firm asserted that in all but one of its locations, Wal-Mart was the largest nonfood retailer in the community.

The stores were located in leased facilities, most of which had been built to the company's specifications. Some were freestanding with their own parking area; others were in shopping centers. The rents paid by the company for half of the stores were fixed annual sums; for the other half, rents were a percentage of sales. For fiscal 1970 (Wal-Mart's fiscal years end on January 31) total rent was approximately $500,000—an average of 97 cents a square foot. Landlords were responsible for real estate taxes, insurance, and exterior maintenance.

Wal-Mart stores were open from 9:00 to 9:00, six days a week. Those in Oklahoma also were open on Sunday afternoons from 1:00 to 6:00. Shopping was self-service, with sales personnel available to assist customers. Purchases were made on a cash-and-carry basis, although the firm honored national credit cards, which in 1969 accounted for approximately 3 percent of sales. The stores carried a wide assortment of department-store merchandise. Hard goods included housewares and home furnishings, hardware and paint, small appliances, automobile accessories, garden equipment and supplies, toys, sporting goods, photography equipment, health and beauty aids, and jewelry. Major categories of soft goods included wearing apparel for men, women, and children; shoes; handbags; and curtains and draperies. Except for clothing, most of the merchandise consisted of nationally advertised brands. Only a limited number of lines carried the company's own name. By 1970 the firm was leasing 17 footwear, 13 jewelry, and 2 pharmacy departments. The distribution of sales by category of goods is shown in Table 3-2.

TABLE 3-2. Distribution of Sales by Category, as of 31 January 1970

PRODUCT CATEGORY	PERCENT OF SALES
Soft goods	33
Hard goods (hardware, housewares, auto supplies, small appliances)	18
Sporting goods and toys	13
Health and beauty aids	10
Stationery and candy	7
Photography and miscellaneous items	7
Gifts, records, and electronics	5
Footwear	5
Jewelry	2

Source: Wal-Mart Stores, Inc., Preliminary Prospectus, filed with the U.S. Securities and Exchange Commission 30 March 1970, 8.

Because Wal-Mart experienced competition from department stores, specialty stores, drugstores, and other discount chains, management deemed low prices and customer satisfaction crucial to its success. With the exception of the "negligible" amount of goods covered by fair-trade laws, the company endeavored to sell all of its merchandise below the manufacturers' suggested retail prices and to meet or undersell the prices of competitors. The firm asserted that its prices were uniform throughout the chain except where it was necessary to lower prices to meet local competition. To fulfill its commitment to customer satisfaction, the company offered an "unconditional money back guarantee" on all of the items it sold.[21]

Walton realized that the efficient distribution of merchandise was central to the firm's stated objective of "maximizing sales volume and inventory turnover with minimum overhead expense." He knew that

K mart and Woolco enjoyed the benefit of using the same large distribution systems that supplied their thousands of variety stores, but he lacked access to such a system because no major distributors were willing to supply his remote market area. Nor were trucking companies, which gave excellent service to Memphis, Kansas City, and St. Louis, accustomed to providing frequent service to the country towns in which Walton's discount stores were located. Under these circumstances, Walton determined that the only way to ensure a cost-effective, reliable means of supplying his stores was to construct his own distribution facility. "In the boondocks, we didn't have the distributors falling over themselves to serve us," he said. "Our only alternative was to build a warehouse so we could buy in volume."[22]

In November 1969 construction was completed on a 72,000-square-foot general headquarters building on a 12.5-acre site with a rail siding, about a mile south of downtown Bentonville. Walton apparently never considered establishing his headquarters elsewhere. Years later, when asked why he stayed in Bentonville, he responded: "Move from Bentonville? That would be the last thing we [would] do unless they run us out. The best thing we ever did was to hide back there in the hills and eventually build a company that makes folks want to find us. They get there sometimes with a lot of trepidation and problems, but we like where we are. It's because of the work ethic, because of the chemistry of the people up there and the support we get. We're much better off than if we had gone to Chicago."

The facility, which cost $525,000 to build, housed a 60,000-square-foot distribution center and 12,000 square feet of office space. The distribution center was intended to supply a constant flow of goods to the Wal-Mart stores, all of which were located within a 250-mile radius of Bentonville. The availability of rail service facilitated buying in quantity and cut freight costs. At the outset, management estimated that the distribution center would handle about 40 percent of the company's merchandise.[23]

During the 1960s Walton began recruiting competent executives to assist in managing the company's increasingly diverse affairs. He would pay his executive officers well, but in return he exacted grueling effort from them. In 1965 he hired Ferold G. Arend to oversee store operations; Arend had been the regional manager in Omaha for the J. J. Newberry chain of variety stores. In 1969 he hired the young Ronald M. Mayer, who had been the chief financial officer at A. L. Duckwall Company, a variety-store chain headquartered in Abilene, Kansas. Mayer would design the centralized distribution process by which all Wal-Mart merchandise was received at the distribution center, where it was assembled and then sent to the various outlets, as well as the firm's first data processing program.[24]

Although Walton was devoting an increasing amount of attention to his discount operation, he continued to operate his chain of variety stores. From its peak of 16 units in 1962 the number of variety stores had declined to 14 by 1965, the year in which Walton opened a fifteenth unit, a Ben Franklin store in Columbia, Missouri—reportedly the largest variety store in the nation. Walton's remaining Ben Franklin and Family Center variety stores were located in Waynesville, Lebanon, Versailles, Boonville, and Kansas City, Missouri; Bentonville, Rogers, Fayetteville, Springdale, Harrison, North Little Rock, and Camden, Arkansas; and Coffeeville and Neodesha, Kansas. He continued to operate his variety stores under franchise agreement with City Products Corporation, which in 1965 was acquired by the Chicago-based Household Finance Corporation. As the retail division of Household Finance, City Products Corporation's mission was to strengthen the Ben Franklin franchised variety chain.[25]

By 1969 the number of units in Walton's variety-store chain had decreased to 14. Of the 9 Ben Franklin units in the chain, 4 were located in Arkansas, 3 in Missouri, and 2 in Kansas. The stores ranged from 4,200 to 7,000 square feet in size and carried the kinds of medium- and low-priced merchandise typical of such outlets. Six of the Ben Franklin units were located in shopping centers, and 3 were in downtown areas. Of the 5 Family Center stores in the chain, 3 were located in Arkansas and 2 in Missouri; all were in shopping centers. Three of these units had originated as Ben Franklin stores and later had been expanded into the larger Family Center units, which ranged in size from 11,000 to 18,000 square feet. The Family Center stores were smaller in size than the Wal-Mart stores, and they generally were located in markets considered too small for a Wal-Mart. The Family Centers offered merchandise that was similar in range and quality to Wal-Mart's, but the selection was more limited. Most of the merchandise was discounted, and margins were midway between those of the Ben Franklin and the Wal-Mart stores.

The importance to the company of the Ben Franklin and Family Center variety stores declined as the number of Wal-Mart outlets increased. In fiscal 1967, for example, the variety stores contributed 42 percent of the firm's sales and 57 percent of its income. Three years later those percentages had fallen to 20 and 26, respectively (see Table 3-3).

Walton's franchise agreement with City Products Corporation was similar to the one originally formulated by Butler Brothers. It required the variety stores to purchase up to 80 percent of their merchandise from

TABLE 3-3. The Changing Character of Walton's Company,
Fiscal 1966–1970

YEAR	TOTAL No. STORES	No. WAL-MART STORES	No. VARIETY STORES	PERCENTAGE OF INCOME, WAL-MART STORES
1966	16	4	12	NA
1967	19	6	13	43
1968	24	8	16	53
1969	27	13	14	59
1970	32	18	14	74

Source: Wal-Mart Stores, Inc., Preliminary Prospectus, filed with the U.S. Securities and Exchange Commission 30 March 1970, 5, 7.

City Products and to pay an annual franchise fee of $1,500 per store. City Products allowed discounts of 2 to 4 percent on the purchase of merchandise, depending on sales volume. In fiscal 1970, for example, Walton's variety stores purchased goods valued at $2.7 million and received the largest discount. During that same year Walton was also leasing eight variety-store locations from City Products Corporation.[26]

By the end of the decade Walton's total workforce numbered 650 full-time and 150 part-time employees, most of whom were sales staff. Included among the full-time workers were 9 supervisors and buyers, 33 store managers, 45 assistant managers, 528 salespeople, and 35 employees in accounting and clerical positions. Supervisory and managerial employees received salaries; in addition, store managers earned a bonus based on store performance. All other workers were paid on an hourly basis. In early 1970 the firm instituted a stock-option plan, but only corporate officers and "key employees" were eligible to participate. All full-time employees were covered by medical insurance. The company reported that it had suffered no work stoppages and that it considered its employee relations to be good.[27]

Walton's company had performed well during the 1960s. The combined number of units in his variety- and discount-store chains had doubled from fiscal 1966 to 1970, and both net sales and net income had shown gains of about 400 percent, as indicated in Table 3-4.

Based on such success, Walton concluded that his discount operation was capable of a more vigorous pace of growth than available funds permitted. Although existing stores had generated some of the money for past expansions, it had not been nearly enough, and Walton had

TABLE 3-4. Financial Results, Fiscal 1966–1970

	1966	1967	1968	1969	1970
Stores in operation	16	19	24	27	32
Net sales	$6,246	$9,279	$12,619	$21,365	$30,863
Total revenue	6,277	9,332	12,703	21,515	31,085
Costs and expenses	5,970	8,780	11,923	20,459	28,886
Income before taxes	307	552	780	1,056	2,199
Net income	247	394	506	651	1,239

Note: Amounts shown are in thousands of dollars
(the last three zeroes have been omitted).

Source: Wal-Mart Stores, Inc., Prospectus, filed with the U.S. Securities and Exchange Commission 1 October 1970, 5.

been compelled to borrow heavily over the years to finance the growth of the chain. To obtain the amount of operating capital he needed for future expansion, Walton realized he had no recourse other than a public sale of stock. In preparation for such a move the firm was incorporated as Wal-Mart, Inc., in Delaware on 31 October 1969. At that time the company was authorized to issue 10,000 shares of preferred stock with no par value and an equal number of shares of common stock with a par value of one dollar. (Par value is a fixed dollar amount per share of stock, specified by a corporate charter, that represents the amount of capital that legally must be maintained by a company for the protection of creditors.) On 2 January 1970 the certificate of incorporation was amended to allow the firm to change its name to Wal-Mart Stores, Inc., and to increase its capital stock to 500,000 shares of preferred stock and 3 million shares of common stock, both with a par value of 10 cents.[28]

Incorporation permitted Walton to reorganize thoroughly his business concerns. Prior to 1 February 1970, Walton's variety stores, Family Centers, and discount stores had been operated by corporations or partnerships owned directly or indirectly in varying proportions by Sam and Bud Walton, their relatives, trusts for their children, and various employees of the company. As an aspect of incorporation, Sam Walton established Walton Enterprises, Inc., an Arkansas corporation of which Walton himself owned 40 percent and his wife owned the remaining 60 percent as a trustee of their four children's trusts. On 1 February 1970 the newly formed Walton Enterprises, Bud Walton, and the others who held interests in the various properties transferred their holdings to Wal-Mart Stores, Inc., in exchange for all of the 1.3 million shares of common stock then outstanding. Of that amount, 300,000 shares, approximately 23 percent, were to be offered for public sale. Of the approximately 1 million shares remaining, company personnel and Walton relatives received approximately 8 percent, and Sam and Bud Walton and their families retained ownership of 69 percent, an amount that ensured their ability to maintain firm control of the company. In 1972, 31 Arkansas, Missouri, and Oklahoma corporations were merged into Wal-Mart Stores, Inc.[29]

Incorporation also necessitated changes in the managerial structure of the firm. A board of directors was elected; its members were Sam Walton, Bud Walton, Ferold Arend, Ronald Mayer, James H. Jones, H. L. Remmel, and Jackson T. Stephens. Serving as the firm's corporate officers were Sam Walton, chairman of the board and president of the company; Bud Walton, senior vice president; Arend, executive vice president; Mayer, vice president and treasurer; Don Whitaker, vice president of operations; Claude Harris, vice president of merchandise; James T. Henry, controller; and Rob Walton, secretary. Although a major figure in the firm, Bud Walton always remained in the shadow of his more outgoing brother, a role he quite obviously favored. He devoted most of his attention to building and real estate operations. Whitaker had been Wal-Mart's first store and regional manager. Harris had been with Sam Walton for ten years in the roles of store manager, buyer, and merchandise manager. A certified public accountant, Henry had been a manger of a local accounting firm before he joined Walton; he subsequently would return to private practice. Rob Walton was a member of a Tulsa law firm. Jones, Sam Walton's long-time financial adviser, was president of the National Bank of Commerce of New Orleans. Remmel and Stephens were representatives, respectively, of the institutional investment banking firms White, Weld & Company and Stephens, Inc.[30]

Stephens, Inc., of Little Rock, the largest and best-known financial house in Arkansas, agreed to underwrite the issue of Wal-Mart securities. The firm submitted the requisite materials to the U.S. Securities and Exchange Commission and scheduled the public sale of 300,000 shares for the spring of 1970. Wal-Mart did not intend to pay cash dividends on its common stock but rather to devote the funds to the development of the business. It planned to use approximately $1 million of the proceeds to retire short-term debts incurred in the process of incorporation and the subsequent reorganization. Some $1.6 million was to be spent for inventory, fixtures, and working capital for the opening of new stores, and most of the balance would be applied to the cost of the recently completed distribution center and its inventory.

Because the market was depressed in the spring of 1970, the Stephens brokerage house decided to delay the sale until later that year. Walton obtained a $2.5 million loan from the Massachusetts Mutual Insurance Company to finance Wal-Mart during the interim. He also recruited White, Weld & Company, a Wall Street firm that had earlier handled the securities of the Pamida discount chain, to join Stephens, Inc., in marketing the Wal-Mart stock. In preparation for the sale, Walton and representatives of the financial houses traveled to several major cities and met with groups of investors and money managers in an effort to stimulate interest. The sale took place on 1 October 1970. The stock, which sold over the counter at $16.50 a share, was well received, although not widely held. Among the approximately 800 shareholders were 44 financial houses in 17 cities from New York to San Francisco; White, Weld & Company bought 52,000 shares, and Stephens, Inc., took 30,000 shares. The stock sale generated a total of $4,950,000. After the underwriters' discount of $348,000, the remaining $4,602,000 went to the company. The stock continued to be traded over the counter until August 1972, when the company was listed on the New York Stock Exchange.[31]

After establishing his first Wal-Mart store in 1962, Walton had found that his idea of opening discount stores in small towns would work, and throughout the remainder of the decade he had steadily shifted the focus of his company away from his variety-store chain to his expanding discount-store chain. At the end of the decade Walton had culminated this restructuring with the consolidation of his business concerns into a single, publicly held corporation as a means of facilitating future growth. In the decade ahead, this action would furnish Walton with the financial resources to accelerate greatly the expansion of his discount operation. In the process, Wal-Mart Stores, Inc., would evolve from a four-state enterprise into a regional colossus.

4

A Billion-Dollar Baby: Wal-Mart during the 1970s

WAL-MART HAD BEEN successful during its formative years, but because the discount chain had remained nestled near its small-town base in the Ozarks, it was regarded by some business experts as little more than a "couturier to the hillbillies." By the end of the 1970s, however, the firm's spectacular growth would transform most scoffers into admirers of both Sam Walton and his company.[1]

Following its conversion into an incorporated, publicly owned firm, Wal-Mart Stores, Inc., expanded rapidly. In fiscal 1971, its first year as a new corporation, the company grew by 6 stores, reaching a total of 38 outlets, 25 of which were Wal-Mart stores and which reported net sales in excess of $44 million and net income of $1.7 million. Such accomplishments failed, however, to earn Wal-Mart a place on *Discount Merchandiser*'s roster of the nation's 71 largest discount firms in 1970, ranked by sales. The top five discounters on the list were K mart, with 488 outlets and sales of $2 billion, followed by Gibson Products Company, Zayre, E. J. Korvette, and Woolco.[2]

In the years that followed, Wal-Mart would add new stores, expand geographically, and register impressive gains in operating results. To accommodate its accelerating rate of growth, in fiscal 1971 the firm established a real estate and construction division to oversee the building of new stores. Its functions included acquiring the land on which the stores would be located, constructing the buildings, and arranging permanent financing for some locations. The properties were either retained by the company or, more commonly, sold to investors and leased back to Wal-Mart. The sale and lease-back arrangement afforded certain advantages: it was faster and more economical than using a developer; it permitted the company greater flexibility in choosing locations; it allowed Wal-Mart to develop a closer relationship with local banks; and it enabled the firm to avoid percentage-of-sales clauses in leases. Of the 25 stores that were built or expanded in fiscal 1974, for example, the real estate and construction division built 10, while lessors constructed 15.[3]

During the 1970s Walton steadily reduced the size of his chain of variety stores. In fiscal 1972 the number of variety stores declined to 12, and in fiscal 1973 the number was down to 10. In fiscal 1974, 2 more Ben Franklin stores were sold and 4 were closed, leaving only 4 variety stores in Walton's chain.[4]

Wal-Mart's growth during the early 1970s paralleled the growth of discount merchandising. As a result of dynamic expansion during the 1960s, discount merchandising had become the largest segment of the retail industry at the beginning of the 1970s, and it continued to grow dramatically during the early years of that decade. In 1973, for example, there were 160 discount chains with 6,500 outlets, and they sold $36 billion worth of goods to 38 million families. Discounting controlled 20 percent of the general-merchandise market, compared with 14 percent for conventional full-service department stores. Despite their success, however, in the mid-1970s discounters began to encounter serious problems. Intense competition came from within the discount industry and from mass merchandisers such as Sears and J. C. Penney. In addition, discounters were adversely affected by the recession of 1974–75 and by inflation. Inflation was especially hard on discounters. Their heating and cooling costs, interest payments, wages, and other overhead expenses increased as fast as the consumer price index, but because they competed so fiercely with one another, they could not always raise prices to keep pace with costs.[5]

In 1974 Sears continued to preside as the nation's leading retailer with annual sales of $13.1 billion, and K mart was the fifth largest with sales of $5.6 billion. The year was difficult for many retailers, as consumers, themselves beset by recession and inflation, postponed many purchases. This caused retail profits to fall, which in turn caused an overall decline in the value of retail stock. Among discounters, some chains were forced to initiate bankruptcy proceedings and others experienced a significant slowdown. Wal-Mart, however, had net sales for fiscal 1975 that had increased a healthy 41 percent over the previous year's to reach $236 million, with the leased shoe, jewelry, and pharmacy departments contributing another $20 million. This kind of success prompted one analyst to conclude that during such periods of "recession and merchandising gloom," Wal-Mart's sales were "nothing short of astonishing."[6]

Wal-Mart's net income for fiscal 1975, which was $6.4 million, also would have increased 41 percent (to $8.7 million) had the company not changed its method of determining inventory cost from a first-in, first-out (FIFO) system to a last-in, first-out (LIFO) system—a change that went into effect 31 January 1975. Under the LIFO method of inventory valuation, the cost of goods sold was based on the most recent prices of raw materials and other inventory items. Wal-Mart converted to this method because the company believed that it would make the firm's costs more accurately match revenue during inflationary periods and that it would generate better cash flow. Following the LIFO adjustment, the company's gross margin declined to 25.2 percent in fiscal 1975 from 26.4 percent in fiscal 1974. For fiscal 1975 total rent costs increased to 2.4 percent of sales from 2.2 percent the preceding year, due to the increase in expenses for buildings, data processing equipment, and trucks. An increase in the cost of acquiring new leases was reflected in the rise in building rentals, which went from 1.8 percent of sales in fiscal 1974 to 1.9 percent in 1975.[7]

Two of the new Wal-Mart units that opened in fiscal 1975 were located in Corinth, Mississippi, and Fulton, Kentucky, marking the firm's entry into those states. By the end of the year the company spanned eight states and consisted of 100 Wal-Mart Discount City stores, 2 Save-Co Building Supply and Home Improvement Centers, and 2 Family Center variety stores. Representing a new venture for the firm, the first Save-Co store had opened in March 1974 in Mountain Home, Arkansas. A second, larger store was opened a month later in Rogers, Arkansas. The two outlets, which had a total of 54,000 square feet, handled home-repair supplies and tools. The Family Centers were all that remained of Walton's variety-store chain. They were located in Bentonville and in Waynesville, Missouri, and were still operated under a franchise agreement with City Products Corporation, which, as the retail division of Household Finance Corporation, continued to strengthen the Ben Franklin variety chain by constructing new units.[8]

During the late 1970s the heightened competition within the retail industry and the weakened national economy continued to affect adversely many of the nation's retailers. One of the most spectacular reversals of the decade was the failure of the W. T. Grant Company in 1976. Significant also were the problems experienced by two of the nation's retail giants, Sears and K mart. When Sears transferred its head-quarters to the tallest building in the world in 1973, the move was symbolic. As the nation's leading retailer, Sears was the envy of its competitors. It obtained innovative products from its vendors at low cost; its mail-order catalog was the largest of its kind; its 860 stores, many located in modern suburban shopping centers, offered the epitome of shopping convenience; and it boasted a huge staff of more than 400,000 employees. For decades Sears's practice of advertising and selling at moderate prices merchandise that carried the Sears brand name as well as its own nationally branded products, such as Kenmore appliances and Craftsman tools, had created for the firm a large base of loyal customers who associated Sears's products with quality. During the early 1970s, however, increased competition from discount chains and a series of marketing mistakes made by the firm threw Sears into a prolonged slump. Earnings would begin to decline in 1973 and, except for small gains in 1975 and 1976, continue to erode for the remainder of the decade.

Sears first erred by attempting to lure a more affluent clientele into its solidly blue-collar customer base by stocking expensive, high-fashion merchandise, but higher-income shoppers showed little interest in purchasing clothing or jewelry carrying the Sears label. At the same time, Sears's traditional, lower-income customers disliked the higher prices and departed to discount operations such as K mart. Seeing its business decline, Sears's management responded with a series of seemingly erratic marketing strategies. Sears moved from more expensive merchandise to budget departments. When that experiment failed, Sears tried to compete directly with the discounters. In 1977 the firm embarked on a price war in an effort to win back customers. Although sales increased 16 percent, the price cuts destroyed profits, and earnings for the merchandise group in 1977 fell more than 10 percent. Suppliers became the next target for Sears's floundering tactics. In 1978 Sears informed its vendors that it no longer would carry products that failed to sell quickly, but those suppliers, such as the Whirlpool Corporation, which made refrigerators, washers, and other appliances for Sears under the Kenmore name, found new customers and expanded their own lines of name-brand merchandise. In 1972, for example, Whirlpool sold 61 percent of its merchandise to Sears; by 1979 Sears accounted for only 47 percent of Whirlpool's business. The decision by some manufacturers to promote their own brand names coincided with the efforts of discounters such as Wal-Mart to offer brand-name products to consumers. In an attempt to regain its image as the leading source of durable goods for the American middle class, Sears returned to its original market approach in the late

1970s and repositioned itself as a middle-of-the-road retailer, but that effort was handicapped by the ailing economy and by retail trends that found customers steadily abandoning the middle of the spectrum in favor of either lower prices or higher quality.

The underlying cause of many of Sears's ill-conceived decisions was a cumbersome management structure that had been continually expanded in an attempt to coordinate the firm's diverse activities—including its insurance subsidiary, Allstate—into a coherent whole. Throughout the 1970s Sears added layers of management. This unwieldy bureaucracy not only hindered timely decision making, but it also imposed on the company an enormous cost burden. At the same time that Sears was adding executives, it was reducing the size of its store-level workforce, and as a result, customer service declined.[9]

Like Sears, S. S. Kresge Company's K mart enjoyed resounding success during the early 1970s. Before his retirement in 1972, Harry Cunningham had built K mart into a retail colossus, and the firm's 80,000-square-foot, low-overhead stores, offering large selections of brand-name merchandise at low prices, were held in high regard by many, including Sam Walton. In his autobiography, Walton revealed an admiration for Cunningham and the discount chain that he had built, and he confessed that through the years he had copied many of K mart's business practices. "I'll bet I've been in more K marts that anybody—and I would really envy their merchandise mix and the way they presented it," he wrote. "So much about their stores was superior to ours back then that sometimes I felt like we couldn't compete." Ironically, while Walton was expanding his discount chain through a strict adherence to the formula that Cunningham had originated—a formula that was based on carrying mainly brand-name merchandise at discount prices all the time—K mart, in pursuit of rapid growth during the 1970s, began to forsake Cunningham's initial concept.

Believing that expansion had been the key to the discount chain's past achievements, Kresge's new management corps pursued an aggressive growth strategy. Signs proclaiming "K" in red and "mart" in blue were installed over new stores at a record rate. K mart's expansion program of the 1970s, however, contained three flaws. First, K mart began to move away from its earlier commitment to brand-name merchandise by carrying an increasing amount of private-brand goods, because they enabled the firm to enjoy a higher margin of profit. Second, in focusing on opening new units, management neglected the existing ones. As a result, by the mid-1970s K mart's older stores, which were poorly lit and often had open cartons of merchandise piled on tables, looked out-of-date and shabby. Consumers, dismayed by K mart's clutter and its tendency to carry products that were of inferior quality and that were too often out of stock, began to shop elsewhere. As America's economy weakened, K mart found itself beset by regional discounters with more attractive stores and more fashionable merchandise, like Caldor in the Northeast, Wal-Mart in the small towns of the South, and Target in the Midwest; by specialty stores that carried such product lines as sports equipment, drugs, beauty products, and shoes; and by catalog showrooms that carried small appliances and jewelry.

Kresge's third mistake with regard to its expansion strategy was the decision on the part of management to abandon Cunningham's big-store format, which had been the basis for the chain's success. Cunningham's successor, Robert E. Dewar, started opening K marts in towns with populations of 15,000 to 20,000, and he was convinced that these smaller markets required smaller stores. Beginning in 1976 many of the new K marts were as small as 40,000 square feet, and they carried fewer lines than the regular-size outlets. Although the continued expansion of the firm, which in 1977 changed its name from the S. S. Kresge Company to K mart Corporation, increased its sales volume, its missteps caused profits to decline. From 1976 to 1980, for example, net profit margins shrank steadily, going from 3.1 to 1.3 percent.[10]

In addition to Sears and K mart, Gibson Products Company, J. C. Penney, and Montgomery Ward also experienced problems during the late 1970s. Wal-Mart, however, continued its successful expansion. During fiscal 1976, for example, the firm grew to 125 outlets; it entered Texas, its ninth state, when it opened a store in Mount Pleasant, a town in the northeastern part of the state.[11]

In two instances during this period Wal-Mart expanded by purchasing existing stores. In 1975 the company bought three Howard Discount Centers from the Howard-Gibco Corporation of Texarkana. Two of the units were located in Little Rock and one was in Fort Smith, Arkansas. In August 1977, in a more significant transaction, the firm bought 16 Mohr Value discount department stores from Wetterau, Inc., of Hazlewood, Missouri. Wal-Mart assumed the leases, paid book value for the fixtures, and book value less a discount for the inventories. The Mohr Value purchase carried Wal-Mart into its tenth state, Illinois, where 6 of the stores were located; the other 10 were in Missouri. Their sales per square foot were only approximately $60, significantly lower than Wal-Mart's more than $100. Two of the former Mohr Value operations, located in Sullivan and Flat River, Missouri, were soon closed, but the other 14 were remodeled and restocked to bring them up to Wal-Mart's standards.

In fiscal 1978 the company abandoned its experiment with the Save-Co Home Improvement Centers. The firm had nurtured great hopes for the venture, but despite considerable efforts to overhaul the stores, they never fulfilled Wal-Mart's sales expectations. As a result, during fiscal 1978 the unit in Rogers was closed, leaving the store in Mountain Home, which was closed at a later date. In that same year Walton also closed the Family Center store in Waynesville, Missouri, his last remaining variety store. After 32 years Walton severed relations with the franchiser that had helped to launch his career in retailing.[12]

Until the late 1970s Wal-Mart had allowed outside firms to lease pharmacies, automotive service centers, and jewelry and shoe departments in his stores as a means of experimenting with those retail areas with a minimum investment. Usually the departments were leased for one year. Wal-Mart received 5 to 12 percent of their sales volume, which translated into only about 1 percent of the firm's total revenue, but the company's only cost was the floor space occupied by the leased departments. In fiscal 1979 Wal-Mart decided to incorporate these leased departments into its own operation. In October 1978 shoes became a company-owned department when the firm acquired Hutcheson Shoe Company of Fort Smith, Arkansas, which had operated the shoe departments in 190 Wal-Mart stores. By 1979 the company was operating 7 pharmacies, and in 1981 Wal-Mart gained 159 jewelry departments that had been operated by the firm Cohen-Hatfield.[13]

During the 1970s Wal-Mart's net sales and net earnings had increased at an annual rate of approximately 40 percent. The firm concluded this remarkable period of growth in fiscal 1980 with net sales of $1.2 billion and a net income of $41.2 million. Existing-store sales had increased 15 percent, which translated into sales per gross square foot of approximately $110, and by this time Wal-Mart was operating 276 stores in 11 states, which now included Alabama (see Table 4-1).[14]

During the 1970s Wal-Mart Discount City stores were fairly uniform in their layout, stock, and size, averaging 45,000 square feet in 1979 (see Figure 4-1). The stores were air-conditioned and fully equipped with modern fixtures, some of which had been manufactured by Wal-Mart itself. An average Wal-Mart store carried about 35,000 items distributed among 36 departments, a greater number than other discount operations, according to company documents. All stores had about the same merchandise mix, although some variations were permitted to meet local tastes. Other than apparel, most products were nationally advertised, brand-name items. Only a few product lines carried the Wal-Mart name.

All stores were open from 9:00 until 9:00, six days a week, and they were open on Sunday afternoon where the law permitted. Wal-Mart's business was basically cash-and-carry, although bank credit cards were accepted at all stores. Wal-Mart did not offer its own credit because

TABLE 4-1. Growth of Wal-Mart Stores, Inc., Fiscal 1971–1980

	1971	1972	1973	1974	1975
Stores in operation	38	51	64	78	104
Net sales	$44,286	$78,015	$124,889	$167,561	$236,209
Total revenue	44,632	78,861	126,447	169,366	238,687
Costs and expenses	41,461	73,292	117,530	157,878	227,116
Income before taxes	3,171	5,569	8,917	11,488	11,521
Net income	1,652	2,907	4,591	5,954	5,995*

	1976	1977	1978	1979	1980
Stores in operation	125	153	195	229	276
Net sales	340,331	478,807	678,456	900,298	1,248,176
Total revenue	344,134	484,200	686,223	909,913	1,258,268
Costs and expenses	322,077	453,343	645,376	853,141	1,183,908
Income before taxes	22,057	30,857	40,847	56,772	74,288
Net income	11,132	16,039	21,191	29,447	41,151

*Company adopted LIFO method of assessing inventory cost.
Note: Amounts shown are in thousands of dollars.

Source: Annual reports of Wal-Mart Stores, Inc.

Walton was convinced that such policies had caused other retail operations, especially department stores, considerable difficulty. Sales were almost all self-service, but store personnel prided themselves on their availability and helpfulness.[15]

In the mid-1970s the company began to upgrade the stores. The first step was a major capital improvement program to replace the harsh blue interiors with softer, more attractive colors; eliminate the last of the old pipe-rack fixtures; and install carpet in selected areas of the stores. Meanwhile, the quality of the firm's apparel improved markedly. Cheaper, private-label lines generally disappeared, and higher-quality brand names replaced them. These changes, which some thought risky, proved highly successful. Shoppers in increasing numbers flocked to the refurbished stores.[16]

Each store was run by a manager and at least two assistant managers, who were responsible for hard goods and soft goods, respectively. In larger stores there also were one or more management trainees. This management staff would supervise the approximately 36 department heads,

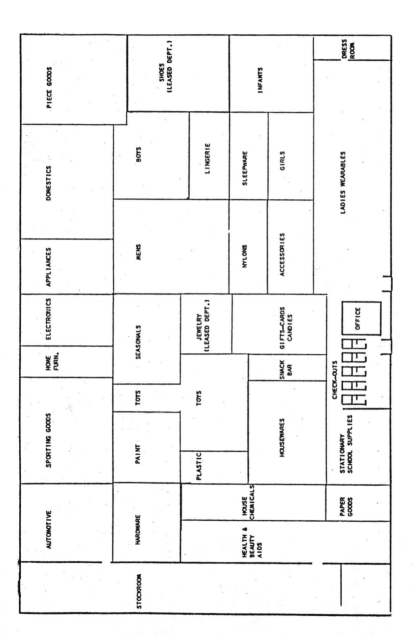

Figure 4-1. Layout of an Early Wal-Mart Store. Source: *Discount Merchandiser* 13 (January 1973): 46.

TABLE 4-2. Distribution of Sales by Category, 1972

CATEGORY	PERCENTAGE OF SALES
Soft goods	33
Hard goods (hardware, housewares, auto supplies, small appliances)	23
Sporting goods and toys	12
Health and beauty aids	9
Gifts, records, and electronics	8
Stationery and candy	7
Footwear	5
Jewelry	2
Pharmaceuticals	1

Note: Sales of footwear, jewelry, and pharmaceuticals were primarily through leased departments. Figures include gross sales of leased departments.

Source: *Discount Merchandiser* 13 (January 1973): 40.

although the number of department managers could vary according to the size of the store. Some departments, such as ready-to-wear and sporting goods, had more than one manager, while other departments, such as hosiery and underwear, were combined under a single supervisor. Store managers reported to district managers, who were each responsible for about a dozen stores. District managers in turn reported to regional vice presidents, who oversaw the work of three or four district managers. The regional vice presidents reported to the firm's vice president of operations (see Figure 4-2). The firm's management structure, which was essentially the same simple organization that Walton had started with, was sparse and efficient. Senior managers were expected to oversee diverse aspects of the business. Their realms of responsibility were substantial and included such things as administration and finance, merchandising, operations, sales promotion and advertising, personnel and public relations, security and loss prevention, and real estate and construction. The sine qua non of the centralized system that emanated from Bentonville was the group of regional vice presidents. Every Monday morning they flew to their respective territories where they stayed through Thursday visiting stores. On site they worked with a store's entire staff, partly to suggest, partly to learn, and, above all, to maintain the free and open communication that characterized Wal-Mart's managerial style.

The vice presidents returned to Bentonville for a day-long merchandising meeting every Friday in which they reviewed performance figures for the week, exchanged information, and made future plans.

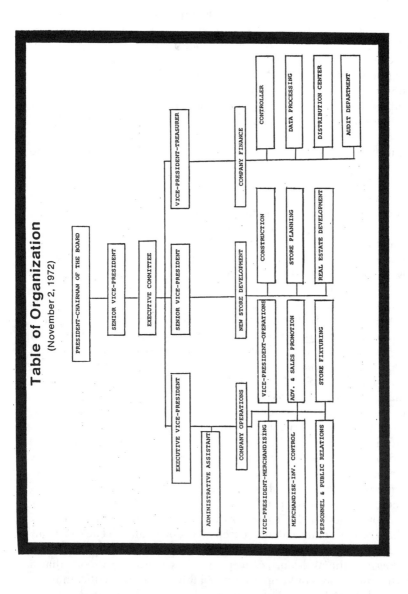

Table of Organization
(November 2, 1972)

PRESIDENT-CHAIRMAN OF THE BOARD

SENIOR VICE-PRESIDENT

EXECUTIVE COMMITTEE

SENIOR VICE-PRESIDENT

EXECUTIVE VICE-PRESIDENT

ADMINISTRATIVE ASSISTANT

COMPANY OPERATIONS

VICE-PRESIDENT-OPERATIONS

VICE-PRESIDENT-MERCHANDISING

ADV. & SALES PROMOTION

MERCHANDISE-INV. CONTROL

STORE FIXTURING

PERSONNEL & PUBLIC RELATIONS

VICE-PRESIDENT-TREASURER

COMPANY FINANCE

CONTROLLER

DATA PROCESSING

DISTRIBUTION CENTER

AUDIT DEPARTMENT

NEW STORE DEVELOPMENT

CONSTRUCTION

STORE PLANNING

REAL ESTATE DEVELOPMENT

Figure 4-2. Wal-Mart's Organizational Chart. Source: *Discount Merchandiser* 13 (January 1973): 41.

On Saturday mornings they were joined by the senior executives, the merchandising staff, the Bentonville headquarters staff, and Walton himself for a 7:30 meeting to review the firm's performance in the past week and to make plans for the coming weeks. An informal tone would be struck at the outset by Walton, who would lead those assembled in the traditional "Wal-Mart cheer": "Give me a W!" Walton would shout. "W!" the group would shout back. "Give me an A!"—and so forth until the company's name had been spelled out. Nonetheless the Saturday morning meetings had a serious purpose, for they enabled company officers to make merchandising decisions based on current information. Walton, in fact, frequently went to his office at three in the morning to study store data in preparation for the event. At the conclusion of the meeting each vice president called his seven or eight district managers to relate what had transpired, and the district managers, in turn, held a conference call with all of their store managers. Before the day was over, each store manager would have passed the information along to his department heads.[17]

In the early 1970s Sam Walton outlined the corporation's plans for the new decade. He listed four major strategies. First, Walton proposed that the company expand steadily by placing full-size discount department stores in towns and small cities within an expanded radius of 300 miles of the Bentonville headquarters. Second, Walton pledged to maintain genuine discount prices and one of the lowest gross margins of any chain in the United States. Third, he emphasized that the firm must make every effort to cut costs in the areas of inventory and operations. Fourth, and most important, according to Walton, was the continued maintenance of loyalty, morale, and enthusiasm in the workforce.

These strategies were enhanced during this era by economic changes in Wal-Mart's territory. Northern Arkansas, southern Missouri, and eastern Oklahoma and Kansas experienced substantial growth in the 1960s and 1970s in terms of both population and per capita income. These developments were fueled by tourism, the establishment of retirement communities, considerable industrial development, and, for a few years, generally satisfactory conditions in agriculture.[18]

A major policy in the 1970s was to put stores in towns and small cities that other retail chains, except Gibson's and TG&Y, usually shunned. "Since its beginning," Walton wrote in the company's 1978 *Annual Report*, "the Wal-Mart concept was based on the theory that a quality discount store could operate profitably . . . in a small community." As already noted, most of the company's stores were located in towns of 5,000 to 25,000 people. County seats were special targets. By the end of the decade, the largest cities with Wal-Mart stores were Little Rock,

Pine Bluff, and Fort Smith, Arkansas, and Springfield and Joplin, Missouri. The company also placed stores near metropolitan areas, such as Dallas, Kansas City, Oklahoma City, Memphis, Tulsa, and St. Louis.[19] It became increasingly apparent that Walton's small-town strategy had been sound and farsighted. While large metropolitan areas began to suffer from too much retail competition during the 1970s, Wal-Mart was virtually unchallenged in the small-town markets in its territory. In most instances a Wal-Mart store was "the biggest thing around," making it the dominant nonfood retailer in the small communities it served. As such, it was capable of drawing customers not only from the town itself but also from a sizable surrounding area. Placing stores in small towns and cities afforded other advantages as well. The cost of land, buildings, and other operating expenses was lower, and the dedication of the workforce was higher.[20]

Expansion of the Wal-Mart chain of stores went forward systematically. Company policy dictated that the firm grow outward in an expanding circle around Bentonville. "We are always pushing from the inside out," said one company officer. "We never jump and then backfill." Since Wal-Mart saturated an area before expanding further, it discouraged competition and ensured that name recognition in new markets would be high. "We have more stores in a tighter geographical area than any other retail chain," explained Walton. "This saves money and increases identification with our customers." By placing stores within a one-day drive of Bentonville, the company was able to resupply stores quickly and avoid empty shelves and excess inventory.[21]

In its pricing policy, Wal-Mart's pledge, reiterated repeatedly, was to provide the "finest quality merchandise at the lowest everyday discount prices." Prices normally were set below manufacturers' suggested retail levels except where fair-trade laws prevailed. Claiming that its prices were uniform throughout the chain except where it was necessary to lower prices to meet local competition, the company did not exploit its dominant retail position in the towns it served. Contradicting the predictions of Adam Smith, it forsook the opportunity to take advantage of monopoly pricing. "Just because we were in west Arkansas we didn't charge the highest price we could get," said Walton. "We charged them the same prices as in Little Rock or Springfield. . . ."[22]

Because Wal-Mart desired to keep its prices low and remain a profitable concern, it had to control costs. Inspired by Walton's zeal for cost cutting, economy of operation was almost a fetish. The firm's general headquarters in Bentonville, with its inexpensive decor throughout, was symbolic of Walton's devotion to frugality. Subsequent to its construction, the installation of conveniences such as an elevator and carpeting in some areas provoked complaints from Walton. The elevator was too slow, he fussed, believing that personnel should demonstrate their initiative by using the stairs. And he considered the carpeting an outright waste of money. Walton, moreover, would not include liquor and entertainment costs in business expenses.

Wal-Mart was known for driving a hard bargain with vendors. The cordiality that sometimes characterized the relationship between buyers and manufacturers in other firms did not exist at Wal-Mart. It was a company rule, for example, that Wal-Mart buyers could not accept free meals or gifts from vendor representatives, thereby eliminating a potential source of conflict of interest. Wal-Mart's demand that suppliers who desired to do business with the company send their emissaries to remote Bentonville reflected a "you come to us, we don't come to you" attitude that shaped the firm's overall relationship with its vendors. The company's growing buying power gave it a strength with manufacturers not enjoyed by smaller firms, and company buyers were grimly determined to capitalize on this leverage by getting the lowest possible prices. An officer of one firm that did business with Wal-Mart remarked: "These people [Wal-Mart buyers] are as folksy and down-to-earth as home-grown tomatoes. But when you start dealing with them—when you get past that 'down home in Bentonville' business—they're as hard as nails and every bit as sharp. They'll drive as hard a deal as anyone anywhere."[23]

The firm constantly sought ways to reduce expenses by such means as increasing inventory turnover, reducing freight costs, maintaining timely and accurate information, and speeding merchandise deliveries. One of Walton's cost-cutting innovations, which he apparently adapted from the Ben Franklin variety stores, was the use of distribution centers. As the company grew, Walton realized that it would be more economical for Wal-Mart's suppliers to ship merchandise in bulk to centralized distribution facilities, where receiving and processing procedures could be consolidated, than to parcel out goods to individual stores. The firm's first distribution center had been constructed in Bentonville in 1969. It was enlarged in stages, and by the mid-1970s it had a total of 238,800 square feet. The center was designed to ensure a constant supply of merchandise to the stores. In addition, a portion of the facility was devoted to the inspection and pricing of some clothing and accessory items, thus allowing the company to exercise careful supervision over the quality of merchandise.[24]

Wal-Mart's method of processing soft goods provides a good illustration of the efficiency and cost-control advantages of its warehouse and distribution facilities. All apparel arrived in flat boxes. Without hanging the merchandise on racks, the workers inspected and ticketed the items, and then put them back into the same boxes for shipment to the stores. This centralized process had certain cost-cutting advantages. It allowed the firm to return immediately any merchandise that was received past the cancellation date; the inspections ensured quality control; and goods that failed to meet company standards could be returned to the vendors, with the freight and extra labor costs charged back to the shipper. Economies such as these ensured that the firm's central-distribution costs amounted to only about 2 percent of sales during the early 1970s.[25]

In January 1975 a new 150,000-square-foot distribution center began operation in Bentonville. This second unit was located within two miles of the firm's original facility. Its purpose was to consolidate case-pack merchandise that previously had been shipped directly from vendors to the stores. It was designed not to serve as a warehouse but to function solely as a redistribution point for bulk merchandise received in truckload and carload lots. In a procedure known as "cross-docking," merchandise frequently was not even stored in the distribution center but was instead placed on outbound company trucks directly from incoming rail cars and trucks.[26]

In 1978 Wal-Mart completed construction of its first major distribution center outside Bentonville, a 390,000-square-foot facility in Searcy, Arkansas. The distribution center was built to provide merchandise to the approximately 40 percent of the firm's stores that were located in the eastern and southern portions of its trade territory. It also was intended to facilitate further expansion. In 1979 Wal-Mart completed a third distribution center in Bentonville, also 390,000 square feet in size. Late in the decade a fifth distribution center was under construction in Palestine, Texas, to serve the southern part of that state.[27]

By 1975 some 80 percent of all of Wal-Mart's merchandise flowed through its distribution facilities. The remaining 20 percent continued to go directly from suppliers to the individual stores. Because the distribution centers could handle large orders and make use of cheap modes of transportation, they created a sizable savings for the firm. Within the distribution centers, a high degree of automation, exemplified by huge conveyor belts that could move merchandise at about 200 feet per minute, allocated goods properly and further reduced costs. The centers also provided speedier and more certain deliveries to stores. By assuring individual stores of resupply from a central, company-owned facility, Wal-Mart could better control its inventory.

Large shipments usually arrived at the distribution centers by rail. The merchandise was moved by truck to the stores. Each store received from one to three truckloads of merchandise a week, and on their return trip to the distribution center, approximately 60 percent of the trucks brought back goods that the firm had purchased from vendors located along their routes. Initially Wal-Mart leased delivery trucks, but by 1978 the company had its own trucking operation consisting of 73 tractors, 288 trailers, and 115 drivers, who logged about 9 million miles that year.[28]

Another area in which Wal-Mart was able to reduce costs was advertising. The firm spent the equivalent of less than 2 percent of sales on advertising, a smaller percentage than most retailers. Its orderly pattern of expansion and the resulting ready recognition of the firm among customers contributed to this economy. Most advertising was by company circulars and local newspapers. The firm attributed some of its savings on advertising to the fact that its circulars were issued only about once a month rather than weekly, as was the practice of many competitors. The 12-page circulars were designed to saturate Wal-Mart's trade territory, going to every city and rural delivery route. The company generally ran one- to two-page newspaper advertisements weekly on a companywide basis, with additional advertisements for seasons such as Christmas and Easter. Individual stores often advertised on Mondays and Fridays. At Bentonville the firm maintained an advertising department with its own printing plant that produced circulars, newspaper inserts, and formats for local advertising as well as materials for in-store promotions. Radio and television were utilized to a lesser extent. During the early 1970s radio accounted for about 9 percent of Wal-Mart's advertising budget. The use of television increased in the late 1970s, rising to 29 percent of total advertising expenditures in 1979.[29]

The use of advanced electronic technology also helped to minimize costs and facilitate the growth and management of the company. The computer (along with the airplane) was vital to the success of Wal-Mart. Like other major retail chains of the late twentieth century, Wal-Mart was in part a product of the new computer technology that revolutionized the retail industry by allowing expansion on a grand scale. Wal-Mart had entered the computer age in 1969 when it leased an IBM 360 computer system to maintain inventory control at its new distribution center in Bentonville. By the mid-1970s the firm was leasing a more advanced IBM 370/135 computer system for inventory control, payroll, financial records, and the generation of statistical data for analysis of store and department performance. Increasingly the stores were equipped with electronic cash registers that provided point-of-sale data for speedy inventory replenishment.

The chief architect of Wal-Mart's full-scale entrance into the computer age was the firm's executive vice president for finance, David Glass, and not Sam Walton, who apparently was skeptical of the new technology. According to one Wal-Mart executive, "Sam never did like computers.

He thinks of them as overhead." Glass was responsible for the installation of a companywide computer network, which was completed in 1977. Capable of transmitting information such as payroll data, messages from buyers, and reorders, this technology provided faster direct communication between corporate headquarters and the stores and distribution centers, thereby ensuring faster restocking of merchandise and improved store operations. In 1979 Wal-Mart completed a highly sophisticated 16,000-square-foot data processing and communications center at the Bentonville headquarters. Designed to house the firm's burgeoning computer network, the facility provided around-the-clock communications throughout the company.[30]

An obvious strength of Wal-Mart Stores was the dedication of its workforce, which increased from 1,500 employees in 1970 to 21,000 in 1979. In fact, company officers maintained that the commitment of its personnel, more than any other factor, explained Wal-Mart's success and made the company unique among American retail firms. According to Wal-Mart's 1978 *Annual Report*, the secret of the firm's success was "nothing more than the bringing together of men and women who are completely dedicated to their jobs, their Company, and their communities. Our organization has become a team that acts with one purpose, deriving its strength from the many individuals who constitute our Board of Directors, our management, and our associates throughout our Wal-Mart organization."[31]

In the nomenclature of the company, hourly employees of Wal-Mart were not called employees, but associates, a term first used by the firm in fiscal 1973. They were treated as equals and kept well-informed of company developments, both good and bad. In the back of every outlet, for example, a chart was posted showing employees how their store compared in sales with other Wal-Mart stores. Store managers received statistical information monthly, including the cost—by department—of every item purchased, a copy of every invoice, and a computer printout of sales.[32]

All associates were invited to make suggestions or other comments on company policy and practices. They were made to feel that their contributions were important and that their voices could be heard by anyone in the organization. When an hourly associate came up with the idea of a "people greeter," one of the firm's most popular and successful innovations was born. An employee usually drawn from the ranks of older local retirees, the greeter's job was simply to greet customers and hand them a shopping cart and a sale circular. Lower-level management at first resisted the concept because of the additional expense involved. Sam Walton, however, liked the idea, so it was tried and subsequently implemented throughout the chain.[33]

A sense of esprit de corps was promoted in a variety of ways. The company launched a monthly employee magazine, *Wal-Mart World*, which kept all employees informed about the firm's progress and permitted the company to praise those stores, departments, and associates who excelled. A handbook spelled out company policies and associates' responsibilities and benefits. The first annual picnic for company personnel in Bentonville was held in 1975. According to the firm, the event was a resounding success, helping to create a feeling of "one big family" and generating "much enthusiasm and dedication." Orientation meetings conducted monthly at the company's headquarters in Bentonville and periodically in the stores afforded opportunities for associates to ask questions, and they were assured that they would get "intelligent" answers. As an example of the spirit of equality that prevailed at Wal-Mart, no one, including Walton (who for several years drove the same pickup truck to work), had a reserved space in the parking lot at the headquarters office building.[34]

The company sought to win and keep the allegiance of its associates through financial rewards as well. Some workers were paid the minimum wage or very little above it, but department heads, assistant managers, and store managers were well remunerated. The company also provided a generous benefits package. In addition to such benefits as health and life insurance, an important benefit was a liberal profit-sharing trust, a plan by which employees shared in a portion of the company's profits each year. The program was instituted in fiscal 1972, when the company made its first contribution of $172,000 to the plan and there were only 128 participants in the program.

Beginning in February 1976 the eligibility requirement for participation in the profit-sharing plan was changed to one year of continuous employment instead of two. Employees were fully vested in the program after five years. The plan was funded by the company and was based on a formula that increased contributions as a percentage of a participant's wages when the firm's pretax profits as a percentage of sales increased. A significant portion of the contributions were invested in Wal-Mart stock, with the remainder placed in other investments. Not only did the program encourage personnel to feel that they were participants in the ownership of the company, but it also provided an excellent retirement fund for many employees.

Another employee benefit was the firm's stock-purchase plan. Adopted in 1972, this voluntary investment program permitted associates to purchase Wal-Mart stock through payroll withholding, with the company contributing part of the cost. This program allowed many workers to amass sizable holdings, making millionaires of several executives, including some at the middle-management level. Additionally, in 1978 the firm instituted individual deferred compensation agreements with some corporate officers and members of management.[35]

Walton and other of the firm's senior executive officers were determined that there would be no labor unions at Wal-Mart, and the company's various employee benefits, combined with the scant currency enjoyed by organized labor in the small towns in Wal-Mart's trade territory, doomed all efforts on the part of labor unions to organize company personnel. Although on occasion such attempts were made by construction unions at building sites, by the Teamsters union at some distribution centers, and by the retail clerks' union at some stores, such as those located in Clinton and Mexico, Missouri, the efforts failed, and Wal-Mart remained a staunchly nonunion firm.[36]

Wal-Mart maintained comprehensive training programs so that employees, such as managers, assistant managers, department heads, and sales personnel, could advance in the organization. It was company policy to promote from within whenever possible, at times giving individuals who failed to obtain a desired promotion a second opportunity to get the job. While some of Wal-Mart's store managers, for example, were hired away from other retail firms or recruited among college graduates, Wal-Mart maintained that many were products of the firm's management training program, having been drawn from the ranks of assistant managers. Believing that it knew best how to train its personnel, Wal-Mart established a training department in 1975 to design a professional training and development program for employees. This department produced monthly audiovisual programs that were presented at stores by district managers. Focusing on the practical, everyday concerns of associates, the programs dealt with such matters as the checkout process, accident prevention, merchandise ordering and display, customer relations, and employee motivation and benefits.[37]

The company offered employees financial incentives to perform well. An example of this was seen in the firm's war against "shrinkage." The retail term for the loss of merchandise, shrinkage includes everything unaccounted for during inventory, whether it disappeared as a result of inaccurate record keeping, damage, shoplifting, or internal theft. By the end of the 1970s, the firm had adopted an incentive program whereby employees were encouraged to "shrink the shrink." Viewing associates as the solution rather than the problem, the company agreed to share savings on shrinkage equally with the workforce. The first year the plan was in effect, shrinkage dropped to 1.8 percent of sales, and in 1984 it was estimated to be only 1.4 percent, compared with an industry average of 2.2 percent.[38]

Customer satisfaction also ranked high among company goals. Based on the belief that "customer goodwill is our best investment for future successful growth," Wal-Mart offered customers an "unconditional money-back guarantee" and pledged to provide "quality service." In practical terms, the money-back guarantee meant that any item could be returned without a sales receipt for any reason whatsoever, and the pledge of quality service meant that the customer was always right. Weekly surveys of customers' perceptions and reactions alerted management to problems and usually led to prompt action to correct them.[39]

Most important, however, for the remarkable growth of Wal-Mart were the abilities and personality of Sam Walton. An entrepreneur in the classic sense, Walton was a manager and a risk taker who combined the economic elements of distribution and marketing to create a dramatically successful firm. For Wal-Mart, Walton was more than a corporate manager; he was the inspiration and the personification of the company. During the early 1970s Walton had led Wal-Mart as chairman of the board of directors and president of the firm, but in November 1974 Walton implemented a major change in management. He relinquished his leadership position to Ronald Mayer, who became chairman of the board and chief executive officer. Mayer, who had been assistant secretary and executive vice president for finance and administration, had played a key role in the development of some of the vital data processing, distribution, and transportation systems used by the company. Walton also appointed Ferold Arend, who had been executive vice president for operations and merchandise, as president and chief operating officer. Walton assumed the role of chairman of the executive committee.

Following Mayer's promotion, disagreement developed between Walton and Mayer over Mayer's management of the firm. Walton was disturbed by Mayer's tendency to encourage corporate cliques, which resulted in the emergence of rival factions in the senior management corps, as some executives expressed loyalty to Mayer while others supported Arend. But Walton also attributed some of his difficulties with Mayer to his own reluctance to give up control of the company he had built. Walton termed his retirement from the leadership of Wal-Mart at the age of 56 a "mistake." He explained that he "wasn't able to assume a passive role" in corporate affairs and indicated that much of the friction with Mayer had stemmed from his own inclination "to say, 'Why don't you do this now?'"

When Walton informed Mayer in June 1976 that he wished to return as chairman of the board and chief executive officer, Mayer resigned, although Walton urged him to remain with the company as a senior executive. Mayer accepted a position as president and chief executive officer of Ayr-Way Stores, at that time a larger discount chain head-quartered in Indianapolis. Mayer's sudden departure was followed by what came to be known as the "exodus," a critical time during which several key executives—including the financial officer, the data processing manager, and the head of the distribution centers—left with Mayer, and another group of managers exited soon thereafter, leading Walton to estimate that one-third of Wal-Mart's senior executives had departed during that period.[40]

Following Mayer's resignation, Walton resumed his former position as chairman and chief executive officer, and Arend remained president and chief operating officer. In 1978 Arend resigned due to health considerations, and Jack C. Shewmaker replaced him. Shewmaker had been executive vice president for operations, personnel, and merchandise since 1976. After joining the firm in 1970 as a district manager, Shewmaker had also served as vice president for security and loss prevention from 1973 to 1976. Following this final management change, for the remainder of the decade the firm's executive officer group consisted of Sam Walton, chairman and chief executive officer; Shewmaker, president and chief operating officer; Bud Walton, senior vice president; David Glass, executive vice president for finance; and Rob Walton, senior vice president, secretary, and general counsel.

During the 1970s the firm's board of directors had been drawn mainly from its senior executive group. Four of the original directors—Sam and Bud Walton, Ferold Arend, and James H. Jones—served throughout the decade. By fiscal 1980 Ronald Mayer and H. L. Remmel had left the board, and David Glass, Jack Shewmaker, J. R. Hyde III (chairman and president of Malone and Hyde, Inc., of Memphis), Rob Walton, and Sidney A. McKnight (a former president of Montgomery Ward) had joined it.[41]

According to Walton, a business manager's primary task was "simply to get the right people in the right places to do a job, and then encourage them to use their own inventiveness to accomplish the job at hand." Although some company officers had been brought in from other firms, a majority had come up through the ranks. Walton's talent for choosing able people, even when they lacked retail experience, at times defied all logic—let alone conventional business wisdom. The story of how Walton hired his first store manager, Bob Bogle, was typical. According to one long-time observer, Bogle, who at the time had been the sanitarian for Bentonville, was checking septic tanks and grading dairy barns when Walton recruited him to manage Walton's Bentonville variety store. Admittedly Bogle had a novel background for a career in retailing, "but Sam saw in the fellow something he liked," said the observer. "That man went on to become one of his greatest managers and employees. And Sam hired them all that way. Some were in merchandising, some weren't, but he put them together and it worked. He had that ability." From the earliest days, when Walton selected potential managers, he looked "for a person who has energy, who's determined to succeed, willing to work and who's loyal" to the firm. He preferred to hire men who had a family, believing them to be more stable and motivated, and those with a strong church affiliation, since such an affiliation showed that they could "identify with something outside of themselves" and "work for a common good."[42]

In addition to his business acumen, Walton possessed personal charisma and social skills that he used to good advantage in fostering the growth of Wal-Mart. An observer reported that Walton "meets people very well" and that he could make "people feel he really cares. His eyes don't go blank and drift off when you talk to him." In fact, Walton did care, and when he would get out, interact, and ask questions, he was doing what was central to his personal management style.[43]

One of Walton's prime means of interacting with his employees was his store visits. He was firmly convinced that it was essential for him and the other executives to spend several days a week visiting the stores. "We like to let folks know that we're interested in them and that they are vital to us. 'Cause they are. Those department heads are the ones who *really* know what's going on out there in the field, and we've got to get them to tell us," he reported. Indeed, many good ideas first came to the attention of senior management during those store visits. They would then be discussed at the Saturday morning executives' meeting in Bentonville and perhaps adopted as company policy.[44]

During the 1970s Walton spent two or three days a week visiting the stores. He tried to visit each unit at least twice during a year. During these visits it was Walton's practice, on arrival, to gather his employees around him and lead them in a rousing corporate cheer. Then he toured the store, eliciting information from hourly associates and department heads alike. After the tour, he met with the store's personnel. In those meetings he rarely criticized. Instead, he complimented the associates on what they were doing well and challenged them to do better.[45]

The Wal-Mart cheer became one of the most colorful aspects of Walton's store visits. The cheerleading device reflected Walton's ability to relate, on a personal level, to his employees—many of whom, like himself, were residents of small towns—and it provided him with an excellent means of eliciting a high level of performance from his personnel. On observing for the first time this singular interaction between Walton and his employees, one associate later confessed that he considered the spectacle "queer as hell," but he went on to attest to its effectiveness: "It was rather bizarre to see [Walton] leading a pep rally personally to motivate hourly employees. . . . I was somewhat embarrassed by the whole thing, but I was also in the minority. This man was selling himself and his store to his employees. . . . Immature as I thought it was, it worked. . . . I knew he [Walton] was a genius at getting the only purpose of retailing accomplished: selling merchandise."[46]

Walton once stated that he had not set out to establish a large chain of discount stores. When the first Wal-Marts prospered, however, he had seen it as a challenge to establish others, a challenge that the merchant in him could not ignore. He disliked publicity and seemed to be little interested in the wealth that Wal-Mart generated for him and his family. He attributed his success to circumstances and luck, and especially to the support of the firm's associates, for whom he possessed a genuine affection. As the firm grew, it became impossible for Walton to know the associates and their families personally as he once had, but his personal touch remained very much in evidence. When Ol' Roy, Walton's favorite bird dog, who had frequently accompanied him on trips to stores, died in 1981, Walton announced his loss in *Wal-Mart World*, much as one would write to a friend.[47]

During the late 1970s Sam Walton and his company were the recipients of various honors and awards that reflected Wal-Mart's status as the nation's leading regional discount chain. In 1977 Wal-Mart received its first national ranking by *Forbes* magazine. In a survey conducted by *Forbes* comparing the performances of the nation's major discount, department, and variety-store chains, Wal-Mart was named the leader in the categories of return on equity, return on capital, and growth in sales and earnings. Each year for the remainder of the decade, Wal-Mart would continue to garner this first-place ranking. In 1979 *Retail Week* named Walton man of the year for the retail industry. The next year he was selected by a panel of 50 securities analysts as the most outstanding chief executive officer in the country in the annual competition sponsored by *Financial World* magazine to honor America's leading executives.[48]

As the 1970s drew to a close, Wal-Mart could look back on 10 years of remarkable retail growth. In fiscal 1970 the company's 18 Wal-Mart and 14 Ben Franklin stores had accounted for less than a million square feet of retail space. Ten years later the old variety stores were gone and there were 276 Wal-Mart outlets, with a total of 12.6 million square feet of retail space. The firm's more than 40 percent annual compound rate of growth for sales and earnings during the decade reflected a precedent-setting rise in net sales from $31 million in fiscal 1970 to more than $1 billion in fiscal 1980. That increase made Wal-Mart the youngest retail firm in the United States to exceed $1 billion in net sales and the only regional retailer ever to reach that volume.[49] Such accomplishments confirmed that the company was indeed the fastest-growing regional discounter in the nation. Impressive as it was, however, Wal-Mart's success during the 1970s would be merely a prelude to its record of achievement during the 1980s.

5

Wal-Mart Becomes a National Discount Chain

AS A RESULT OF ITS impressive growth during the 1970s, in fiscal 1981 the Wal-Mart chain consisted of 330 stores and enjoyed a net income of $83 million on net sales of $1.6 billion. Because of its regional status, however, its sales volume in that year ranked only thirty-third among the nation's retailers, with sales that were a mere 9 and 11 percent, respectively, of Sears Merchandise Group's nearly $17 billion and K mart's $14.2 billion. Wal-Mart's rate of growth, however, far exceeded that of its competitors. Wal-Mart's sales were 31.6 percent above those of fiscal 1980, while K mart had gained only 9 percent and Sears's sales had stagnated.[1]

During the 1980s Wal-Mart would couple its tremendous sales capability with an expansion drive that would convert the regional discount chain into a national giant. In fiscal 1982 Wal-Mart launched its expansion program with a rare departure. In what constituted only the second major acquisition in the company's history, Wal-Mart purchased Kuhn's Big K Stores Corporation, a southern discount chain headquartered in Nashville, Tennessee. Founded 68 years earlier as a variety-store operation, the once-profitable firm was in financial difficulty. For the year ending in January 1981, for example, Kuhn's had suffered a loss of $5 million on sales of $287 million. It had become overextended partly as a result of spending $8.9 million in 1977 to acquire Edwards, Inc., a chain of 34 discount and variety stores in South Carolina and Georgia, as well as by constructing a massive corporate headquarters and distribution center in Nashville.

Wal-Mart agreed in December 1980 to acquire Kuhn's for an exchange of cash and Wal-Mart preferred stock totaling about $17 million. At that time Wal-Mart operated stores in rural communities that stretched from Texas to Alabama and north into Kansas and Illinois. According to David Glass, then Wal-Mart's vice chairman and chief financial officer, the purchase was viewed as an "excellent opportunity for our company to expand its marketing area" farther into the Southeast, since Kuhn's consisted of 106 discount department stores located throughout nine southeastern states. In seven of those states Wal-Mart already had stores and planned to open additional ones, while expansion into the new states of South Carolina and Georgia was consistent with the firm's long-range plans. The agreement was subject to a reduction in the purchase price if Kuhn's net worth dropped below $19 million by 3 July 1981. When Kuhn's net worth fell to $13.2 million, Wal-Mart revised its offer. Wal-Mart agreed to pay $7.5 million in preferred stock in exchange for all of Kuhn's common stock. It acquired the firm on 11 August 1981.

Wal-Mart moved quickly to recast the former Big K operation in the Wal-Mart mold. It closed the Nashville headquarters and 14 stores that were in direct competition with existing Wal-Mart stores. It then began to renovate and remodel 50 of the remaining 92 outlets. Wal-Mart maintained that the acquisition allowed the firm to gain stores immediately that otherwise would have required years to develop, and at lower rent costs than would have been available under new leasing arrangements. Undeniably, the transaction was a bargain for Wal-Mart. Compared with the cost of opening an equal number of new stores, Wal-Mart saved $68 million, according to one estimate. As a result of the acquisition, Wal-Mart, with a total of 491 outlets in a 13-state area that stretched from Texas through South Carolina and north to Illinois, became the nation's second largest discount chain, superseded only by K mart.[2]

Although discount merchandising remained the dominant form of distribution for popularly priced general merchandise during the early 1980s, the recession of 1981–82, combined with such factors as spiraling inflation, rising costs for labor and energy, increased competition as regional chains expanded nationally, and a high rate of consolidations as healthy firms absorbed weaker operations, critically affected the discount industry. By 1982 two pioneers of the industry, E. J. Korvette and Mammoth Mart, were out of business; Caldor had been acquired by Associated Dry Goods; and Ayr-Way had merged with Dayton Hudson's

Target chain. Then in the fall of that year another once-great discounter, Vornado, closed its doors, and Woolworth ended its 20-year effort to become a successful discounter when it liquidated its Woolco stores. Badly hurt by the recession, K mart saw its earnings decline during the early 1980s. In fiscal 1983, for example, it had only a minimal sales increase and a return on income that was less than a third of Wal-Mart's.[3]

In fiscal 1983 Wal-Mart's record of performance was superior to that of many other retailers. Sales in comparable stores per gross square foot, for example, advanced to $145 from $133 the year before, while the industry average was only $105. By this time the firm's trade territory included 15 states that spanned the country from Nebraska to Florida, but its focus was the South. According to Sam Walton, "about 50 percent" of Wal-Mart's expenditures were in Oklahoma, Louisiana, and Texas, which Walton considered the "best state we have ever opened." To ensure an uninterrupted flow of goods to its stores, Wal-Mart expanded the number of its distribution centers to six.

The secret of Wal-Mart's success during the early 1980s was simply the application, on a broader scale, of Sam Walton's fundamental business precepts of efficient management—as manifested in the high level of productivity the firm derived from its existing stores and the improved performance it elicited from the recently acquired Kuhn's Big K Stores—and a shrewd location strategy that allowed the company to expand aggressively by continuing to open new stores in towns and smaller cities that other major retailers ignored. As Walton wryly observed, "There's a lot more business in those communities than people thought."[4]

Over the next two years Wal-Mart not only accelerated its pace of growth, but it also embarked on a program of expansion through diversification. In fiscal 1984 the firm inaugurated two new retail formats, Sam's Wholesale Clubs and dot Discount Drugs. The following year it launched another innovation, Helen's Arts and Crafts.

In fiscal 1985 Wal-Mart's net sales were $6.4 billion, and its net income was $271 million, increases of 400 and 327 percent, respectively, over the past five years. The firm's Wal-Mart stores, which now numbered 745, were located in 20 states, now including Iowa, New Mexico, Indiana, North Carolina, and Virginia. During fiscal 1985 more than 7.5 million square feet of store space were added. At the same time, sales productivity per gross square foot of store space advanced to $166 from the previous year's $150.[5]

Fiscal 1985 represented a turning point in Wal-Mart's program of expansion. Over the preceding 10 years the company's sales and profits had increased at annual compounded rates of 39 and 43 percent, respectively. This sustained growth confirmed Wal-Mart's dominance of its regional market area. During the mid-1980s more than half of Wal-Mart's stores still were located in towns with populations between 5,000 and 25,000. About one-third of the firm's outlets were located in areas that were not served by any competitor. In towns and small cities where Wal-Mart had no competition, it often claimed 10 to 20 percent of total retail sales.

Wal-Mart's preeminence in the small cities and towns throughout the South and Midwest convinced the company's executives that expansion into the remainder of the nation was not beyond Wal-Mart's capabilities if it continued to rely on its proven formula of opening stores within an enlarged, 400-mile radius of existing distribution centers. In its first step outside its regional base, the firm built a distribution center in Mount Pleasant, Iowa, in 1985 to serve future stores in Illinois, Iowa, and Indiana. The location of distribution centers, in fact, had become the clearest indication of Wal-Mart's plans for future expansion.

As its field of operations became more national in scope, Wal-Mart continued to resist the temptation to skip over states in establishing a market presence or acquiring new properties. In both such cases the company would take care to ensure that its new stores and its rare acquisitions were contiguous with areas in which it already was located. At the same time, Wal-Mart accelerated its expansion into larger cities. The company's growing interest in more densely populated areas was manifested in the expanded size of its stores, which went from an average of 47,000 square feet in 1980 to 63,000 by 1985. This increase reflected Wal-Mart's commitment to developing even larger stores, in the 85,000-square-foot range, in order to enter urban markets.

Wal-Mart's rapid growth during the 1980s was built on America's shifting demographic and living patterns. To achieve market saturation, Wal-Mart tackled larger cities by surrounding them with several suburban stores. This approach reflected the company's wish to capitalize on the trend of a mass exodus of Americans from the cities to the suburbs, which was still in ascendance during the 1980s. In 1984, for example, Wal-Mart had four stores in Springfield, Missouri, which had a population of 150,000, and at least five more within 30 miles of the city. David Glass put this strategy in perspective, explaining, "In our areas there is still flight from the inner cities to the suburbs. The suburbs have been and continue to be growth areas. For that reason, we have always surrounded cities."[6]

Wal-Mart's rapid pace of expansion continued during the mid-1980s. In fiscal 1986 the firm had stores located in 22 states, having added the states of Wisconsin and Colorado. In that year Wal-Mart continued to lead the retail industry in the construction of new stores. Unlike the two leaders in square-footage increases, Ames Department

Stores and K mart, Wal-Mart's additions, which totaled more than 8 million square feet, did not rest largely on acquisitions, but rather on the actual building of new stores. While diversification into different retail formats had become increasingly important to the company, Wal-Mart's discount stores still accounted for 91 percent of its net sales and 96 percent of its pretax profits in 1985.[7]

During the early 1980s Wal-Mart had modified its real estate policy by abandoning its practice of leasing its stores from the developers who had financed and constructed them. Instead, the firm had reestablished its own real estate and construction division, which then selected the cities for the prospective stores and contracted for and supervised their construction. Wal-Mart financed these activities internally until the stores were completed; it then sold the buildings and leased them back. In fiscal 1986, however, Wal-Mart ceased building its own stores and reverted to its former policy of leasing the outlets from the developers who had constructed them, believing that this practice better fitted its long-range expansion plans.[8]

In fiscal 1987 Wal-Mart's net sales surged to $12 billion, making it the nation's seventh largest retailer and fourth largest general-merchandise retailer, behind Sears, K mart, and J. C. Penney. This sum represented an increase of 41 percent from the previous year, a growth rate that far outdistanced the retail industry as a whole, where, excluding automobiles, sales had risen only a torpid 2 percent. But such an increase was not unusual for Wal-Mart, since its 10-year compounded growth rate in sales had been 38 percent. The company's net income on its earnings was $450 million, an increase of 37 percent above the previous year. This increment was also consistent with its 10-year compounded growth rate on net income of 40 percent, a rate that overwhelmed K mart's 9 percent, Penney's 8 percent, and Woolworth's 6 percent for the same period. During fiscal 1987 the firm opened 121 new stores, giving it a total of 980 outlets in 23 states, including the added state of Minnesota. To serve as bases for future growth, Wal-Mart opened 3 new regional distribution centers, located in Douglas, Georgia; Brookhaven, Mississippi; and Plainview, Texas. Wal-Mart's network of 10 distribution centers now totaled more than 7 million square feet.[9]

Beginning in fiscal 1988, annual growth rates for both sales and income declined from the 40 percent range of the preceding 10 years to a range of 30 percent. Because of a sluggish national economy, the retail industry in general failed to post good earnings that year. Wal-Mart's outlets, however, earned the company a pretax profit of 7 percent and a 33 percent return on investment, according to Sam Walton, who attributed this success to Wal-Mart's controlled pattern of expansion. "We've done it," he said, "by putting them [Wal-Mart stores] in only 23 states."[10]

In fiscal 1988 total retail space in all Wal-Mart divisions (including a new retail format, Hypermart USA) was 78 million square feet, representing a 23 percent increase from the previous year and the fifth consecutive year in which retail space increased in excess of 20 percent. Sales productivity for all Wal-Mart operations averaged $213 per gross square foot of store space, an increase of $19 from the previous year. Wal-Mart added 1.5 million square feet to its distribution centers through the expansion of three existing facilities and the opening of an eleventh distribution center, located in Laurens, South Carolina, in January 1988.[11]

In fiscal 1989 Wal-Mart stores were located in 25 states, now including Arizona and Ohio. In addition, Wal-Mart inaugurated a new retail format, the Supercenter. Total sales productivity in all Wal-Mart divisions averaged $231 per gross square foot of store space. The number of distribution centers increased to 13 when 1 was opened in New Braunfels, Texas, and a second distribution center was opened in Laurens, South Carolina. Wal-Mart became the nation's third largest retailer, despite the fact that it operated in only half the states. It also continued to be the nation's fastest-growing retailer, again adding more gross square footage than any other major retail organization. In fiscal 1990 Wal-Mart concluded a decade of record-breaking expansion with 1,402 discount stores in operation in 29 states, including the added states of Michigan and Wyoming. Net sales were $25.8 billion and net income was $1 billion, representing increases over the previous five years of 306 percent (see Table 5-1). For the first time, gross square footage in all retail divisions exceeded 100 million (see Table 5-1).[12]

Wal-Mart's spectacular growth during the 1980s occurred in a highly competitive retail environment. For much of the decade consumer spending soared, fueling a frenzy of business expansion that, by the end of the decade, far exceeded consumer demand. This overexpansion, combined with other factors, such as recession, large takeover debts, and demographic and social change, forced many retailers out of business. During the 1980s certain retail trends that had started in the 1970s accelerated as consumers continued to abandon the three leading national department stores, Sears, Penney's, and Ward's, in favor of more efficient retail operations where they could find lower prices, a wider selection of products, and better service. One retail sector that benefited from this trend was the specialty store, which claimed a growing share of the general-merchandise market during the decade. A significant type of specialty chain that evolved during the 1980s was the "category killer." Modeled after Toys "R" Us, category killers were single-line stores with in-depth inventories in such areas as sporting goods, office supplies, and electronics.

TABLE 5-1 Growth of Wal-Mart Stores, Inc., Fiscal 1981–1990

	1981	1982	1983	1984	1985	1986
Stores in operation	330	491	551	642	745	859
Sam's Clubs	—	—	—	3	11	23
Net sales	$1,643,199	$2,444,997	$3,376,252	$4,666,909	6,400,861	8,451,489
Total revenue	1,655,262	2,462,647	3,398,687	4,702,940	6,453,028	8,506,616
Costs and expenses	1,555,983	2,313,910	3,174,131	4,345,793	5,951,608	7,903,024
Income before taxes	99,279	148,737	224,556	357,147	501,420	603,592
Net income	55,682	82,794	124,140	196,244	270,767	327,473

	1987	1988	1989	1990
Stores in operation	980	1,114	1,259	1,402
Sam's Clubs	49	84	105	123
Net sales	11,909,076	15,959,255	20,649,001	25,810,656
Total revenue	11,993,699	16,064,038	20,785,868	25,985,300
Costs and expenses	11,147,673	14,995,368	19,460,401	24,277,800
Income before taxes	846,026	1,068,670	1,325,467	1,707,500
Net income	450,086	627,643	837,221	1,075,900

Note: Amounts shown are in thousands of dollars.

Source: Annual reports of Wal-Mart Stores, Inc.

Discount merchandisers also profited from the decline in market share experienced by national department stores during the decade. From 1978 to 1988, for example, department stores suffered a 2 percent reduction in inflation-adjusted sales per square foot, while discount-store sales jumped 46.7 percent, adjusted for inflation. Within discount merchandising, however, liquidation and consolidation continued to characterize an industry choked with too many stores. The shakeout among discount firms aided the large chains, as marginal operations were either forced out of business or absorbed by successful competitors. Two large . chains that benefited from the shakeout were Target and Ames Department Stores. Target's expansion was prompted in part by the demise not only of Ayr-Way, but also of Fed-Mart, Gemco, and Gold Circle, while Ames bought Neisner, King's, G. C. Murphy, and Zayre.[13]

As retailing became more fragmented, some firms, including Sears and K mart, turned to diversification as a means of shoring up their sagging performance. During the early 1980s Sears underwent a major restructuring. The firm became a holding company with three subsidiaries: Allstate Insurance Company; the Seraco Group, a realty and financial services company whose chief duty was to oversee Homart Development Company, which developed shopping centers; and the Merchandise Group, its retail division. By giving all three divisions equal status, the reorganization signalled a shift away from retailing as the primary focus of the firm. During the mid-1980s K mart diverted resources from its discount operation and diversified into specialty retailing. In 1984–85, a period when Wal-Mart opened 217 new discount units, K mart had a net increase of just 31 outlets. Instead of opening additional discount stores, K mart's chief executive officer, Bernard M. Fauber, devoted that time to acquiring Walden Book Company, Inc., the nation's largest retail bookstore chain; Builders Square, Inc. (formerly Home Centers of America), a chain of discount home-improvement warehouses; and Pay Less Drug Stores Northwest, Inc., one of the nation's largest drugstore chains.[14]

The move toward diversification on the part of Sears and K mart was an indication that problems continued to beset both retail giants. In an effort to stop the further erosion of its business and to reclaim customers lost to discount and specialty stores, during the late 1980s Sears experimented with a number of strategies designed to improve its business performance. Unlike J. C. Penney, which effectively repositioned itself in the market by eliminating many of its hard goods, expanding clothing and home fashions, and replacing much of its private-label apparel with brand names, for most of the decade Sears retained its extensive inventory in hard goods and eschewed brand-name apparel, attempting instead to develop its own fashion names through endorsements from celebrities such as Cheryl Tiegs and Arnold Palmer. After this strategy proved unsuccessful, in 1988 Sears belatedly began to carry trendy women's fashions and to sell brand-name products other than its own. Under the leadership of Chairman and Chief Executive Officer Edward A. Brennan, the firm also moved to freshen the bland appearance of its stores. On 1 March 1989 the company resorted to an even more drastic measure when it adopted a policy of everyday low prices; that day it closed all 824 of its stores to reduce the prices on 50,000 products. Sears also laid off numerous employees in an effort to decrease its costs, which were nearly double Wal-Mart's.[15]

Although K mart remained the leading discount chain in the nation throughout the 1980s, it suffered disappointing gains in sales and earnings. A renovation program undertaken during the early 1980s had done little to relieve K mart of its "polyester palace" image, and by 1987, when Joseph E. Antonini became chief executive officer, the chain was mired in problems. Its stores were dilapidated, cramped, and often out of stock on advertised items; its inventory control system was outdated; customer service was poor; and competitors like Wal-Mart and Target had lower prices. Antonini addressed these difficulties by implementing a program to rebuild the dowdy chain. His strategy included automating the firm's internal-control systems and also refurbishing K mart's image by modernizing aging stores, adding more expensive merchandise to compliment the firm's lower-end lines, carrying more brand-name merchandise, and recruiting celebrities, such as race-car driver Mario Andretti and author Martha Stewart, to endorse K mart products. In 1989 K mart, like Sears, followed Wal-Mart's example and switched to a strategy of everyday low prices on all of its merchandise. Despite the efforts by Sears and K mart to become more efficient retail operations, by the end of the 1980s Wal-Mart was rapidly narrowing the gap in sales volume that existed between it and the two largest retailers.[16]

The performance of Wal-Mart stock during the 1980s mirrored the firm's phenomenal success. Fiscal 1990 capped a decade of growth during which shareholders' equity had increased to $3.966 billion from $248 million in fiscal 1981. It also marked the fifteenth consecutive year that annual increases in shareholders' equity and the return on shareholders' equity were at least 30 percent. The stock's remarkable rate of growth made it popular with Wall Street analysts and investors alike. In 1990, for example, the stock's appeal was reflected in the selection of Wal-Mart by the United Shareholders Association, a nonprofit organization designed to protect shareholders' rights, as the nation's leading company among 1,000 publicly held corporations in terms of stock performance and management's responsiveness to shareholders' interests.

Throughout the 1980s many securities analysts had recommended Wal-Mart stock as a stable, long-term investment because of the company's growth prospects, high return on equity, and consistent growth in earnings. By the end of the decade, however, Wal-Mart securities seemed to have lost some of their luster on Wall Street. In September 1990 the Salomon Brothers brokerage firm joined a small minority of critics who were no longer willing to recommend the purchase of Wal-Mart stock. The decision was based not on any loss of confidence in the company's record of performance, which it judged to be excellent. Salomon Brothers withdrew its recommendation to buy Wal-Mart stock because it believed the securities were overpriced. The firm asserted that even though Wal-Mart's sales and earnings prospects remained bright, there was "considerable" risk that the earnings potential of Wal-Mart stock might decline, since investors' confidence in Wal-Mart's future growth had caused them to purchase the securities at prices that left "little room for disappointment." Other economic experts disagreed. They conceded that Wal-Mart's rate of growth was likely to decline from its amazing level in the 1980s, but they believed that the anticipated 22 percent rate of growth in the per-share earnings of the company's stock for the early 1990s still made it a desirable long-term investment (see Table 5-2).[17]

Wal-Mart's record of sustained growth, particularly its ability to thrive during bad economic times, amazed many financial experts. After citing the company's sales increases during the recessions of 1974–75 and 1981–82, one analyst proclaimed the company virtually recession-proof, explaining that during those periods customers in need of consumer necessities had frequented the chain because of its low prices. Equally impressive was the company's demonstrated ability to survive economic downturns in agriculture and the petroleum industry, despite the fact that those enterprises were the economic mainstays of a significant portion of Wal-Mart's market area.[18]

On the strength of sales growth that was at an annual compounded rate of 36 percent from February 1980 through January 1990, Wal-Mart was indisputably the nation's fastest-growing retailer during the 1980s. Throughout the decade Wal-Mart also enjoyed a steady decline in operating expenses and gross margins. Operating, selling, and administrative costs as a percentage of sales moved downward from the vicinity of 20 percent during the early 1980s to 18 percent in fiscal 1986, 16 percent in fiscal 1988, and 15 percent in fiscal 1990. Wal-Mart reduced its gross profit margins as a percentage of sales to keep pace with its dropping operating expenses. At the start of the decade, Wal-Mart's gross profit margin was 27 percent, already one of the lowest in the discount industry. It increased slightly by 1982 due to a weak economy and the cost of remodeling and upgrading the stores acquired from Kuhn's Big K Stores Corporation; the following year Wal-Mart's gross margin declined slight-

TABLE 5-2. Shares of Preferred and Common Stock
Outstanding, and Dividends

FISCAL YEAR	PREFERRED STOCK	COMMON STOCK	DIVIDEND PAID PER SHARE
1971	—	6,000,000	—
1972	—	6,000,000	—
1973	—	6,513,000	—
1974	—	6,542,000	$.05
1975	—	6,660,000	.10
1976	—	13,418,000	.065
1977	—	13,650,000	.085
1978	—	14,868,000	.16
1979	—	15,079,000	.22
1980	—	15,121,000	.30
1981	—	32,342,000	.20
1982	296,489	32,420,000	.26
1983	296,278	67,212,000	.18
1984	247,909	139,916,000	.14
1985	222,860	140,222,000	.21
1986	181,229	281,045,000	.14
1987	—	282,183,000	.17
1988	—	565,112,000	.12
1989	—	565,591,000	.16
1990	—	566,135,000	.22
1991	—	1,142,282,000	.14
1992	—	1,149,028,000	.17

Source: Annual reports of Wal-Mart Stores, Inc.

ly. By 1985 Wal-Mart's gross margin had dropped to 25 percent, and by
the end of the decade it was in the vicinity of 23 percent. The downward
trend in the gross margin was caused in part by the expansion of the
Sam's Club division, whose gross margin was 10 percent lower than that
of the discount stores.

During the 1980s Wal-Mart nearly doubled its sales volume every
three years. On the strength of such a record, Sam Walton projected that
Wal-Mart would more than quadruple its annual sales volume by the end
of the century, reaching $130 billion. The firm confidently predicted that
while its sales volume would continue to rise, its gross profit margin

would continue to decline. In response, some analysts cautioned that, since Wal-Mart probably would find it increasingly difficult to lower its expense ratio in the years to come, a lower gross margin would be difficult to achieve without a willingness on the part of the company to accept a lower level of profitability.

The experts had little doubt, however, that Wal-Mart would continue its growth in sales volume. Predicting that the increase in consumer spending would be slow during the 1990s, some analysts indicated that Wal-Mart's growth would come at the expense of weaker competitors, since there would not be enough consumer dollars available to satisfy the needs of less efficient retailers after Wal-Mart claimed its portion. According to this rationale, businesses with higher expense ratios would be compelled to charge prices higher than Wal-Mart's. As a result, they would be unable to obtain sufficient sales growth and would fall even further behind Wal-Mart in price competition.[19]

Several factors contributed to Wal-Mart's ability to cut expenses and reduce gross margins during the 1980s. The company's considerable sales volume gave it massive buying power. This capacity to buy products cheaply was passed along to customers in the form of Wal-Mart's widely heralded "everyday low prices," which, in turn, built customer loyalty and led to even greater increases in sales. Exacting standards of efficiency and cost cutting, which were imposed by company executives on every aspect of Wal-Mart's operation, also contributed to the firm's declining operating expenses and gross margins.

The expansion of Wal-Mart's sophisticated distribution system during the 1980s was central to its cost-cutting strategy. By the end of the decade, Wal-Mart had a total of 16 distribution centers located throughout the company's trade territory. The huge facilities (some as large as 27 acres under one roof) continued to process at least 75 percent of the merchandise sold in Wal-Mart stores. The distribution centers were fully automated, and their 10,000 workers utilized such innovations as conveyor belts and laser scanners to route 300 million cases of merchandise annually, with 99 percent of the orders filled correctly, according to the company. Wal-Mart's distribution costs, for example, by the end of the 1980s were only 1.3 percent of sales, a figure significantly lower than those of K mart and Sears, which had distribution costs of 3.5 percent and 5 percent, respectively.

At the foundation of Wal-Mart's distribution system was its process of cross-docking. Through this intricate procedure, merchandise was continuously delivered to Wal-Mart's distribution centers, where it was rapidly repacked and sent to stores. Instead of languishing in the warehouses themselves, many goods crossed from one loading dock to another at Wal-Mart's distribution centers in 48 hours or less. This process enabled Wal-Mart to economize by purchasing merchandise in bulk while avoiding the customary inventory and handling costs. Wal-Mart's large truck fleet played a vital role in ensuring that the flow of merchandise from its distribution centers to its outlets was uninterrupted. In fiscal 1991 Wal-Mart's trucks traveled more than 190 million miles and delivered more than 315,000 trailerloads of merchandise. At a typical distribution center, for example, 150 outbound and 160 inbound Wal-Mart trucks were loaded and unloaded daily. Its insistence on the frequent, often daily, delivery of merchandise set Wal-Mart apart from rivals such as K mart, which generally delivered merchandise to its stores once every five days, and Target, which averaged a delivery every three to four days. Acknowledging Wal-Mart's ability to outdistance its competitors in keeping stores well-stocked with merchandise, David Glass said, "Our distribution facilities are one of the keys to our success. If we do anything better than other folks, that's it."[20]

Because Wal-Mart's complex distribution process was dependent on the accurate and speedy transfer of inventory-control information, the firm continued to invest vast resources in technology and communications. At the heart of a technological system regarded by many as one of the most sophisticated in retailing was the firm's high-speed computer system. Housed in a 16,000 square-foot facility at the corporate headquarters, the system linked all retail outlets and distribution centers to Bentonville. The system logged every item sold at checkout counters, automatically kept warehouses informed of merchandise to be ordered, and directed the flow of goods not only to the stores but also even to the proper shelves.

Another important component in Wal-Mart's inventory-control process was the firm's use of point-of-sale electronic scanning and the Uniform Product Code (UPC). In 1981 Wal-Mart began testing bar-code scanning by installing equipment that would read the UPC at checkout counters in selected stores. Although manufacturers initially had placed the UPC on merchandise for the benefit of the supermarket industry, Wal-Mart and other discount chains realized that they could use the technology too, since many of the products that carried a UPC, such as candy, tobacco, and panty hose, also were sold by discounters.

After two years of testing, Wal-Mart demonstrated its commitment to the UPC technology by expanding the system to 25 stores, followed by an additional 70 stores in 1984. In 1985 Wal-Mart installed bar-code scanning in more than 200 stores in the first phase of the company's plan to place scanners in all of its stores. By the end of the decade, scanning was in use throughout Wal-Mart's entire operation, including every distribution center and the receiving departments of all stores.

Wal-Mart's decision to adopt UPC scanning anticipated its emergence during the 1980s as the prevailing marking technology for the retail industry. Discount chains, especially, came to prefer bar-code scanning to the alternative of keying in inventory information by hand. Not only was scanning quicker, ensuring the customer a faster checkout time, but it was also a more accurate method for capturing detailed information at the point of sale that could be utilized to accelerate the reordering of merchandise.

Wal-Mart also used bar-code scanning for inventory management and merchandise handling throughout its operation. Laser scanners were used in distribution centers to speed the flow of merchandise to stores, while at the stores themselves, a check-in system known as "automated receiving" was designed to take advantage of containers' bar-code labeling by allowing stocking crews, with the assistance of handheld laser scanners, to get freight onto the sales floor faster. Installed in the back room of every Wal-Mart store by the summer of 1987, this procedure, according to the company, saved 60 percent of the man-hours required by previous freight-processing methods. Handheld portable computers with bar-code scanners attached also were used in stores for monitoring inventory levels on the sales floor. These units recorded such information as the description, quantity, cost, and selling price of current stock. The system's ability to acquire this information directly from shelf labels allowed the firm to project inventory needs more quickly, thereby saving time in the company's reordering process.

During the late 1980s Wal-Mart was in the vanguard of stores using advanced computer technologies to forge direct electronic linkage systems with vendors. These links were designed to provide a more rapid replenishment of merchandise at a reduced cost. In an effort to minimize paperwork, Wal-Mart adopted the Electronic Data Interchange (EDI) system. This system provided for the electronic transmission of business documents, such as purchase orders, invoices, shipping notices, and point-of-sale information, thereby allowing suppliers to respond promptly and accurately to sales trends. By 1990 Wal-Mart had initiated EDI arrangements with some 1,810 of its approximately 5,000 vendors, making it the nation's largest user of the technology.

Wal-Mart also experimented with more advanced computerized systems such as Quick Response and Retail Link. Instead of relying on purchase orders, these systems utilized bar-code scanning and satellite communications to move sales, shipping, and reorder information directly from stores to suppliers on a daily basis. Through the use of such technology, Wal-Mart's suppliers received a constant flow of specific sales results and inventory needs, including details such as colors and sizes. As a result, the appropriate merchandise could be promptly dispatched to stores, sometimes arriving in as few as nine days.[21]

In 1987 Wal-Mart launched its own satellite communications network. The largest privately owned system in the United States, it cost Wal-Mart $20 million, an amount that staggered Walton. "It blows my mind that we spent $20 million for a satellite outfit," he said. The company's commitment to the technology proved to be a worthwhile investment. Inaugurated with a live broadcast from Walton to all Wal-Mart associates, the six-channel satellite network provided two-way voice and one-way video communication to every operating unit. The company found the network's video capabilities especially useful, since they facilitated the face-to-face communication between corporate management and associates that the firm had always deemed crucial to its success. The semiweekly programs were considered to be an electronic extension of the trips Walton and other company executives continuously made to stores and distribution centers. They were broadcast from a television studio at the Bentonville headquarters to the stores, which could tape them or view them live. *Wal-Mart Week in Review* was a 10-minute program designed for all associates, but most of the programs were more narrowly focused. Mainly they presented rapidly changing, up-to-date inventory and merchandise information, such as previews of new products. The satellite system also fulfilled other important functions for the company. With it, Wal-Mart could communicate with its operating units simultaneously and as many times a day as it desired, which reduced telephone costs. The system also gathered sales and inventory information for the company's master computer, handled credit-card approval in approximately five seconds, and kept track of the company's complex distribution process.[22]

Wal-Mart's efficient distribution and technology systems allowed the company to sustain its commitment to keeping its stores well-stocked with merchandise. The nature of this merchandise changed dramatically during the 1980s, however, as Wal-Mart significantly modified its merchandising strategy. Early in the decade, Wal-Mart decided to revise its "cheap and deep" approach to stocking its stores by emphasizing brand-name goods. While this innovation did not transport the company into the realm of upscale discounting exemplified by Target, it did greatly enhance the quality and selection of Wal-Mart's products.

In apparel, and especially women's wear, Wal-Mart realized that to be more competitive with other discounters it had to upgrade its offerings. The firm enhanced its overall clothing presentation by focusing on a wider selection of goods, paying greater heed to style, improving displays, and emphasizing value-priced brand names such as Brittania and

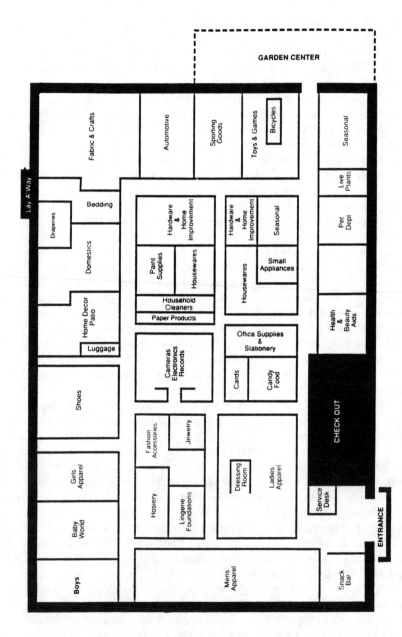

Figure 5-1. Layout of a Modern Wal-Mart Store

Gitano. In other categories, such as domestics (bed and bath products) and hard goods (hardware, automotive goods, small appliances, and housewares), Wal-Mart moved away from a merchandising strategy based on cheap imports, seconds, irregulars, and private labels to one founded on a wider selection of brand names, such as Cannon sheets and towels and Dutch Boy and Glidden paints. In consumer electronics, Wal-Mart also upgraded its merchandising by exchanging cheap imports for brand names and by adding big-ticket items like fax machines and personal computers.[23]

In its advertising, cost cutting remained the norm. Except for store openings, the firm minimized its use of television and newspaper advertising and relied instead on its prices to lure customers to its stores. The firm preferred to build traffic on an individual-store basis by using small, local promotional events, such as Moon Pie–eating contests and gerbil races in the pet departments of its stores.[24]

During the 1980s Wal-Mart garnered a variety of industry and other awards for performance and excellence. It was ranked by *Forbes* magazine as the leading retailer in the United States from 1977 to 1987 in the categories of return on equity, return on capital, earnings growth, sales growth, and profitability; it was recognized in 1982 as one of the 5 best-managed companies in America by *Dun's Business Review*; and it was recognized by *Business Month* magazine in 1988 as one of the 5 best-managed companies in the nation from 1972 to 1987. Wal-Mart received the Gold Medal Award from the National Retail Merchants Association in 1988 for having the most distinguished retail performance of 1987; it received a special "Retailer of the Decade" award in 1989 from *Discount Store News*, which devoted an entire edition to the firm, entitled "Wal-Mart's Decade of Excellence"; its 250,000 associates were collectively named the mass-market retailers of the year in 1989 by the trade publication *Mass Market Retailers*; and it was included on *Fortune* magazine's list of America's 10 most admired corporations, where some 8,000 of the nation's business executives ranked it ninth in 1988, fifth in 1989, and in 1991 fourth overall and first in the quality of its management. Sam Walton was the recipient of numerous individual honors as well, including being named CEO of the Year in 1986 and CEO of the Decade in 1989 by *Financial World* magazine.[25]

To the publicity-shy Walton, possibly the decade's most dubious honor came in 1985, when *Forbes* magazine named him the richest man in the United States by placing him at the head of its annual "Forbes Four Hundred" list of wealthiest Americans. According to *Forbes*, Walton, who along with his family owned 39 percent of Wal-Mart Stores, Inc., through a family investment firm, Walton Enterprises, was worth $2.8

billion. Walton was accorded the same honor in 1986, 1987, and 1988, when *Forbes* reported his worth at $4.5 billion, $8.5 billion, and $6.7 billion, respectively. The $1.8 billion drop in 1988 was the result of the stock market crash in 1987. When trading ended on 19 October 1987, Wal-Mart securities had plunged 31 percent. The loss did not seem to faze Walton, however. After learning of the drop in stock prices, he told the Associated Press the next day, "It's paper anyway. It was paper when we started and it's paper afterward." That Walton seemed untroubled, even of good cheer, on the day following the crash did not surprise one long-time observer, who noted that it was typical of Walton to be more concerned with his company than his stock portfolio. After Walton divided his fortune with his children by converting Walton Enterprises into a partnership to avoid double taxation on dividends, in 1989 *Forbes* ranked Walton and his four children twentieth through twenty-fourth on its list, with $1.8 billion each; they were ranked eleventh through fifteenth, with a combined fortune of $12.5 billion, in 1990.[26]

To cope better with his company's phenomenal growth, Walton moved to assemble an executive staff capable of guiding the rapidly expanding firm. At the beginning of the 1980s Wal-Mart's senior management corps consisted of Walton himself as chairman of the board and chief executive officer, Jack Shewmaker as president and chief operating officer, and David Glass as vice chairman and chief financial officer. Donald G. Soderquist was executive vice president of administration and distribution. As a senior vice president and a member of the board of directors, Bud Walton, who owned approximately $300 million in Wal-Mart stock, remained active in corporate affairs and continued to oversee the purchasing of sites for Wal-Mart stores. Rob Walton held the title of vice chairman, secretary, and general counsel.

The membership of the board of directors remained remarkably stable during the 1980s, although the number of directors gradually increased to 15. Sam, Bud, and Rob Walton served on the board throughout the decade. Others who continued on the board included James H. Jones, Glass, Shewmaker, and Soderquist. Jackson T. Stephens and Ferold G. Arend, both long-term directors, departed in the mid-1980s. Among the members who joined the board in mid-decade were William H. Seay, the retired chairman of Southwestern Life Insurance Company of Dallas; Charles Lazarus, chairman and chief executive officer of Toys "R" Us, Inc.; and Hillary Rodham Clinton, a partner in a Little Rock law firm and wife of then governor Bill Clinton.

Throughout the early 1980s Walton remained active in corporate affairs. His days typically began at six in the morning and lasted into the evening, although on at least one occasion he visited a distribution center at four in the morning to have coffee and doughnuts with his employees. Frequently piloting his twin-engine airplane himself, he continued visiting stores at least four days a week—sometimes as many as six per day.

By the mid-1980s Walton realized that, despite his hands-on involvement, the time had come for him to name a successor, and he had two candidates in mind for the job. Jack Shewmaker and David Glass were commonly considered the leading contenders to one day succeed Walton. In 1984 Walton asked the two men to exchange jobs. Glass replaced Shewmaker as president and chief operating officer of the firm, while Shewmaker assumed Glass's positions of vice chairman and chief financial officer. Although Shewmaker thereafter reported to Glass, both men made identical six-figure salaries and each executive's stock holding was valued at more than $23 million by 1987. Walton downplayed the action by calling it a routine cross-training exercise, consistent with his frequent practice of asking his managers to switch jobs to ensure that they were well informed regarding various aspects of corporate affairs. The curious move, however, merely heightened the aura of competition that had surrounded the two men for some time.

Finally, on 1 February 1988 the 69-year-old Walton ended the suspense and anointed his successor. He relinquished the job of chief executive officer to David Glass, who was 52, retaining the title of chairman of the board. On 28 February the 49-year-old Shewmaker resigned, leaving Glass, along with Walton, to lead the company. Walton rounded out his senior management team with two additional appointments. He promoted Donald Soderquist to vice chairman and chief operating officer, and Paul R. Carter, formerly executive vice president for finance, replaced Shewmaker as chief financial officer.[27]

Walton's choice of David Glass was a sound one. Glass had come to Wal-Mart with a solid background in retailing. After graduating from Southwest Missouri State University in Springfield with a degree in accounting, he had joined a small drugstore chain headquartered in Springfield. He had been serving as an executive at a small supermarket chain, also located in Springfield, when Walton, impressed by his tenacious managerial style, asked him to join Wal-Mart in 1976 as executive vice president for finance.

The reserved Glass exhibited little of the flamboyance that characterized Walton's colorful leadership. Walking a pig down the street, as Walton had done in Dallas in 1986, clearly would not be his style. His intense nature was not inclined toward Wal-Mart's promotional gimmickry, and on those occasions when he did attempt the down-home demeanor that came so naturally to Walton, such as the time he donned overalls and rode a donkey around the parking lot of a Wal-Mart store in Harrison, Arkansas, his performances seemed awkward and contrived.

In the matter of providing leadership for Wal-Mart, however, Glass was ably qualified to serve in Walton's stead, since both his philosophy of retailing and his corporate values were similar to Walton's. His innately conservative style, moreover, was well suited to the frugality that was Wal-Mart's trademark. Although it had been Glass who had first convinced a reluctant Walton to embrace computer technology in the 1970s, his willingness to commit vast expenditures to state-of-the-art electronics was to him merely an expedient in the pursuit of efficiency. In fact, possibly his greatest achievement had been his ability quietly to transform Wal-Mart into a paragon of technological wizardry without disturbing the company's folksy image. Glass's influence also could be seen in the aggressive expansion strategy pursued by the company.[28]

Through the years, there had evolved at Wal-Mart a novel and innovative set of values that had fostered the company's success. This informal, yet firmly held, system of rules by which business was conducted was known as Wal-Mart's "corporate culture." At the foundation of this corporate culture were the firm's principles of management, which had been fashioned by Sam Walton at the outset. Over the years, Walton's gift for staffing key positions with individuals who naturally subscribed to Wal-Mart's corporate philosophy allowed him to assemble a senior management staff fully committed to perpetuating the fundamental precepts on which the company had been built. Already firmly in place as the 1980s dawned, Wal-Mart's management methods would reap astounding results for the firm during the years that followed.

A hallmark of Wal-Mart's management style was its flexibility. Walton avoided unnecessary layers of bureaucracy by delegating a broad range of responsibilities to his versatile senior executives. In 1984 Donald Soderquist, for example, was in charge of categories as varied as personnel, training, warehouse management, legal services, government and public affairs, and the firm's aviation department. In fulfilling their diverse duties, Walton allowed his executives a large measure of autonomy. This tendency to encourage independent thinking permeated every level of the organization, from top managers down to hourly associates.[29]

To save his company from the ossification that frequently afflicted large corporations, Walton relied on vigorous internal communication between the upper levels of management and hourly personnel. Wal-Mart continued to be truly exceptional in the amount of daily contact it maintained between corporate officers and the firm's retail outlets. David Glass, like Walton, seldom spent an entire week in Bentonville. Instead, he, as well as other senior officers, spent several days a week visiting stores, finding out what was on workers' minds, and listening to ideas that might improve operations. These trips no doubt played a key role in maintaining the high energy and enthusiasm that characterized Wal-Mart's employees.[30]

The store visits made by the firm's regional vice presidents were central to the success of Wal-Mart's communications system. Although headquartered in Bentonville, the 12 executives continued to depart every Monday morning by airplane for their respective territories, in each of which approximately 75 stores were located by the late 1980s. This system was at sharp variance with that of competitors such as K mart and Target, where the regional vice presidents' counterparts actually lived in their geographical territories, which were three to four times larger than Wal-Mart's. The expense of maintaining regional offices possibly cost those companies as much as an additional 2 percent of sales.

The vice presidents continued to visit stores through Thursday, gathering information from managers, employees, and customers. Ever thorough, they also visited stores belonging to competitors. They then flew back to Bentonville for the traditional Friday and Saturday meetings. On Saturday mornings, senior management officials were joined by some 250 to 300 store managers. While these 7:30 gatherings increasingly had taken on the aura of pep rallies and featured Wal-Mart cheers, awards, and appearances by such groups as the singing truck drivers, serious business was also conducted. The executives reviewed computer information charting the performance of every store for the week, discussed the activities of competitors, and made merchandising and advertising plans for the coming weeks.

No detail was small enough to escape the attention of Wal-Mart's corporate officers. If the sales of a particular product—garden hoses, for example—were sluggish, quick action would be taken; a decision such as changing displays or lowering prices would be made and implemented. As always, at the conclusion of the Saturday meeting, information such as this, as well as the overall merchandising strategy for the upcoming week, was relayed to every store. After the satellite network became operative, the Saturday morning meetings were broadcast directly to all stores.[31]

Wal-Mart was considered by some observers the "finest managed" retail firm in the United States, with one group of financial analysts terming it the "finest managed company we have ever followed." But while corporate America was impressed, it was also bewildered by Wal-Mart's unorthodox methods. To Walton, however, the secret of Wal-Mart's success was beguilingly simple. It lay in attracting people well suited to their jobs. For Walton, this meant hiring individuals who exhibited the fundamental values of loyalty and, especially, hard work.[32]

Walton prized the work ethic above all other standards. He was aware that retailing was a labor-intensive industry, and his demands on personnel, in terms of time and effort, were immense. Commenting on the experience of one 53-year-old senior executive who, weary of the grueling regimen of store visits, resigned after only one year on the job, an observer said, "He just burnt out. Sam doesn't let up."[33]

Although hard work was required, it was also rewarded. A Wal-Mart store manager, for example, could keep up to 5 percent of his store's pre-tax profits. This translated into as much as $130,000 a year for some store managers, but managers' salaries were typically just over $40,000 in the mid-1980s.[34]

The firm apparently believed that women were not particularly adapted to the arduous toil required of those who desired to rise through the corporate ranks. In fiscal 1991, for example, only two women served as corporate officers: one of the women was on the board of directors, and the other woman was one of the firm's 12 vice presidents. There were no women at the senior management level. The company's rejoinder to those who reproached it for the noticeable absence of women in its senior management circle was that the rigors of the job in terms of time and travel were just too demanding. This disclaimer failed to satisfy the critics, however, who continued to rebuke the company for its apparent reluctance to promote women.[35]

The firm did work to enhance the career opportunities of its associates by means of continuous training through such instructional programs as the Walton Institute. Taught by Wal-Mart managers, faculty from the University of Arkansas, and guest lecturers and authors, the institute sponsored five-day training sessions for the firm's store managers. In addition, the company conducted numerous seminars for associates who aspired to join the ranks of management. As a result, in fiscal 1988, for example, Wal-Mart promoted 1,100 associates to management who previously had worked in nonmanagement positions.

Even as Wal-Mart expanded beyond its small-town base during the 1980s, it retained its ability to imbue its associates with what Walton called "Wal-Mart fever." The high degree of motivation among Wal-Mart personnel was due in part to generous financial incentives. These included an employees' disaster-relief fund; a scholarship program for employees' children; shared savings when store stock losses were reduced; a payroll-deduction plan for purchasing stock; so-called stretch-incentive bonuses, which were designed to "reward each associate's involvement"; and a profit-sharing plan. In fiscal 1990, for example, Wal-Mart's benefits plans, combined with store-management bonus and compensation programs, enabled employees to earn more than $100 million over and above their wages and base compensation. Moreover, because many associates were stockholders, explained one analyst, they were inclined to "feel it's their company as much as management."[36]

Yet Wal-Mart's ability to motivate its employees extended beyond its pecuniary compensations. The motivation related directly to the firm's focus on people, which remained the cornerstone of its corporate culture. As the company's operations became more extended and technologically complex, senior executives went to great lengths to bolster workforce morale by continually stressing that the true key to the company's success lay in the efforts of its personnel. By demonstrating a respect for employees' opinions and including them, even down to the departmental level, in the corporate decision-making process, management made personnel feel a genuine sense of participation in the company. As David Glass explained: "Most people give lip service to the idea that 'we are what we are because of our people,' but here that actually is the case. Sam said when he first started, 'If you can create a partnership rather than an employer-employee relationship, obviously it will work a lot better.'"[37]

The high level of energy and loyalty that Wal-Mart's personnel exhibited toward the firm was due in large measure to what the company termed its "environment of open-door communication," which provided for the "free flow of ideas from every possible source" in the firm. Corporate policy allowed every employee to meet annually with management to discuss anything from working conditions to the direction of the company, as well as to ask questions and make suggestions. Associates at all levels were encouraged not only to express their ideas to management but also to vent their concerns and complaints. Moreover, they were made to feel that their opinions mattered. According to one observer, "[Walton] listens to his employees. Not just store managers and clerks, but the janitors tell him what's going on."[38]

Management gave associates a wide range of freedom and responsibility in the performance of their jobs and then held them accountable for their actions. In fiscal 1987, for example, Wal-Mart announced its new policy of creating "a store within a store," which encouraged department managers and assistant managers to operate their departments just as they would run their own businesses. The company supported its department managers in this enterprise by providing them with weekly figures on sales, profits, losses, markup, and inventory. This information indicated precisely how their departments compared with other departments in their own store as well as in other stores in the chain.[39]

The firm's senior managers continued to insist that its employees were its best resource for innovation and change. This ideal, which was first stressed by Walton, was reiterated by Glass, who said: "We believe nothing constructive happens in Bentonville. Our grass-roots philosophy is that the best ideas come from people on the firing line." As proof of its commitment to employee participation, Wal-Mart continued its practice of implementing suggestions made by hourly associates. During the late 1980s, for example, a marketing student at the University of Florida, while working one summer at a Wal-Mart distribution center, devised a more efficient method for filling orders from stores. Wal-Mart not only adopted the plan, which, according to the company, resulted in a substantial annual savings for the firm, but it also recognized the inventive employee by establishing a five-year retail scholarship in his name at the University of Florida.

The speed with which Wal-Mart implemented such innovations was typical of the firm's adaptability. Calling the company's low resistance to change a "trademark," Walton said: "We are willing to change. I would just like us to continue to make changes as they need to be made, and every day is a different situation in this retail business. . . . But change and the willingness to change, to try anything, try anyone's idea, it might not work. But it won't break the company when it doesn't."[40]

Wal-Mart's approach to philanthropy was consistent with its corporate precepts of employee involvement and thrift. The company's charitable priorities were education, community service, and support for the American free-enterprise system, and in 1981 the firm establish the Wal-Mart Foundation to oversee the bulk of its philanthropic activities. Although the foundation contributed to established national causes, such as the United Way and the Children's Miracle Network, an annual telethon that raised money for children's hospitals, it gave priority to local programs that directly touched the lives of Wal-Mart's customers. The best example was the foundation's community scholarship program, in which each Wal-Mart store annually awarded a college scholarship of $1,000, payable over two years, to a high school senior living in the store's trade area. The company maintained that in 1989, for example, 1,244 such scholarships were awarded through the foundation. In addition the foundation coordinated three other scholarship programs. One served the children of Wal-Mart employees, another was for high school seniors who worked part-time for Wal-Mart, and the third was for college students who worked part-time for the Sam's Clubs.

The Wal-Mart Foundation also supported Students in Free Enterprise (SIFE), a program that recruited college students to teach elementary and high school students about the virtues of the American free-enterprise system. In 1987, for example, SIFE received a $68,500 appropriation from the foundation. SIFE also served as a convenient labor pool for Wal-Mart, since some of its young workers, having proved themselves compatible with the firm's corporate values, were regarded as ideal future employees.

Wal-Mart encouraged individual stores to be actively involved in community affairs by adopting causes or raising funds in response to local needs. Through its grant program, the foundation would then match the amount that individual stores raised for local charities or community projects. (Most of the grants were for $2,000 or less.) Wal-Mart maintained that in 1987, for example, the Wal-Mart Foundation assisted 1,018 communities with more than 2,650 projects as diverse as installing playground equipment and purchasing bulletproof vests for law-enforcement agencies.

By widely publicizing such activities at the local level, Wal-Mart managed to maintain a high profile that was embellished with huge dollops of community goodwill and customer loyalty. Overall, however, in comparison with other firms, Wal-Mart was parsimonious when it came to corporate giving. In 1987, for example, according to the standard gauge of corporate philanthropy, the percentage of pretax earnings a firm donates to charity, Wal-Mart ranked last among the major discounters. Rival K mart contributed 3.6 times as much. In that same year, the Wal-Mart Foundation, with total assets of $6.1 million, ranked nowhere near the top 100 corporate foundations in charitable expenditures.[41]

The acclaim that Wal-Mart received in the national news media in 1989 in the aftermath of Hurricane Hugo demonstrated the firm's ability to reap the maximum favorable publicity from its measured charitable activities. Wal-Mart received total credit in the news media for donating $1 million worth of goods to the hurricane's victims in the Carolinas. In reality, the donation was a joint effort with some of the firm's vendors, but Wal-Mart got the credit because the goods were shipped in Wal-Mart trucks. When queried about the incident, Wal-Mart refused to name the vendors involved or to disclose how much of the $1 million it had donated.

Wal-Mart always was quick to point out that its employees were urged to be good citizens and to contribute to their communities by becoming involved in local affairs. Many store managers, for example, were members of local chambers of commerce. Employees, especially those aspiring to management positions, were also expected to contribute directly to charitable causes endorsed by the company and, more important, to raise money for local projects from customers through in-store cash solicitations and through such fund-raising enterprises as car washes, rummage sales, and fried-pie and bake sales. Wal-Mart touted the leadership role its associates assumed in fund-raising activities as a sterling example of its emphasis on employee involvement in community affairs. Also to be considered, however, was the benefit to the company:

in using the associates to solicit contributions from Wal-Mart shoppers, the firm was able to garner a significant portion of its philanthropic expenditures from its customers.

In addition to the Wal-Mart Foundation, the company sponsored two other active charitable foundations, the Walton Foundation and the Sam M. and Helen R. Walton Foundation, which, in 1988, for example, spent $605,000 and $441,000, respectively. Initially the entire thrust of the Walton Foundation was educational. It granted college scholarships in the amount of $6,000, payable over four years, to approximately 100 children of Wal-Mart associates, who were known as "Walton Scholars." Beginning in 1988, it also began to extend grants to miscellaneous educational and community-service organizations, such as the Arkansas Business Council Foundation and Planned Parenthood. The Sam M. and Helen R. Walton Foundation, in conjunction with personal contributions from Walton himself, funded a scholarship program for 180 students from seven Central American nations to allow them to study the American way of life at three universities in Arkansas. At Harding University, for example, a Christian school located in the small Ozark town of Searcy, 60 students received four-year scholarships of $9,000 per year. Begun in 1985, the program, according to Sam Walton, was designed to expose the participants to the "benefits of a free society" so that they might "encourage democratic traditions and private development in their countries."[42]

After David Glass became CEO, Sam Walton remained active in corporate affairs. He continued his hectic schedule, spending at least four days a week visiting stores. Walton also emerged as the leading symbol of his firm's folksy image. Ironically, as he began to relinquish day-to-day operations to his handpicked senior managers, the growing fame of his company increasingly focused on Walton a high-profile spotlight that he often found disconcerting. He remained reticent about corporate affairs, usually declining interviews. As honors and awards were thrust upon him, he endeavored to deflect the glare of publicity from himself and onto his employees, who he continued to insist were the source of his firm's success.

He continued to preside at the traditional Saturday morning management meetings in Bentonville and at the annual shareholders' meetings, which, by the late 1980s, had taken on the trappings of a religious revival for Wal-Mart's ardent supporters. These robust gatherings had grown to such proportions that the 1989 affair attracted more than 7,000 people. At this meeting, the proceedings began solemnly enough with the Pledge of Allegiance and a prayer. Then, for two hours, exuberant shareholders were treated to a rollicking program of songs, awards, and, of course, price comparisons indicating that Wal-Mart's prices were lower than its competitors' on selected merchandise.[43]

The element of unpredictability in Sam Walton's style of leadership often enthralled Wal-Mart employees and customers alike. His habit of making unannounced store visits and leading associates in a rousing Wal-Mart cheer had become as much a part of the growing Walton legend as his old pickup truck. On one occasion, however, Walton's penchant for the spontaneous gesture came back to haunt him. In a moment of unbridled enthusiasm, Walton had pledged to Wal-Mart's associates that if the company achieved an 8 percent pretax profit in fiscal 1984, he would perform a hula dance in the heart of New York's financial district. Bolstered by his knowledge that the retail-industry average at that time was only 3 percent, Walton had believed his bet to be a safe one. "There's not a chance," he said, "but if you [associates] achieve those ridiculous figures, I'll dance a hula on Wall Street." When profits for the year turned out to be 8.04 percent, Walton resolutely kept his word. In March 1984 he donned a Hawaiian shirt and grass skirt over his business suit and, looking every inch as uncomfortable as he no doubt felt, briefly danced on Wall Street.[44]

Walton's greatest priority was to instill the essence of Wal-Mart's corporate culture in the firm's increasing number of associates. Both in person and via the company's private telecommunications network, Walton ardently preached the gospel of customer service. Confessing that he was "totally obsessed" with the subject, Walton, in one video presentation, urged associates to go out of their way to accommodate the needs of customers. He concluded the broadcast by asking his associates to raise their right hands and repeat the pledge: "From this day forward, I solemnly promise and declare that every customer that comes within ten feet of me, I will smile, look them in the eye, and greet them, so help me Sam."[45]

Despite its rapidly swelling size, the company endeavored to maintain its common touch. An easy informality, symbolized by the use of first names for everyone from Walton—whom employees addressed as "Mr. Sam"—on down, continued to characterize the firm. According to one analyst, even after a decade of tremendous growth, many of the company's associates continued to "feel as if they are part of Sam Walton's extended family." One employee held the firm in such high esteem that she got married in the Wal-Mart store in Monroeville, Alabama.[46]

Undergirding this sense of family was the gratitude of many associates, especially those in poorer states like Arkansas and Mississippi, who were thankful to the firm for providing them with a higher income than they otherwise might have achieved. Such economic realities typically led to high levels of employee satisfaction, but there were exceptions. For example, on three occasions employees at the distribution center in Searcy, Arkansas, contemplated joining the Teamsters union. Among their complaints were low wages, unsafe working conditions, and a failure on the part of the company to recognize seniority and provide compensation for work-related injuries. In a meeting with his disgruntled employees, Walton moved forcefully to thwart this threat to Wal-Mart's nonunion tradition. According to a union official who was present, Walton told employees that if they voted in favor of the union, he would curtail their profit-sharing program. He also reminded the workers that he had on file 500 applications for their jobs.

When he informed Wal-Mart's other personnel of the episode, Walton applauded the satisfactory resolution of the problem. He wrote in the February 1982 edition of *Wal-Mart World*: "Last Friday, our good associates at our Searcy distribution center rejected the union by the overwhelming margin of over three to one. Bless them all. . . . We will never need a union in Wal-Mart if we work with and for one another and keep listening to each other." While rare, contretemps such as the Searcy incident indicated that although senior management liked to rhapsodize about Wal-Mart's being one big, happy family, such was not always the case.[47]

Wal-Mart's family image was further tarnished by other complaints about its labor policies. From time to time the firm was criticized for its low entry-level salaries and, especially, its heavy reliance on cost-effective part-time labor. In 1988, for example, Arkansas state senator Jay Bradford took Wal-Mart to task for its unwillingness to provide some of its employees with enough hours to lift them out of poverty. Citing evidence from a source at the Arkansas Human Services Department indicating that many of Wal-Mart's workers earned such meager salaries that they had to rely on public assistance to make ends meet, Bradford accused Wal-Mart and other companies that pursued similar cheap-labor policies of "dumping their overhead" on the taxpayers by failing to allow part-time personnel to work enough hours to redeem themselves from welfare. Wal-Mart responded by stating that the use of part-time help was standard practice in the retail industry and that the number of such workers employed by Wal-Mart was not excessive.[48]

In one instance Wal-Mart's effort to highlight the family values with which it so closely identified itself plunged the firm into unanticipated controversy. In the summer of 1986 Wal-Mart banished some 32 adult and teen magazines, including *Playboy* and *Rolling Stone*, from its stores. The firm acquired a certain notoriety in some circles when the action was linked to a sermon delivered earlier by televangelist Jimmy Swaggart, who had criticized Wal-Mart and K mart for carrying magazines that might adversely affect children. Critics maintained that in purging the offending literature from its racks, Wal-Mart had yielded too readily to the pressures brought to bear by the broadcast and by a subsequent letter-writing campaign inspired by Swaggart. Wal-Mart denied that Swaggart's fulminations had played any role in the decision. The firm asserted that the action was merely an aspect of its long-standing policy of removing from its stores any merchandise that might be considered in the least obscene. One record-company executive took a different view, insisting that the action reflected the firm's Bible Belt mentality. "You're talking about hard-core fundamentalism," he said. Ironically, Wal-Mart's rectitude with regard to rock music magazines did not extend to banning the music itself. The firm routinely stocked controversial heavy-metal albums and also promoted them in television and radio advertisements that stated that Wal-Mart had low prices on the latest hits.[49]

Wal-Mart found itself mired in further controversy as a result of its relationship with its vendors. As an aspect of its ongoing campaign to extract the lowest possible prices from suppliers, in the early 1980s Wal-Mart had adopted a policy of excluding independent manufacturers' sales representatives from business transactions and ordering directly from suppliers. Wal-Mart then demanded that the manufacturers cut their prices 2 to 6 percent, an amount equal to the typical sales representative's commission. If a company refused, Wal-Mart often would not order any more merchandise.

The policy, which the firm declined to acknowledge publicly, was effective. In the face of Wal-Mart's awesome purchasing power, many manufacturers acceded to its wishes and sent senior sales executives, rather than sales representatives, to Bentonville. Although determined to humor Wal-Mart, some suppliers did concede that their purported savings from the elimination of the independent representatives was nonexistent, since someone had to be paid to perform their task.

Faced with the loss of such a lucrative account and fearing that the practice would spread, the manufacturers' representatives fought back. In 1986 some 1,000 of them formed the Organization of Manufacturers Representatives. Through this organization, they began a campaign of denouncing Wal-Mart's actions in the national press. In December 1986, for example, the organization sponsored a full-page advertisement in the *Wall Street Journal* condemning Wal-Mart's policy of bypassing manufacturers' representatives.[50]

The accusations they leveled at Wal-Mart, together with the company's already formidable reputation among vendors as a tough negotiator on price (an official at one consumer-goods firm called Wal-Mart "the rudest account in America"), convinced the firm that it needed to improve its overall relationship with suppliers. Besides, by the late 1980s fortuitous advances in technology afforded the company a far more effective means of pursuing its cost-cutting aims with vendors without the unsavory publicity that had attended its drive to eliminate manufacturers' representatives. In an effort to convert its adversarial relationship with suppliers into a more cooperative one, Wal-Mart began to establish what it termed "partnerships" with vendors, based on sharing information through such systems as EDI and Retail Link.[51]

Further evidence of Wal-Mart's efforts to forge partnerships with select suppliers was its in-store vendor shops, which allocated space in conventional Wal-Mart stores to key vendors, and its even bolder experiment, Wal-Mart vendor stores. Located in Janesville, Wisconsin, and Charlotte, North Carolina, the vendor stores featured a more limited number of brands than a typical Wal-Mart store. Begun by Wal-Mart in 1989, both of these new ventures allowed such suppliers as Gitano, Cannon, and Rubbermaid considerable control over the presentation of their merchandise in the marketplace. By giving individual suppliers the freedom to design their own display areas, Wal-Mart hoped to create within the stores a more appealing and specialized shopping environment that would lure customers away from department stores and specialty stores.[52]

Wal-Mart's efforts to establish partnerships with its key suppliers were well received. Some vendors, in fact, credited these mutually advantageous alliances with revolutionizing the entire business relationship between manufacturers and merchants. As one supplier explained: "Years ago, we prayed for orders to come from our customers. Today, we are partners with our customers. We feel they are part of our company, as we're part of theirs. This is something not even considered a possibility six to eight years ago."

Although Wal-Mart may have refined its tactics, the firm did not relinquish its hard-bargaining ways altogether. The company stressed that since suppliers now were partners in providing customers with the lowest possible prices, they had to abandon archaic practices of packaging and shipping in favor of methods that would encourage sales. In addition, if a vendor failed to maintain an acceptable standard of product quality or keep its prices at a reasonable level, Wal-Mart would terminate its relationship with the offending manufacturer.[53]

While some of Wal-Mart's practices may have subjected the firm to disparaging public scrutiny, other policies were greeted with widespread approval. One of the company's most popular projects was its so-called Buy American program, which was designed to replace foreign goods with domestic goods. Walton realized the stigma that imports had among rural Americans, particularly in small towns in the South, where some local economies had been damaged when textile jobs shifted overseas. In 1985 he sent an open letter to 3,000 manufacturers in the United States, inviting them to take part in the Buy American program and offering to work with them to produce goods that were competitive with imports in price and quality. Wal-Mart did not wait for manufacturers to come to it. In some instances it sought out American suppliers. Fieldcrest Cannon, a manufacturer of towels and linens, was asked by Wal-Mart if it could replace a line of low-priced washcloths being made in China. The company produced the washcloths for the same retail price and made them 25 percent thicker than the imports they replaced.

As a public relations device, the idea was a windfall, earning for Wal-Mart the loyalty of blue-collar shoppers who had lost their jobs because of imports. But inspiration for the policy was genuine and reflected a concern on the part of Walton not only for the displaced American worker, but also for a domestic manufacturing sector that he believed was losing its competitive edge. As Walton envisioned it, the program was broader than just saving jobs; it was a way of encouraging manufacturers to strengthen their place in the world economy by following Wal-Mart's lead and forging a profit-sharing partnership with their workers.

Although the Buy America program was based in part on a strain of old-fashioned patriotism that was much in evidence at Wal-Mart, it was not simply a sentimental undertaking. While the firm was interested in creating jobs in the United States, it was not willing to subsidize inefficient American suppliers by paying higher prices for domestic goods than for imports. Indeed, at times Wal-Mart moved purchases back overseas when it became clear that American manufacturers could not compete.[54]

Wal-Mart was also quick to capitalize on the growing sensitivity of American consumers to environmental issues. In 1989 the company took out a full-page advertisement in the *Wall Street Journal* and *USA Today* that proclaimed, "We're looking for quality products that are guaranteed not to last." The advertisement went on to say that the company would feature in its stores products that had been environmentally improved by manufacturers, with special signs placed alongside those products. The information would give shoppers the choice of purchasing environmentally improved products over those that were not. One manufacturer, Rubber Queen of Dublin, Ohio, responded to Wal-Mart's pleas for environmentally safe products by producing an automobile floor mat made in part from shredded plastic bottles. True to its word, Wal-Mart, which retained exclusive rights for several months to sell the new item, allocated display space for the mats at the end of store aisles, a high-visibility location where merchandise could readily be spotted by shoppers.[55]

Wal-Mart also strongly endorsed recycling. During the era when competitors were abandoning paper bags for nonbiodegradable plastic sacks, Wal-Mart had not. Instead, the firm steadfastly stayed with paper bags made from recycled paper. In 1989 the company asked its 7,000 suppliers to provide it with more recycled or recyclable products. The company drove home the point at its Bentonville headquarters by stationing large cardboard receptacles throughout the facility in which personnel could deposit reusable paper. The firm further demonstrated its commitment to recycling by establishing recycling centers in the parking lots of some stores to make recycling more accessible to customers and the general public. In 1990 Wal-Mart announced that its *Sam's Buy-Line*, a newspaper mailed to the business customers of Sam's Clubs, was being printed on 100 percent recycled paper. The company maintained that for a single issue of the newspaper, recycling had saved 3,026 trees, 1,246,000 gallons of water, and 729,800 kilowatts of electricity, "not to mention the amount of landfill space saved by recycling."[56]

To most of its customers, Wal-Mart's virtues far outweighed its faults. Its sensitivity to popular causes, folksy values, attention to detail, emphasis on satisfying customers, and everyday low prices engendered a level of customer loyalty that was the envy of competitors. Indeed, Wal-Mart was virtually unique among large retail chains in terms of the high esteem and popularity it enjoyed with its clientele. In a poll conducted in 1987, Wal-Mart shoppers said that they spent more money and rated their store significantly higher overall than did K mart shoppers.[57] By the end of the 1980s, for its personnel and for the public it served, the firm had evolved into more than just a job or a store. In the eyes of its growing legion of admirers, Wal-Mart had become a cultural phenomenon.

*Walton in 1972.
Courtesy of Discount
Merchandiser*

The interior of a Wal-Mart store in Broken Arrow, Oklahoma, in the early 1970s. Note the extent to which the decor reflects Sam Walton's variety-store origins. *Courtesy of Discount Merchandiser*

Wal-Mart Stores' senior management committee in fiscal 1973 was made up of (from left to right): Jim Elliott, administrative assistant to the executive vice president and merchandise inventory control manager; Jim Rountree, administrator for public relations and personnel; J. L. (Bud) Walton, senior vice president; Ferold G. Arend, executive vice president; Sam Walton, president; Ronald M. Mayer, vice president for finance and treasurer; Keith Binkleman, advertising and sales promotion manager; Claude Harris, vice president for merchandising; John Hawks, vice president for operations; Robert Thornton, distribution center manager. Not pictured: James C. (Jim) Walton, real estate manager. *Courtesy of Discount Merchandiser*

The grand opening of a Wal-Mart store in Savannah, Georgia, in 1984. The exterior is typical of Wal-Mart stores during the 1980s and into the 1990s. Following Sam Walton's death in April 1992, the hyphen in Wal-Mart's name was changed to a star in his memory.

(top) A Sam's Wholesale Club in the late 1980s. Note the plain, warehouse-like appearance. *Courtesy of* Discount Merchandiser

(bottom) A checkout line at a Sam's Club in Wisconsin. Note the boxes of merchandise stacked nearly to the ceiling on metal shelves in the background, the industrial appearance of the interior, and the bulk purchases in the shopper's cart in the foreground. *Courtesy of* Mass Market Retailers

Sam Walton and Wal-Mart executive Thomas N. Smith (foreground) leading associates in the Wal-Mart cheer at the grand opening of the Wal-Mart store in Johnson City, Tennessee, on 20 October 1987, the day after Walton lost $1.8 billion in the stock market crash. Walton and Smith are shown doing the "squiggly," a downward, wriggling movement that was performed at midpoint in the cheer to represent the hyphen in the Wal-Mart name.

Sam Walton addressing Wal-Mart associates two days before the grand opening of the first Hypermart USA in Garland, Texas, in December 1987. *Courtesy of* Discount Merchandiser

An American flag, symbolic of the firm's emphasis on patriotic values and focus on American-made products, and a banner touting Wal-Mart's low-price policy ("True One Stop Shopping at the Lowest Prices EVERY DAY!") displayed inside a Wal-Mart Supercenter. *Courtesy of* Discount Merchandiser

Merchandise displayed in a Wal-Mart store. Note the banner in the background promoting the company's low-price policy ("Always the Low Price, *Always*"). The sign reflects the firm's shift away from advertising the "lowest" prices (as depicted on the Supercenter banner pictured on the preceding page) to "low" prices. Wal-Mart made this modification as it moved into urban areas and encountered competition from other discount chains. The new slogan embodied the company's belief that although individual items on a given day might be bought cheaper elsewhere, a Wal-Mart customer could be assured of consistently finding low prices overall at Wal-Mart. *Courtesy of* Mass Market Retailers

David D. Glass, who joined Wal-Mart Stores in 1976, became the firm's chief executive officer in 1988. Courtesy of Mass Market Retailers

Sam Walton addressing associates and their families during one of his many store visits. *Courtesy of* Mass Market Retailers

Sam and Helen Walton in 1987. *Courtesy of* Discount Merchandiser

6

Wal-Mart's Diversification during the 1980s

AS WAL-MART'S STORES had continued to increase in number during the early 1980s, Sam Walton had become anxious to diversify the firm's standard discount format to allow expansion at an even faster pace. Walton's attention was drawn to a number of enterprises that intrigued him: arts and crafts, the pharmacy business, and, especially, the lucrative grocery business, which he was anxious to incorporate into his existing general-merchandise operation.

Walton's interest in these new ventures was at least twofold. First, he believed that diversification would better enable him to move his company beyond its small-town base into larger urban areas. Second, and, above all, he was fascinated by the prospect of carrying discount merchandising into the challenging realm of deep discounting. A concept that evolved during the early 1980s in supermarkets and super drugstores (a format that included pharmacies, health and beauty aids, cosmetics, and general merchandise), deep discounting referred to operating at even lower gross margins—usually a maximum of 18 percent—than those of typical discount operations. This could translate into savings for customers of 40 to 60 percent below suggested retail prices. Deep discounting appealed to Walton because it would allow his company to provide customers with a broader array of products at lower prices that few competitors could match.[1]

Wal-Mart thus embarked on a program of diversified expansion by means of deep discounting, based on the testing of three new concepts: dot Discount Drugs, Helen's Arts and Crafts, and superstore retailing. In December 1983 Wal-Mart opened its first dot Discount Drugs in Des Moines, Iowa. The 24,000-square-foot store was designed to be a high-volume operation specializing in health and beauty items. At that time health aids were not new to Wal-Mart's operation: the company operated 100 leased pharmacy departments in its stores as well as the 100 company-owned pharmacy departments. Then, in October 1984, Wal-Mart opened its first Helen's Arts and Crafts in Springfield, Missouri. Named for Sam's wife, Helen Walton, the 17,000-square-foot store featured a wide variety of craft-related merchandise.[2]

Although Wal-Mart ultimately opened 14 dot Discount stores and 3 Helen's Arts and Crafts outlets, both ventures failed to meet the company's stringent return-on-investment expectations, and both were sold. The Helen's stores were sold in May 1988 for $2.3 million to a 97-store arts-and-crafts chain, Michaels Stores, Inc., of Irving, Texas. The dot Discount chain, which operated in four states, was sold in February 1990. Although abortive, that experiment taught Wal-Mart about the pharmacy business and the deep discounting of drugstore prices. One analyst explained that dot Discount's performance had been lackluster because most of the stores had been located in markets where the income level of shoppers was lower than that of typical Wal-Mart customers and also because a large percentage of its sales had been low-margin food items. The dot experience reaffirmed Wal-Mart's belief, however, that pharmacies should be an integral part of its discount package. The firm was interested not only because of the inherent profitability of pharmacies but also because they were perceived as a stimulus to store traffic. The company believed that a pharmacy encouraged a loyal customer base, since patrons came on a regular basis to have prescriptions filled.

In 1980 pharmacy departments had accounted for only 1 percent of Wal-Mart's total sales. By 1989 their contribution had increased to 4 percent, or approximately $825 million. The company expected these figures to grow substantially in the years ahead. This prediction was based mainly on the anticipated aging of the population and the realization that older Americans would need more pharmaceuticals as well as related health-and-beauty-aid products. With the future growth of its pharmacies in mind, in 1989 Wal-Mart changed drug wholesalers. After having done business for four years with FoxMeyer Drug Company of Dallas, it returned to its former wholesaler, McKesson Drug Company, the largest drug wholesaler in the nation.[3]

Wal-Mart's next new departure, warehouse clubs, was based on Sam Walton's desire to find a retail concept capable of moving his company beyond its small-town base and into larger urban areas. Warehouse clubs were part of a new, rapidly growing retail category known as superstores. Designed to be one-stop shopping magnets, these superstores were large outlets that housed both food and general merchandise—everything from appliances and automobile supplies to detergents and canned ham—under one roof. They were predicated on the theory that shoppers, in their quest for value and convenience, would willingly pile a wide variety of goods into a single shopping cart.[4]

Warehouse clubs engaged in deep discounting by selling merchandise to members only, at wholesale prices. Their leading customers were small businesses, such as restaurants, convenience stores, mom-and-pop retailers, and gas stations, that paid a fee to be able to shop there, usually $25 annually for a primary membership and $10 each for a maximum of four secondary memberships. This entitled them to make small purchases more cheaply than they normally could from conventional wholesalers. While these businesses accounted for only 12 percent of the membership, their purchases generally amounted to 60 percent of the volume of a typical warehouse club. To expand their customer base, the clubs also solicited memberships among select consumer groups, such as employees of state and federal governments, schools, and hospitals. Initially these groups paid no annual fee but paid an additional 5 percent for the merchandise. Increasingly, however, the clubs adopted paid-membership policies that allowed individuals in qualifying member groups to pay the $25 annual fee, which permitted them, like the business members, to pay the posted wholesale price for products. Selling to members only served to eliminate casual shoppers and marginal purchases, while alleviating the worry of small businesses that their customers would forsake them and buy directly from the warehouse club.

The warehouse clubs sold vast quantities of limited-assortment merchandise. Groceries (packaged, canned, and frozen) accounted for the largest percentage of sales, followed by appliances and housewares, hard goods (automotive supplies, tools, and office supplies), and sundries (candy, health and beauty aids, tobacco, and cleaning and paper products). Soft goods accounted for only a small percentage of sales. Fresh meat and produce were excluded from the food selections, which were available in institutional sizes or in multiple packs of consumer-size containers, reflecting the desire of warehouse clubs to sell in large amounts. In hard goods, merchandise was restricted to the best-selling one or two brands in each category, such as Black & Decker tools, Du Pont paint, Michelin tires, and Nike shoes.

Warehouse clubs generated $600 in sales per square foot. They operated at an average gross margin of 10 to 13 percent, well below the average gross margins of their leading competitors, supermarkets and conventional discount operations, which had gross margins in the vicinity of 18 and 25 percent, respectively. Their pretax profit margin was 4 percent, half that of conventional discounters. Such low margins could translate into savings of up to 30 and 40 percent below retail prices for individual and group members, respectively. Inventory turned over an average of 11.3 times a year, although it could turn as often as 19 times a year. By comparison, traditional retailers and supermarkets annually turned their inventory 4 to 5 times and 10 to 15 times, respectively. To generate such high inventory turnover rates, clubs generally were located in large metropolitan areas with populations of 400,000 to 500,000.

Because the clubs discounted so deeply, efficiency of operation was a necessity. To restrain labor costs, the format was self-service, and staff was kept to a minimum. Clubs eliminated jobbers and other middlemen by buying directly from manufacturers. By routinely ordering great quantities of merchandise, they demanded and received huge volume discounts. Since clubs, moreover, were often able to sell their merchandise before payment was due (usually within 30 days of receipt), they could operate with little investment in stock. Warehouse clubs restricted their inventory to a limited number of preselected items. This allowed truckload quantities of merchandise to be shipped directly to clubs, significantly reducing distribution expenses. The enterprises had to be particularly adept at receiving and stocking inventory. Merchandise was moved mechanically rather than by hand throughout the operation, with forklift trucks used even to restock shelves. Since the clubs were such good customers, suppliers were willing to modify their standard vending practices to fit the unique demands of the warehouse-club business. They prewrapped items in three-packs and six-packs or preticketed items on pallets that could be placed directly on the sales floor. Warehouse clubs were hailed by some analysts as the most innovative merchandising concept in recent years, and due to their lower margins and overhead, they increasingly threatened to supplant traditional discount stores as the low-cost distributors of general merchandise.[5]

During the 1980s eight firms dominated the warehouse-club business. The four leading firms, all of which did in excess of $1 billion in sales in fiscal 1989, were Price Club, Sam's Wholesale Club, Costco Wholesale Corporation, and Pace Membership Warehouse, Inc. Price Club of San Diego originated the warehouse-club concept when Sol Price and his son Robert established the first club in 1976. By the end of fiscal 1989 the 47-unit chain enjoyed sales of $4.9 billion. Costco, headquartered in Seattle, was founded in 1983 by Jeffrey Brotman, whose background was in the apparel industry, and James Sinegal, the former executive vice president of operations for Price Club. In fiscal 1989 Costco operated 62 clubs, mostly in the West, and did $2.94 billion in sales, an increase of 48 percent from the previous year's $1.99 billion. Pace was founded in 1982 by Henry Haimsohn, former vice president of Handyman, a do-it-yourself (DIY) home-improvement chain. Established in a suburb of Denver, the chain grew rapidly, and by the end of fiscal 1989 Pace operated 47 units and had an estimated $1.5 billion in sales. In November 1989 K mart entered the warehouse-club business when it purchased Pace for $322 million. The remaining major clubs were BJ's Wholesale Club, Price Savers, the Wholesale Club, and the Warehouse Club.[6]

Sol Price, considered the father of the warehouse-club industry, was no stranger to discount merchandising, having run the Fed-Mart chain from its inception until 1975. From the outset, Price Club concentrated on generating high sales volumes and excellent profits in existing stores rather than rapid expansion. A typical Price Club averaged 108,000 square feet and had average annual sales of $110 million; in 12 of the oldest units sales reached $130 million. The company was entrenched on the West Coast, with 27 units in California at the end of 1989 and another 2 stores planned in its aim to establish dominance in its home-state market, where competitive warehouse clubs recently had opened more than three dozen units. It also operated 6 clubs in Arizona and 1 in New Mexico. Later the company established stores in Canada; its subsidiary, Price Club East, expanded to the East Coast in 1984.

Price Club preferred to hold its own real estate, and at the end of 1989 it owned all but two of its warehouse-club sites. The company devised a shrewd real estate strategy to facilitate expansion. It would acquire excess acreage whenever possible in low-cost, semi-industrial areas that had no proven traffic draw. It then developed these company-owned sites into shopping centers, or "power centers," with other high-volume, low-markup specialty retailers as co-tenants. In partnership with a Los Angeles–based shopping-center developer, the company was pursuing approximately 30 such projects in 1990.

Price Club was the model for subsequent warehouse clubs during the industry's formative years, and as the warehouse-club business matured, it remained the undisputed leader. Its sales of $4.9 billion in 1989 put the 47-unit chain slightly ahead of the $4.8 billion generated by Wal-Mart's warehouse-club division. Price Club also maintained its preeminent rank in other areas: its $116 million in sales per outlet, its $1,116 in sales per square foot, its 19.5 annual inventory turns, and its

45.7 percent return on inventory. Price Club's ability to outdistance its competitors consistently in sales and profitability moved one analyst to laud it as the "the most disciplined retail organization I have ever seen."[7]

Wal-Mart launched its warehouse-club division in April 1983 when it opened its first Sam's Wholesale Club in Oklahoma City. Located in a former 100,000-square-foot discount store, it lacked the warehouse look of subsequent outlets but afforded the company an inexpensive means of testing the format. Named for Wal-Mart's founder, for the first eight years of their existence the stores were called Sam's Wholesale Clubs. In 1990 the name was changed to Sam's Club: Members Only in response to a lawsuit in North Carolina filed by the Better Business Bureau. After ruling that most Sam's customers bought goods for their own use, the court decreed that Wal-Mart was in violation of a state law specifying that a business using the word "wholesale" in its name had to sell the major portion of its goods for resale.

Sam's Club was patterned after Price Club. Sam Walton's interest in the warehouse-club concept was first aroused in the early 1980s when he was invited to invest in such a venture and was provided with a financial analysis of a club. He grew more interested after he was given a personal guided tour of Price Club by Sol Price. Wal-Mart acknowledged Price Club as the model for Sam's. One of several innovations borrowed from Sol Price was his checkout procedure, wherein a clerk unloaded merchandise and called out prices to a cashier, a process that enhanced both security and efficiency.

Wal-Mart was quick to point out, however, that salient differences existed between the two enterprises. Sam's leased its warehouses, cutting the initial investment in each by about $4 million; it emphasized soft goods and broadened its membership base to include Wal-Mart stockholders. The company also claimed that due to its discounting expertise and broad financial base, Sam's, unlike competing warehouse clubs, could afford to enter smaller urban markets, such as Greenville, South Carolina, and Jackson, Mississippi, which had populations of 125,000 and 175,000, respectively. One Wal-Mart executive observed: "This business looks simple, but it is very complicated. It not only takes painstaking planning, sophisticated data processing and complex logistics in the purchase and movement of merchandise, it takes enormous capital."[8]

Sam's Clubs were markedly different from Wal-Mart discount stores. The division's gross margin, estimated at 13 percent, was lower than Wal-Mart's 23 percent, and its $401 in sales per square foot was higher than Wal-Mart's $150. Averaging 109,000 square feet, Sam's Clubs were significantly larger than Wal-Mart stores, yet inventory was confined to an average of 3,500 items versus the 70,000 items carried in a typical Wal-

Mart. Inventory turns averaged 16 to 18 times a year, compared with 5 at Wal-Mart. Inventory purchases were made independently of Wal-Mart's conventional ordering operation, and they were far more limited in assortment and continuity. Due to special purchases, inventory often varied, and a significant amount of seasonal merchandise, such as beach equipment, was featured. This practice allowed Sam's Clubs not only to utilize their selling space more efficiently but also, according to one analyst, to create an aura of excitement for customers, who would not "know what they will find from one month to the next."

Wal-Mart and Sam's, according to David Glass, were designed for different markets—Wal-Mart for small towns and Sam's for cities. While both Sam's and conventional Wal-Marts could be found in the same markets, sometimes even adjacent to each other, Glass insisted that they did not compete with each other. Instead, he said, they actually complemented each other because of their different market strategies and customer bases. As evidence, Glass noted that in the three markets in which a Sam's and a Wal-Mart operated side by side in 1986, sales volume had been above average, due to increased consumer traffic. Glass stressed, however, that despite their dissimilarities, both formats were based on Wal-Mart's abiding operating principle: selling high-quality, brand-name merchandise at low prices.[9]

While traditional wholesalers offered such services as credit terms, a wide selection of merchandise, and delivery, Sam's Club was strictly a no-frills operation where such amenities as delivery, credit, sales clerks, and eye-catching merchandise display were nonexistent. There was little or no advertising. Store hours were limited, usually from late in the morning until about eight in the evening, and the clubs were located on the "wrong side of the tracks," on sites that no conventional retailer would consider. The stores themselves were cavernous warehouses with very limited signage to direct customers. Frozen-food items, which accounted for about 10 percent of sales, were contained in large banks of freezers, while general merchandise could be found in cut-open packing cases or piled on steel shelves that extended from the concrete floor nearly to the exposed ceiling. Despite its Spartan environment, Sam's Club boasted an undeniable appeal: high-quality, brand-name products at rock-bottom prices. One caveat, however, generally prevailed—customers had to be willing to buy merchandise in multiple-pack quantities and industrial-size containers, which tended to increase the dollar amount of their purchases.

On any given day Sam's customers could be seen arriving in pickup trucks and Mercedes automobiles, often coming from several miles away. They would show their membership card at the door and then ply the seemingly endless aisles ferrying their stacks of merchandise—ranging from car batteries to butter—in huge shopping carts or even on large dollies. After enduring the inevitable lines at the numerous checkout counters, they would pay by check or cash and haul their bargains out to the parking lot.[10]

Wal-Mart was pleased from the outset with the performance of its new format and promptly began to expand it. Having begun with 3 stores in 1983, the division totaled 11 stores the next year, 23 stores in 1985, 49 stores in 1986, and 84 in 1987, due in part to the acquisition that year of another warehouse chain, Super Saver Wholesale. Based in Monroe, Louisiana, the Super Saver chain had been in direct competition with Sam's in 10 cities. After losing money in each of its three years of operation, the chain agreed to sell its 21 stores to Wal-Mart, which subsequently closed units in the 3 cities where Sam's Clubs were already in operation (Memphis; Jackson, Mississippi; and Greenville, South Carolina) and converted the remaining units into Sam's Clubs. In 1988 the number of stores had reached 105 in 21 states. Eighteen units were added the following year. This growth was funded by $223 million in capital expenditures, an 85.5 percent increase from the $120 million budgeted in 1988.[11]

Because of its immediate success, by the late 1980s the impact of Sam's Club on its parent company was profound. Its sales volume grew at a faster rate than that of the traditional Wal-Mart stores, as evidenced by the increase in the division's share of total corporate revenue from 14 percent in 1986 to almost 18.5 percent in 1988 and 18.8 percent in 1989. While the lower gross margin of the Sam's Clubs caused Wal-Mart's cost of sales as a percentage of sales to remain constant or increase slightly, it contributed to a decrease in the firm's overall operating expenses as a percentage of sales, since Sam's expense ratios were significantly lower than those in the balance of the company. This decline in the ratio of Wal-Mart's operating expenses to its sales volume during the 1980s, in turn, enabled the company to lower its gross margins overall. Consistent with Wal-Mart's commitment to price reduction at every opportunity, these lower margins were translated into lower prices for the company's principal operation, the Wal-Mart discount stores. This ability to reduce prices accounted in large measure for the steady advance made by Wal-Mart during the 1980s on its competitors, who, lacking the edge provided by warehouse clubs, did not enjoy the same expense-ratio advantage.

Sam's Clubs were first opened in major metropolitan centers in the South and Southwest. In 1986 the division moved into the Midwest. In that same year it also began opening in smaller cities that it could dominate, thereby applying the market-saturation policy that had been central to the expansion of the Wal-Mart stores. By 1989 Sam's Club was pursuing both its large- and smaller-city strategies, while at the same time edging into new geographical territory—the Northeast. The first Sam's in that region opened in late 1989 in Delran Township, New Jersey, and the company planned to open at least 19 more over a two-year period in the 11-state mid-Atlantic and New England region. (Projections called for 10 in Pennsylvania, 6 in New York, and at least 1 each in Delaware, Maine, and New Hampshire.) This move was a departure from the company's pattern of having Sam's Clubs follow Wal-Mart's discount stores into areas where the latter was already firmly established.[12]

Along with Sam's, Price Club, Costco, and BJ's also looked to the Northeast—which had seen little warehouse-club activity—for future growth, making it the first region in which all of the major warehouse clubs would vie for business. Adding spice was the fact that the Northeast would be the first area in which the two giants of the business, Price Club and Sam's, would face one another in direct competition. By 1990 Price Club East was already an established presence in the region, with three stores in Virginia, two each in Maryland, New York, and Washington, D.C., and one each in New Jersey and Connecticut. Its expansion plans included two more stores each in Maryland and Virginia and one each in New Jersey, New York, Pennsylvania, and Rhode Island. The Costco chain targeted Massachusetts, Connecticut, and New York for clubs, opening its first warehouse store in Springfield, Massachusetts, in 1990. The Costco stores in the Northeast were modeled after Costco's newest prototype, an expanded 120,000-square-foot unit that featured a fresh-food format consisting of meat, produce, a delicatessen, and a bakery.

These aggressive competitors represented a challenge for Wal-Mart, since the Sam's Club average store volume in fiscal 1989 was $43 million, less than half of Price Club's $116 million, about $14 million under that of Costco, and about even with BJ's. Aware of the intensive competition that lay ahead, Wal-Mart continued to fine-tune its successful warehouse-club format. For example, the company began testing its own new, 130,000-square-foot outlet, which included a "made-from-scratch" bakery as well as fresh meat and produce.[13]

Warehouse clubs had begun by confining themselves to cities in their original geographical areas, but the expansion into the Northeast by Price Club, Sam's, Costco, BJ's, and others underscored what analysts perceived as the major stumbling block for the industry in the future—head-to-head competition in the same urban markets. Since there were only about 100 metropolitan areas in the nation with populations of half a million or larger in the late 1980s, and since one market could provide only one or two clubs with the tremendous sales volume needed to spur inventory turnover and profitability, the questions to be answered were: which participants would survive this same-market rivalry, and what impact would such deadly competition have on the industry at large?

Unlike other branches of retail, in the warehouse-club business the first company to enter a market usually dominated it; newcomers did not enjoy the same ease of entry. To gain a competitive edge, some newer clubs determined to make the concept more accessible by offering such innovations as increasing the level of customer service; extending the hours of operation; and opening stores in more desirable locations, such as shopping centers. There was a danger, however, that such modifications would dilute the warehouse club's deep-discounting advantage. As one industry analyst explained, "the history of retailing shows that more aggressive merchandising and advertising lead to higher costs and higher prices."[14]

Such dire predictions had not materialized by 1990. Despite a sluggish national economy overall, warehouse clubs had become the fastest-growing segment of retailing, with annual revenue increments of approximately 30 percent over the preceding several years. By January 1990 Wal-Mart clearly had established its numerical superiority over its rivals through the rapid expansion of the Sam's division to 123 stores in 25 states. In November 1990 Wal-Mart extended its lead by buying the Wholesale Club, which by then consisted of 27 units in 6 midwestern states, for stock and cash valued at $172 million. The purchase brought Wal-Mart's total number of stores to 168, virtually triple the number of any other warehouse club. In an atmosphere in which competing warehouse chains were scrambling to establish territorial hegemony over one another, the transaction was a shrewd one. It furnished Sam's with an established customer base in a region that it scarcely had penetrated. As one analyst pointed out, "Rather than expanding into the Midwestern market one or two stores at a time, it's logical for them to do it very quickly and cheaply with an acquisition."[15]

By January 1991 there were 148 Sam's Clubs in 28 states. The division's growing significance in Wal-Mart's overall operation could be seen not only in its vigorous expansion but also in the sales revenue it generated. Sam's added an additional $1.7 billion in sales in fiscal 1991. With the increase, Sam's Club sales volume jumped to $6.6 billion, and it overtook Price Club to become the national leader in sales as well as number of stores.[16]

Perhaps inspired by the success of Sam's Club, Walton's appetite for experimentation was whetted by an even more daring form of superstore retailing—hypermarkets. Significantly larger than warehouse clubs, hypermarkets combined full-scale supermarket offerings with a large number of general-merchandise categories, all under one roof. The typical supermarket was about 40,000 square feet; hypermarkets were usually in excess of 200,000 square feet. At a cost that could exceed $50 million, they were expensive to build when compared with construction expenses of only $5 million for a typical supermarket. Because of their size, they required annual sales volumes between $75 million and $100 million to break even.

The success of the concept hinged on product mix, with bargain-priced food as the main attraction. Hypermarkets were designed to lure consumers who were disaffected with the perceived high prices of typical supermarkets. To do so, they had to be highly efficient food operations, since it was difficult to undercut conventional grocery operations in price. While it occupied only 40 percent of the space in most hypermarkets, food accounted for approximately 60 percent of the revenue. It ordinarily sold at a gross profit margin of 10 percent, but in some instances the margin dropped as low as 1 percent. General merchandise usually consisted of smaller items that were compatible with food and could fit into a single shopping basket, such as compact discs, cameras, garden tools, jewelry, and hair dryers. While prices were discounted throughout the operation, the profit margins of the general merchandise had to compensate for the extremely low margins of the food items.

The gross profit margin overall for a hypermarket was approximately 15 percent, as opposed to an 18 percent average for the supermarket industry. Labor costs had to be held to about 5 percent of sales, or about half of what a typical K mart spent on labor. Because of such narrow margins, a high turnover of goods was essential. Food, again, was the key, since it could turn over as many as 20 times a year. Breakfast cereal, for example, usually sold within two weeks, while big-ticket items like patio furniture might not sell for more than three months.

To provide the high inventory turnover required to make the venture profitable, hypermarkets had to be located in major urban areas. According to one analyst, to succeed, a typical hypermarket required easy highway access and at least 500,000 households within a 20-minute drive. He further stated that the hypermarket needed potential customers who were in their twenties and thirties, who earned $25,000 to $55,000 annually, and who had at least two children. During the late 1980s only 37 metropolitan areas in the nation had more than 1 million people and only 19 exceeded 2 million; thus suitable markets seemed limited.[17]

Originated in 1962 by the French retail firm Carrefour, the hypermarket concept took root in France and spread to several European countries. Over the years the hypermarket became a shopping institution in France. This was largely due to the support of the French government through such practices as enacting zoning laws designed to keep rival retailers away from the stores. In 1988 there were more than 780 hypermarkets in operation, including the 73-store Carrefour chain. According to the Paris-based International Association of Chain Stores, French shoppers made nearly half of their $96 billion in food purchases at hypermarkets. But the enthusiasm of the French government for hypermarkets began to wane because of the mounting outcry from the nation's small shopkeepers. According to one spokesman, the shopkeepers were protesting that the hypermarkets were "taking business away from them," and, as a consequence, the government was "beginning to have second thoughts."[18]

In the United States the hypermarket was viewed by some analysts as the apotheosis of the retail progression that had begun a century earlier with the department store and then evolved into the general variety store, the supermarket, and the discount chain. Many American retailers, however, were skeptical of the European concept from the outset. They stressed that the difference between the American and European markets was the prior existence in the United States of the large supermarket. Since most European cities contained mainly small food stores, outlying areas were ideal for the hypermarket. Europe, in effect, had jumped from the 1930s to the 1960s with the hypermarket, while in America during this period the size and scope of the supermarket gradually had been enlarged to meet customer needs, and discount merchandising also had been born. Most American retailers believed the nation was too saturated with supermarkets and discount stores for the hypermarket to have much appeal. They also believed that since the amount of retail space dedicated to each person in the nation had more than doubled between 1972 and 1990, there already were far too many stores for the available business.

The hypermarket evolved in the United States as an aspect of superstore retailing, which was pioneered by two veteran discounters, Fred Meijer of Grand Rapids, Michigan, and Fred Meyer of Portland, Oregon. In the mid-1960s Meijer had begun experimenting with the European concept of combining food and general merchandise under one roof and discounting both. Under the name Meijer's Thrifty Acres, by 1990 his firm consisted of 53 stores, averaging more than 100,000 square feet, in Michigan and Ohio. In addition to groceries and general merchandise, the upscale stores also had restaurants, pharmacies, movie rentals, in-store bakeries, and dental services. Meijer was followed by Meyer, whose firm in 1988 consisted of 93 stores located in the Pacific Northwest, averaging approximately 115,000 square feet and collectively doing $1.7 billion in sales volume. Because of their smaller store sizes, however, neither firm could be said to be operating a genuine hypermarket.[19] Several attempts were made at creating hypermarkets in the United States and Canada in the 1970s—by such firms as Fed-Mart, Gemco, Modell's, and Laval's—but all failed, and by the 1980s the idea lay virtually dormant. Then the French firms Euromarché and Carrefour, as well as America's two largest discount chains, K mart and Wal-Mart, decided to give it another try. Euromarché, which operated in the United States under the name of Bigg's, opened the first of its American hypermarkets, a 200,000-square-foot store, in 1984 in the Cincinnati area, followed by a second store with 250,000 square feet in 1988. Although situated in a city dominated by the Kroger supermarket chain, the Bigg's operations did well, due mainly to their ideal locations. Within 10 miles of the stores were 565,000 households with an average annual income of $33,000. Because of good freeway access, they could easily draw customers from a radius of 60 miles. Although the initial store struggled during its first two years of operation, decisions by management to redefine the product mix—deemphasizing such goods as automobile tires and books, for example, and expanding inventories in such things as sporting goods and patio furniture—caused the enterprise subsequently to prosper.

The experience of Carrefour, the largest hypermarket operator in the world, in the American market was not so fortunate. The French firm opened a 330,000-square-foot unit in early 1988 in Philadelphia. In 1989 it managed to generate only about $64 million in sales volume, far short of the $100 million some analysts had forecast. Many of its problems were caused by its location. While there were 800,000 potential households in the Philadelphia area from which to draw, 85 percent of the 35,000 weekly shoppers came from the working-class neighborhoods immediately surrounding the store. As a consequence, Carrefour's average purchase amount was a scant $40, and its sales of $200 per square foot were disappointing.

Carrefour's product mix was dominated by general merchandise. Its 64,000 products were roughly comparable in number to that of a typical discount operation. In food, however, its 16,000-item selection was smaller than the typical supermarket's 25,000 items. Since half of its square footage already was devoted to food, company executives did not believe that enlarging food offerings would stimulate sales. Instead, the firm eventually was able to turn a marginal profit by keeping inventories low and increasing inventory turns to 6 times a year, primarily by adding more food-compatible items such as compact discs and tapes. Company executives calculated, however, that the firm would have to increase its annual inventory turns to 10 times a year to achieve stable profitability. Carrefour had planned to build five American stores, but it abandoned plans to build its second hypermarket in Brookhaven, New York, and postponed plans for the other three as well.[20]

Since the early 1970s some analysts had predicted that the hypermarket would define American retailing in the last quarter of the century. This prediction was based on two assumptions. The first was that with 53 percent of women working, those primary shoppers would not have time to go to different stores and would embrace one-stop shopping, especially at discount prices. The second assumption was that American consumers were increasingly value-conscious, as evidenced by the success of large discount operations and supermarkets. The idea of combining both retail formats under one roof had flowed naturally from those findings, and the hypermarket was born. The heyday of the hypermarket, however, never materialized, and by the late 1980s the sprawling superstores had, in the words of one analyst, "done as well as the Edsel."[21]

At 200,000 to 330,000 square feet, hypermarkets were just too big. Certain groups of consumers, such as the elderly, found the shop-'til-you-drop emporiums intimidating. Although the hypermarket was envisioned as a time-saving panacea for busy shoppers, paradoxically, the stores' size worked against the very convenience they were designed to provide. Unlike the supermarket, the hypermarket had little appeal to harried customers who only wanted a few items. As one analyst explained, "In a hypermarket, by the time you've bought some aspirin, some Kleenex, and a bottle of milk, you could easily walk a mile." Some authorities insisted that hypermarkets were merely ahead of their time and would ultimately find their market niche; others felt that their size doomed them. One marketing consultant, for example, predicted that without major changes they would be like "beached whales" that would "flop around and get a lot of attention, but eventually die."[22]

In 1990, of the 10 hypermarkets in operation nationwide, 5 were owned by Wal-Mart and K mart. The discount chains had turned to hypermarkets in part to offset the supermarket industry's encroachment on their retail domain. Supermarkets had evolved into superstores by combining their traditional food offerings with expanded categories of nonfood merchandise, such as health and beauty aids, paper goods, and household cleaners—product lines that had been found mainly in discount stores. To compete more effectively, the discounters decided to sell food.[23]

Although some analysts initially had scoffed at the one-stop-shopping idea, maintaining that the discount store and the grocery store were two separate excursions, the warehouse club, albeit with restricted membership, had confirmed that busy consumers would indeed combine food and general merchandise into a single shopping trip, especially if the savings were substantial enough. In experimenting with hypermarkets, both Wal-Mart and K mart deduced that size rather than concept would determine the ultimate success of superstore retailing. Both companies began superstore retailing for the general public with hypermarkets, but after discovering that there was a direct correlation between square footage and struggle—the larger the store, the more difficult for it to succeed—they reduced the size of their later stores. They apparently concluded that superstore retailing could be profitable if the concept were scaled down to a more manageable range of 125,000 to 150,000 square feet.

K mart launched its hypermarket format in a 51 percent partnership with Bruno's, Inc. A supermarket chain headquartered in Birmingham, Alabama, Bruno's operated about 150 stores throughout the Southeast under the names FoodMax and Food World, and in 1988 it did approximately $1 billion in sales volume. Under the name American Fare, K mart opened its first hypermarket in Atlanta in January 1989. It employed 600 people and would need $80 million to $85 million in sales to break even its first year in operation, although the company hoped to generate $100 million in sales. The 244,000-square-foot store promised "everyday low prices" (meaning prices consistently lower than the discount-industry average) on all of its 45,000 items, in contrast to the typical 86,500-square-foot K mart, which carried about half as many items and practiced everyday low pricing on only 3,000 of them. The store's categories of inventory were narrow but deep, with food accounting for 12,000 items, or stock-keeping units (often referred to as SKUs); apparel and shoes for 12,000; and durable goods for 15,000.

With American Fare, K mart hoped to transcend the hypermarket's discount image and at the same time refurbish its own reputation for drabness. The warehouse look of other hypermarkets was avoided by using splashes of color and glass to give the store's exterior a bright, cheerful appearance. Inside, its warehouse-inspired concrete floor was offset by colorful signs in the form of oversize, vertical banners. In both the selection and the presentation of merchandise, the store was upscale rather than discount. Apparel, for example, consisted of "off-price" merchandise, which is defined as current, in-season stock, as opposed to standard "discount" fare, which refers to older, out-of-season merchandise offered at greater reductions in price. The store's clothing labels were exclusively brand names, such as Bugle Boy and Duckhead pants. Unlike a traditional K mart store, it did not carry the chain's private label.

K mart had high hopes for the Atlanta operation, but its performance was disappointing. It simply was unable to attract a sufficient number of customers. This was probably because of the public's dislike of its gargantuan size and poor product mix. One disenchanted customer, who called the store "very bizarre," explained that the selection was not "good enough to warrant all of the walking." After a year of sluggish sales, K mart removed 20 of the store's 81 cash registers and filled the space with an expanded selection of existing and new lines. Despite these shortcomings, the store remained faithful to the company's pledge to provide a wide selection of products at very low prices, prompting one analyst to state that American Fare's food prices were "probably the lowest . . . in Atlanta."[24]

K mart initially intended its American Fare stores for metropolitan areas in excess of 250,000 people, but after the Atlanta operation failed to meet corporate expectations, the company adapted by reducing the size of the stores and opening them in smaller markets. In 1990, also in conjunction with Bruno's, Inc., it opened two additional American Fare outlets, one in Charlotte, North Carolina, and another in Jackson, Mississippi. These units, however, were more appropriately classified as superstores rather than hypermarkets, since their size was approximately 150,000 square feet. In fact, the Atlanta operation remained the company's only true hypermarket.

Realizing that the hypermarket idea was flawed, K mart was forced by the combined pressures of high overhead expenses and high sales-volume demands to make adjustments quickly. By the time the third American Fare opened, the company not only had scaled down the concept but also its role in it. Unlike the two earlier stores, Bruno's, rather than K mart, owned 51 percent of the Mississippi operation. The outlet consisted of 147,000 square feet, with a 50,000-square-foot grocery area and a 97,000-square-foot general-merchandise area. Greater attention was given to decor: white tile, for example, replaced the polished concrete floors of the earlier units. The store employed between 300 and 350 people and had only 27 central checkout counters, not including the checkout stands in the garden shop, pharmacy, and delicatessen. At an estimated construction cost between $12 million and $15 million, and with a need to generate only $30 million to $40 million in annual sales, K mart had reduced American Fare's expenses and sales-volume expectations with this unit. In June 1992 K mart bought out Bruno's, which was losing money in the American Fare venture, and changed the name of the three units to Super K mart Center. The firm indicated that it planned eventually to open 25 Super K mart Centers across the country.[25]

Typical of Wal-Mart's willingness to experiment with new retail concepts, the firm had preempted K mart by entering the hypermarket business more than a year ahead of its rival. Sam Walton hoped that hypermarkets would provide a means of expanding superstore retailing to include the general public and at the same time allow him to enter the food business, in which he had been interested for a number of years. Wal-Mart's aim with hypermarkets was to provide "malls without walls" that, in addition to supplying deeply discounted groceries and general merchandise, also would include a variety of noncompeting service retailers and a twenty-four-hour convenience store and gas station. Wal-Mart pinned its hopes for the new format upon the same features that had caused the Sam's Clubs to succeed—low overhead and buying and selling in volume, which would translate into rock-bottom prices for customers. Little advertising beyond grand-opening announcements was used. The company's stated hypermarket policy was, "Absolutely the lowest prices in the market area every day; no sales gimmicks or weekly advertised specials." It also promised to match competitors' advertised prices and accept coupons. While Wal-Mart had gained valuable experience from its warehouse clubs in deep discounting general merchandise, the hypermarket remained a new venture since Sam's limited food offerings gave the company no expertise in the traditional supermarket business.[26]

Wal-Mart joined with Cullum Companies, Inc., a supermarket chain headquartered in Dallas, to open hypermarkets in a fifty-fifty joint venture under the name Hypermart USA. Because of the hypermarket's troubled reputation, Hypermart USA was widely anticipated and closely watched by financial analysts. If the concept could be made to work, the experts reasoned, surely Wal-Mart had the best chance of success. Wal-Mart opened its pilot Hypermart USA in December 1987 in Garland, Texas, a suburb of Dallas. The 220,000-square-foot unit had 2,000 shopping carts and a giant parking lot. It employed 500 full-time, nonunion workers and 100 part-time workers. Its merchandise mix was 35 percent food and 65 percent nonfood items, with a general-merchandise assortment that exceeded that of a typical Wal-Mart. Designed to be the last word in one-stop shopping, the store had 35 merchandise departments, including a complete apparel department with accessories; fine jewelry; an automobile department with a comprehensive tire and battery center; a large health-and-beauty-aids department, complemented by a pharmacy; a photo-processing center; a large electronics department; the first homemade tortilla factory in a Dallas–Fort Worth grocery; a bakery and on-site bread factory; a delicatessen; a seafood shop; and full-line meat, produce, frozen-food and dairy departments. The size of the store itself was only 150,000 square feet, with the peripheral space devoted to independently owned service centers like a bank, a shoe-repair shop, and fast-food outlets.

In merchandise display Wal-Mart applied some of the lessons it had learned from its Sam's Clubs. General merchandise was often piled 20 feet high, and canned goods usually were sold from their cut-open cartons. Compared with a traditional Wal-Mart, Hypermart USA carried more brand names. In apparel, for example, there were no private labels, and well-known brands like Guess jeans and Oshkosh predominated. Brands and selection for most products were limited. In an update of the Henry Ford legend, Hypermart USA customers could have any color of paint they liked, so long as it was white.[27]

In the first year of operation, Hypermart USA customers' purchases were split evenly between food and nonfood items. The average sale was $40, and 70,000 people within a 30-mile radius shopped there weekly. In his hypermarket venture Walton had vowed that he would "not be undersold," and prices that averaged as much as 40 percent below prevailing retail levels made good that claim. In at least one instance Wal-Mart even sold a product at no markup. The company had built a combination gas and convenience store, called Wal-Mart Super USA Convenience Store, in conjunction with Hypermart USA. Seeing gasoline as a loss-leader, Wal-Mart sold it at cost to entice customers to its hypermarket operation. Wal-Mart's willingness to "give away gas" created consternation among local gas stations. One petroleum jobber in the area predicted that Hypermart USA, where lines at its pumps were as much as a block long, would "in time, destroy the market." While conceding that outlets in other parts of Dallas had not been affected, he said that for stations within a four- or five-block radius, the hypermarket meant "death."[28]

To avert potential customer disenchantment, Wal-Mart made a concerted effort to make shopping in the sprawling store, which was as big as five football fields, as palatable as possible. Color-coded floors, numerous information telephones, and clerks who zoomed around on roller skates were provided to aid weary shoppers, while amenities such as a playroom for customers' children, wheelchairs for those who needed them, park benches, and complimentary coffee and cider were available to bolster their morale. Finally, mindful of anticipated large purchases, 48 central checkout stands were installed to hasten shoppers out the door.[29]

In 1988 Wal-Mart opened two additional hypermarkets in Topeka, Kansas, and the Dallas suburb of Arlington. Wal-Mart had planned to open a hypermarket in Ferguson, Missouri, but opened a Wal-Mart store next to a Sam's Club instead. The company changed its plans due to a lack of adequate parking facilities, having decided that the more than 1,200 allotted parking spaces would be insufficient. Indeed, one of the earliest lessons learned by the company pertained to parking. The traffic at the grand opening of the Garland store had been overwhelming; about 70,000 people had shown up. To avoid such a rush, the Topeka opening was extended over several days.[30] Wal-Mart soon realized that more serious problems existed with its hypermarkets. The company's estimated gross margin on its stores was approximately 15 percent, and it found that making money at that margin level was difficult. One analyst estimated that Wal-Mart's hypermarkets only just broke even in 1989, although they met sales goals of $80 million to $100 million per store. Ironically, the difficulties with profits were not in the untried realm of food but in general merchandise. Specifically, sales were lower than anticipated on hard goods and apparel. Those categories had been expected to stabilize the more volatile food business, which was bargain-priced at a gross profit margin of 10 percent to generate traffic. With the opening of its fourth hypermarket in Kansas City, Missouri, in February 1990, the company sought to correct the problem by expanding the general-merchandise assortment in the 268,230-square-foot store from the narrow-and-deep format found in the Sam's Clubs to the broader offering found in the traditional Wal-Mart stores. The company hoped that providing a greater variety of items would increase sales.

This action harbingered the company's later decision to recast Hypermart USA even more in the image of a typical Wal-Mart store. Company executives concluded that they had erred initially by departing from the "Wal-Mart way" and selling higher-priced items such as grandfather clocks (priced at $400, while they would cost $1,500 in a jewelry store), cars, and boats. By 1990 the company had decided to incorporate the struggling Hypermart USAs into the Wal-Mart merchandising system by deleting the big-ticket items and carrying typical Wal-Mart merchandise instead. With the opening of its Kansas City unit, the company made official this subsumption of the hypermarket by changing its name to Wal-Mart's Hypermart USA.

While the hypermarkets presented other problems, such as the high costs of cooling and heating the huge spaces and the difficulty of finding adequate land for parking, customer dissatisfaction with the overall format proved the greatest disillusionment for the company. Consumers shopping for electronics, for example, often were found to prefer stores where the choices were greater and the sales staff more knowledgeable. Being forced to buy items in large quantities was another complaint. At the Garland store, for example, Kellogg's Special K cereal could be purchased only in giant-size boxes. Worst of all, in the eyes of many shoppers the stores were just too big. The reaction of one fatigued customer at the Garland store was instructive. After roaming through the behemoth store in search of Canada Dry Club Soda, which he could not find, and waiting for 40 minutes to pay for his other groceries, he exclaimed, "I won't be back until it shrinks."[31]

Wal-Mart's fourth hypermarket was its last, as Sam Walton confirmed in 1990. "We don't have any plans for any more," he said. Rather than merely writing off the swollen stores, however, Wal-Mart had something better in mind. The hypermarkets would become retail laboratories where the company could experiment with the selection, the presentation, and the warehouse-marketing of food. Wal-Mart turned increasing attention to the food business because it hoped to use groceries as an incentive for customers to shop at its stores more often. The firm's challenge was to make food, with its low margins and low returns, as profitable as general merchandise. In this regard, the hypermarkets provided the company with valuable experience in such areas as handling perishables, developing a successful pricing structure to counter the heavy promotions common in the supermarket industry, and mastering the supermarket shopper's great priority, a fast checkout. Despite its claim that the hypermarkets had been merely one aspect of the company's continuing research and development of new marketing ideas and new types of stores, the abandonment of the concept was a rare setback for Wal-Mart.[32]

Wal-Mart apparently concurred with the disgruntled customer who had complained that the hypermarkets needed to shrink, for shrink they did, to be reconstituted as Wal-Mart Supercenters. While the hypermarkets had proved a disappointment, the firm was enthusiastic about its third superstore venture, which appeared three months after the hypermarket. Like Hypermart USA, the Supercenter, which was patterned after the Fred Meyer stores, was a one-stop-shopping concept, combining discounted groceries and general merchandise under the same roof.

Learning from its experiences with the unwieldy Hypermart USAs, Wal-Mart created a more practical and profitable format by scaling down the size to an average of 155,000 square feet. The unexpected problems that had been associated with building and operating the hypermarkets made the smaller Supercenters more manageable. And because of their smaller size, the Supercenters were freed from the hypermarkets' razor-thin gross profit margin of 15 percent and were able to operate in the more lenient, though still low, 17 to 18 percent range, which allowed them to compete easily with their arch rivals, the supermarket chains. The firm's annual volume projection for the format, $30 million per store, also was more attainable.

The company opened its first Wal-Mart Supercenter, a 126,000-square-foot store, in March 1988 in Washington, Missouri. It was the third Wal-Mart operation in 10 years to be established in this small town of 9,200 people. Prior to its opening, a market survey was conducted that revealed that people in Washington were regularly traveling some 50 miles east to St. Louis to buy food. According to a Wal-Mart spokesman, the firm's strategy was to stanch this "leakage of customers" to a nearby major city by providing the community with a "complete supermarket" that offered lower prices than a traditional supermarket.[33]

In November 1988 Wal-Mart opened a second, 96,000-square-foot unit in Wagoner, Oklahoma, a community of about 6,000 people some 35 miles from Tulsa. A third, larger store, which was 186,000 square feet in size, was opened in March 1989 in Farmington, Missouri, a town of about 10,000 people located 70 miles southwest of St. Louis. According to a Wal-Mart spokesman, the "leakage" factor was a primary consideration in the location of these subsequent units, since in both cases there was a high number of people who "regularly shop[ped] out of their respective counties."[34]

The Supercenter was essentially a complete Wal-Mart discount store with a supermarket added to it. While the grocery area carried a narrower assortment of goods than a conventional supermarket, it was better stocked than the hypermarkets had been. In fact, company executives pinned their hopes for the new concept on the strength of its full-line grocery section, along with apparel. The Supercenter was similar both in size and format to a typical Wal-Mart. In its Supercenters, Wal-Mart eliminated big-ticket items, such as refrigerators, and services, such as restaurants, and adhered to the "Wal-Mart way" by keeping nongrocery items more in line with traditional Wal-Mart fare.

There were 36 general-merchandise departments in the Supercenters, the same as in a Wal-Mart discount store. These departments included an extensive fine jewelry department, an automotive center, a lawn and garden center, an electronics and appliances center, a health-and-beauty-aids department with a pharmacy, an optical shop, a full fabric and crafts department, and snack bars. There were no leased departments. Major credit cards were accepted, as well as layaway purchases. The Supercenters stocked approximately 65,000 items. Wal-Mart anticipated doing $30 million per unit in annual sales volume, with about 60 percent of that total in general merchandise and 40 percent in food, although the company's ultimate goal was a fifty-fifty split.

Wal-Mart executives viewed the Supercenter as a versatile concept capable of meeting numerous and varied corporate needs. The company was determined to keep the format flexible by continuing to experiment with such features as market size, store square footage, and product mix. One of the Supercenters' greatest assets was their perceived ability to fit into the kinds of smaller communities where Wal-Mart already had an established presence and a stable customer base from which to draw. As one company spokesman explained, "We look at the Supercenters as an extension of our Wal-Mart stores. Our strategy would be to consider any town [for a Supercenter] where we have a Wal-Mart."[35]

The Supercenters' potential for dominating a small town's economy was enormous. In Washington, Missouri, for example, its impact on retailers both in the community and in the surrounding area was profound. One local competitor, the independent IGA supermarket, elected to close even before the Supercenter opened. After the Supercenter did open, National Supermarket, a subsidiary of Loblaw Companies of Toronto, had its volume drop by more than half, though much of the loss probably was due to the vacancy of the space formerly occupied by the Wal-Mart store that had coanchored the shopping center in which it was located. Donald G. Soderquist, vice chairman and chief operating officer for Wal-Mart, confirmed management's belief in the Supercenters' performance capability in small towns. "The Supercenter does what we thought it would do," he said, explaining that people who had been going to big cities to shop for their food and general merchandise now had "it all right in their home town."[36]

Another advantage of the Supercenters was that they could act as replacements for aging Wal-Marts in need of refurbishing. The company viewed the Supercenters' potential in this regard as unlimited. In fact, company executives envisioned replacing numerous outdated Wal-Mart discount stores with Wal-Mart Supercenters. As a company spokesman commented, "We may build new Supercenters. At the same time, if we are relocating or expanding existing stores, they might give us the opportunity to add food." No one was more aware of the awesome potential of a Wal-Mart with food than Sam Walton, who stated at the grand opening of the first Supercenter, "This is a Wal-Mart, but then again it's not a Wal-Mart, and it may be our future."[37]

In December 1990 Wal-Mart purchased McLane Company, Inc., one of the nation's largest wholesalers of grocery and general-merchandise products. Headquartered in Temple, Texas, the company generated approximately $2.6 billion in annual sales volume; supplied approximately 26,000 customers; and provided candy, tobacco, snack-bar items, and some general-merchandise goods to all of Wal-Mart's discount stores. The acquisition gave Wal-Mart access to McLane's grocery-marketing expertise as well as its extensive distribution system, consisting of 14 centers in 11 states, which it intended to use to supply goods to the Sam's Clubs and the Wal-Mart Supercenters, as well as to continue to provide most of the 250 to 300 grocery items sold in Wal-Mart's discount outlets. The transaction signaled Wal-Mart's intention of expanding its role in the food business, which, according to some analysts, the firm viewed as a future means of sustaining its rapid pace of growth.[38]

Wal-Mart's diversification into new retail formats during the 1980s did more than enhance the firm's growth in the fundamental areas of retail square footage and net sales volume. Diversification also gave the company the opportunity to take risks and experiment in additional ways: by entering the retail food business; by expanding into large urban markets; by enlarging its geographic territory; by launching ancillary service businesses, such as optical, photo-processing, and shoe-repair centers and convenience stores with gasoline; and by embracing state-of-the-art technology. With some of these new ventures Sam Walton and his company succeeded; with others they failed. Through it all, Walton never abandoned his characteristic enthusiasm for discovering innovative ways of discounting or his willingness to admit mistakes and move on. Wal-Mart's bold experimentation would leave an indelible imprint on the world of discount merchandising. In its quest for finding more efficient ways to meet consumer needs, Wal-Mart significantly altered for years to come the ways in which Americans would shop.

7

The Impact of Wal-Mart on Small-Town America

THE INSIGHT THAT Sam Walton had shown in locating his discount stores in small retail markets garnered much favorable attention. Beginning in the 1980s, however, the rural communities in which Walton chose to do business increasingly found themselves the objects of a different type of recognition, as Wal-Mart's impact on small-town America became one of the most widely discussed aspects of the firm's phenomenal success. As shoppers abandoned downtown merchants and flocked to Wal-Mart to avail themselves of the chain's wide selection of merchandise at discount prices, traditional patterns of commerce were disrupted and debate ensued over whether Wal-Mart's overall impact was beneficial or detrimental to the local economies of rural America.

Wal-Mart had gotten its start in the South, and many southerners were grateful to Sam Walton for his willingness to serve the small, rural markets of the region that other major retailers had disdained. To these people Wal-Mart was more than a store: it was a symbol of progress and hope. Its founder was a genuine hero—a retail Elvis Presley—a southerner who had made it to the top while remaining faithful to his roots. "We've got a Wal-Mart, you know," town fathers across the South proudly proclaimed, as though the store's very presence suggested better days to come.

Yet there lurked in the minds of some the suspicion that Wal-Mart's impact on the small towns it inhabited was not as salutary as many believed. Some individuals asserted that local businesses bore the brunt of Wal-Mart's success, causing the focal point of many communities, their once-bustling main streets, to wither away—and with them, a way of life. For example, in Leland, Mississippi, a sleepy Delta town of 6,500 people, the local newspaper editor complained early in 1990 that after Wal-Mart had arrived in two neighboring towns, the last department store in Leland had vanished; and, as a consequence, he could not buy a decent pair of underwear or socks in his hometown. On a more serious note, he argued that the old mom-and-pop stores were best for the rural South, since they kept more profits and salaries in the community, thereby providing a larger tax base.

Indeed, during the 1980s some of Wal-Mart's harshest critics were small-town newspaper publishers and editors who tended to sympathize with the plight of the local merchants on whom they depended for much of their advertising revenue. Even in Wal-Mart's home state, for example, the publisher of the *Advance Monticellonian* in Monticello, Arkansas, stated, "People come by and ask for donations, and the same person goes to Wal-Mart to buy their goods. For the struggling merchant, it gets kind of grating." The editor of another local newspaper, the *Stone County Leader*, reprimanded the local citizens of Mountain View, Arkansas, after they launched a petition drive to persuade Wal-Mart to come to their town. Located in a rural, sparsely populated region of Arkansas that during the 1980s suffered from layoffs in industry and downturns in the timber and agricultural sectors, the town was isolated by the mountains that surrounded it, and its population of 2,430 was static. With their businesses already suffering from these economic adversities, the local merchants viewed the possible arrival of Wal-Mart with consternation. Taking their side, the publisher cautioned local consumers to consider what their enthusiasm for Wal-Mart's low prices ultimately might do to their town. "Is it really worth saving a few bucks to virtually destroy the heart and soul of our small town business community?" he asked.[1]

During the 1980s considerable attention was also given to Wal-Mart's impact on small Texas towns, whose economies were ailing because of the general problems besetting agriculture and industry as well as the downturn in the oil business. Because Wal-Mart's presence in Texas was pervasive, its effect was strongly felt. "You hear people gripe about the economy, Wal-Mart, and the weather," said the co-owner of a local hardware store in Mount Pleasant, Texas. As in other areas, the points of view that small-town Texans manifested toward the discount chain varied. The attitude of many consumers was summed up by one shopper who termed Wal-Mart the "greatest thing that ever happened" to her town, while the feelings of some local retailers were best expressed by a merchant in Livingston, Texas, who said, "If I was a city father and Wal-Mart wanted to move in, I tell you what I'd do. I'd sit out there on the city limits with a shotgun."[2]

As Wal-Mart expanded outside its southern base, it seemed that more and more Americans were becoming alarmed at its potentially negative impact. By the late 1980s this growing concern had made the fight against the "Wal-Marting of America" something of a cottage industry. For example, the owner of two Nebraska clothing stores that were located in towns near a Wal-Mart store became a popular speaker in the firm's new western territory, lecturing on how he had survived the Wal-Mart juggernaut. That commentator maintained that the basic problems were Wal-Mart's buying power and its adverse impact on local businesses. "They do such a tremendous sales volume and their money leaves town almost immediately," he said. "That's money that may have circulated among several businesses in town, but now, once it's gone, it's gone."[3]

As the issue became more controversial, scholars began to examine existing evidence in an effort to analyze Wal-Mart's actual impact on small-town America. Kenneth E. Stone, professor of economics at Iowa State University and an economist with the state agricultural extension service, studied the effects of Wal-Mart on towns in Iowa. Completed in 1989, his study was designed to evaluate the impact of Wal-Mart on firms both in the towns it entered and in competing towns in its operating area. The basis of Stone's study was the *Iowa Retail Sales and Use Tax Reports*, which he used to document sales levels in Iowa towns before and after a Wal-Mart had arrived. The study compared retail sales over a four-to-six year period in three types of Iowa towns: small towns (between 5,000 and 30,000 in population) in which a Wal-Mart was located, competing towns of the same size without a Wal-Mart, and larger Wal-Mart towns (over 30,000 in population).

Stone's findings indicated that after a Wal-Mart opened in larger towns and cities, total retail sales increased from 1.8 percent after one year to 7.9 percent after four years, with only general-merchandise and grocery operations experiencing a decline in sales. The study also revealed that following Wal-Mart's arrival in small towns that had little growth in population, total retail sales for the towns increased from 2.3 percent after the first year to 3.2 percent after the fourth year. Stone attributed the increase in sales to the fact that the presence of Wal-Mart stores had expanded the towns' trade areas by bringing in more shoppers from neighboring towns. This influx of shoppers benefited some local businesses. The report indicated that restaurants, taverns, and lumber yards experienced sales increases, or "spillover" sales, as a result of

Wal-Mart's presence. Since their merchandise was not in competition with Wal-Mart's, home-furnishings operations, such as furniture stores, major household-appliance stores, and floor-covering stores, also were potential beneficiaries of the larger customer base created by Wal-Mart. Stone pointed out, however, that while Wal-Mart towns did experience overall increases in retail sales, such gains could be deceptive, since they generally benefited Wal-Mart at the expense of some local merchants, especially those who found themselves in direct competition with the discount chain. Stone indicated that after Wal-Mart's arrival, many small businesses suffered substantial losses unless they were able to adapt and compete in the changed retail environment. Building-materials firms such as hardware stores and paint stores were in direct competition with Wal-Mart and therefore lost sales to the discount chain. Food stores often lost sales after Wal-Mart's arrival, since Wal-Mart offered such supermarket staples as health and beauty aids, household cleaners, candy, paper products, and canned goods at comparable or lower prices. Even service companies suffered decreases in revenue that ranged from 6.4 percent the first year to 12 percent after four years. It is possible that those losses occurred because people found it cheaper to replace small appliances at Wal-Mart than to have them repaired. Competing general-merchandise firms, which included department stores and variety stores, suffered the greatest losses. Two other categories of stores that suffered a significant decrease in sales, in part because their merchandise was similar to Wal-Mart's, were specialty stores, such as drugstores, sporting goods stores, fabric stores, card and gift shops, and apparel stores, which included shoe stores as well as clothing stores.

The report further indicated that the retail sales gains for Wal-Mart towns came at the expense of neighboring small towns. In the towns surrounding Wal-Mart towns, losses in total retail sales ranged from 0.7 percent one year after the arrival of a nearby Wal-Mart to 2.8 percent after the fourth year. Local merchants in these towns were especially hard hit, with home-furnishings stores, service businesses, building-materials enterprises, and apparel stores suffering the greatest decline in sales.[4]

As a result of his study, Stone became a frequent speaker to concerned merchants in small towns where Wal-Mart had announced it would open a store. He conducted seminars sponsored by groups such as the Mississippi Downtown Development Association, a nonprofit group designed to improve the downtown areas of cities and towns in that state, to educate small-town merchants on how to survive the invasion of Wal-Mart. Based on his research, Stone offered suggestions to local merchants both in his study and on the lecture circuit. He advised local merchants that it was possible for them to "co-exist" with the giant chain if they were willing to develop "new business strategies." One important strategy for local merchants was to avoid competing with Wal-Mart in its areas of undisputed expertise: price and inventory. He told merchants that since they could not hope to contend against Wal-Mart in price, they should forgo carrying the same merchandise that Wal-Mart stocked; that, instead, they should seek out "voids" in the discount chain's inventory and carry merchandise that was "complementary" to Wal-Mart's. He further suggested that small businesses expand their inventory to offer customers a greater variety of products, such as "upscale," or more expensive, merchandise.

A second crucial adaptation was for small businesses to extend their hours of operation. Stone indicated that small-town merchants would have to change such outdated customs as closing on Sundays and closing at 5:00 on weekdays and on Wednesday afternoons, "primarily so everybody can go fishing." Instead, he suggested that stores open later in the morning and stay open longer in the evening, possibly until 6:30, to accommodate shoppers, especially working women. He pointed out that some downtown merchants were experimenting with remaining open until 8:00 one night a week, usually Thursday.

A third key to survival, according to Stone, was for local merchants to hone their personal service skills. Stone alluded to research that indicated that poor customer relations was the main reason shoppers ceased patronizing a business. He noted that while small businesses in the past had enjoyed a reputation for "excellent customer relations," shoppers had come to feel that they were "treated no better in small firms than in larger ones." He urged independent merchants to capitalize on the fact that customer service was generally neglected by large chains. He recommended that merchants seek to foster a loyal customer base by adopting such practices as merchandise deliveries and special orders of specific products desired by customers. He also urged store owners to make their return policies more lenient and to lower prices when possible on standard inventory items (those purchased frequently by customers). Other ways in which local retailers could improve their relationships with their customers included training employees to be friendly and helpful, and soliciting and heeding customer complaints.[5]

A second report, which studied Wal-Mart's effect on rural counties in Missouri, emanated from the University of Missouri at Columbia. The authors of the project were Thomas Keon, associate dean of the College of Business and Public Administration; Edward Robb, director of the College of Business and Public Administration Research Center; and Lori Franz. Although prepared under the auspices of the College of Business and Public Administration, the project was funded by Wal-Mart itself, which paid the university $10,000 for the report. (In 1992 the University of Missouri announced that Sam Walton had pledged a $3 million donation to the College of Business and Public Administration. The money was to be used for student scholarships and to fund an endowed professorship.) Thomas Keon, the coordinator of the project, stated that Wal-Mart selected the College of Business and Public Administration at the University of Missouri to do the study after asking five or six state universities for proposals.

The study, which spanned the years 1979 through 1988, utilized a list provided by Wal-Mart of 14 stores that had opened in rural Missouri counties from 1983 through 1988. The purpose of the report was to determine Wal-Mart's impact on those 14 counties by comparing their economic condition at least three years prior to Wal-Mart's arrival with their economic status following Wal-Mart's arrival.

The report presented a glowing account of Wal-Mart's impact on the rural communities it examined. It indicated that there was "no evidence that Wal-Mart [had had] a negative impact on the economy" of those communities. In fact, according to the authors, the opposite was true. They asserted that the economic factors examined in the report showed that "many of the counties" actually had been "in decline " before Wal-Mart's arrival, and that "almost all showed growth or revitalization after the opening of Wal-Mart."

Among the authors' findings were that both personal and per capita income had increased both in current and constant dollars in every county after Wal-Mart's arrival; that retail employment and salaries had increased in almost every county after Wal-Mart's arrival, even when Wal-Mart's employees and payroll amounts were excluded from the calculation; and that Wal-Mart had had a "significant positive effect on sales tax revenues" for each county. The report further indicated that Wal-Mart's presence had benefited some businesses in the communities studied and that some even had shown "marked improvement" after Wal-Mart's arrival. The authors conceded that the overall number of retail businesses within the 14 counties had declined during the 10 years encompassed by the study, but they stressed that the remaining businesses were "larger, with [a] greater number of employees and larger payrolls" than before Wal-Mart's arrival.

The report then focused specifically on two Missouri towns, Butler and Maryville, in an effort to "illustrate the recovery effect associated with the opening of a Wal-Mart in a rural town." The authors stated that both towns had been in a condition of economic decline before Wal-Mart's arrival, as indicated by the erosion of such economic factors as population, wages and salaries, personal income, per capita income, and the number of retail firms in operation. The report then stated that after Wal-Mart's arrival, economic conditions had improved in both towns, as evidenced by increased sales-tax receipts, and concluded that both towns had "enjoyed growth" as a result of Wal-Mart's arrival. The study failed, however, to indicate that economic improvement in these and the other communities it examined may have been attributable in part to a general improvement in agriculture during the mid-1980s. In fact, the only consideration given by the authors to overall economic conditions in rural Missouri was when they commended Wal-Mart for its willingness to enter small country towns beset by such difficulties as "declining farm incomes, population shifts and loss of employment opportunity."

While the authors denied that Wal-Mart's funding of the project had any effect on its favorable findings, the report's failure to assess the impact of Wal-Mart on neighboring towns was at sharp variance with other scholarly studies. The report's assertion, moreover, that Wal-Mart's appearance seemed to "induce more [retail] establishments to enter or remain in the market" was also a far more optimistic interpretation of Wal-Mart's impact on competing businesses than the general conclusion drawn by Stone and others, who asserted that Wal-Mart's success in rural communities often was at the expense of some existing merchants.[6]

Three other academicians, John Ozment, professor of marketing and transportation at the University of Arkansas, Michael A. Jones, professor of business and economics at Linfield College in McMinnville, Oregon, and Gregory S. Martin, professor of business at the University of Wisconsin at Madison, approached the topic from a slightly different perspective. Rather than focus specifically on Wal-Mart, they conducted studies that analyzed the impact of discount chains in general on small rural communities, although they pointed out that Wal-Mart was a prime example of the type of discount chain that they were examining. The purpose of these studies was to evaluate the impact of discount chains both on the economy overall and the retail environment in particular of the rural counties in which they were located.

The authors asserted that it was possible to gauge the impact of discount chains on rural communities by comparing economic variables over time in rural counties with a discount chain with the same economic variables in counties without a discount chain. Based on census information contained in the 1983 and the 1988 editions of the *County and City Data Book*, published by the U.S. Bureau of the Census, the resulting reports focused on counties in Arkansas, Missouri, and Oklahoma that had populations in 1980 between 8,000 and 50,000. In examining the effect of retail chains on rural economies, Ozment and Jones compared such economic factors as changes in population, the number and value of new houses, per capita income, the number of bank deposits per capita, and the levels of employment and local tax revenues for the years 1977–86 in 182 counties, 104 of which had a discount retail chain and 78 of which did not. In an effort to determine whether or not discount chains damaged the retailing sector of rural communities, Ozment and Martin measured the comparative rates of change during the years 1977–82 of such business indicators as the number of retail establishments in operation, the number of retail employees, and the level of retail sales volume in 164 counties, 92 of which had a discount chain and 72 of which did not.

The studies indicated that the overall economy of rural counties with a discount chain fared no worse than the economy of counties without a discount chain. The authors noted that, if anything, the economy of counties with a discount chain tended to be healthier than that of counties without a discount chain, although the authors conceded that this could be due in part to the fact that discount chains generally prefer to locate in areas with a strong economy initially.

With regard to the retail environment, the studies also indicated that there was no significant difference in the overall number of retail businesses located in rural counties with and without a discount chain. There were, however, significantly more service businesses per capita in counties with a discount chain, and those businesses, such as automobile repair shops and eating and drinking establishments, enjoyed higher sales volumes than the service businesses in counties without a discount chain. The authors also indicated that overall retail sales were higher and that there were significantly more retail employees in counties with a discount chain.

The studies asserted that after the arrival of a discount chain, the structure of retailing in rural areas changed significantly and that local merchants, in particular, were "dramatically affected." Ozment and Martin's report noted that "it may not be possible for independent merchants to survive the effects of large chain store competition in the small-town environment" and cited other studies that indicated that after discount chains arrived in some rural communities, local merchants who could not adapt were forced out of business. In one such study the number of independent merchants in 10 small communities in Ohio had declined by 8 percent over a 10-year period, while the number of discount chains had increased by 11 percent.

The authors maintained, however, that a discount chain would create new business opportunities through its ability to draw customers from surrounding towns, and they suggested that as a result of this altered retail environment, some local merchants driven out of business by the discount chain could make a successful transition to types of businesses that provided services or products that complemented, rather than competed with, the discount chain. Like Kenneth Stone, the authors pointed out that the economies of neighboring towns assuredly would suffer when a discount chain arrived in an area.

The reports cautioned that not all merchants could be guaranteed success in their new business ventures, since some might not be able to generate enough sales volume to offset their operating costs and overhead. The reports stated further that if local merchants were forced out of business, a town's central business district would decay. This, in turn, "could lead to serious problems for the community as a whole," such as reduced population, increased unemployment, an eroding tax base, diminished property values, and a loss of community leadership. The studies maintained that the adverse economic consequences could extend to local banks, accountants, wholesale distributors, and others who supplied goods and services to the local business community.

The three studies indicated that the controversy over the impact of discount chains on rural communities was comparable to two earlier controversial retailing phenomena. With regard to the first, the anti–chain store movement of the 1920s and the 1930s, the studies asserted that the concern voiced by local retailers in rural communities over the potentially negative effects of discount chains on their businesses was reminiscent of the strong opposition voiced by the earlier independent retailers to the rapid growth of retail chains. With regard to the second controversy, the development of suburban shopping centers and their effect on urban downtown business districts during the 1950s and the 1960s, the studies stated that the entry of discount chains into small communities had the "potential to affect small towns in much the same way" that suburban shopping centers had brought about change in the nation's major cities in the 1950s and the 1960s, creating "major controversies" that have had "lasting effects on retailing and society in general."

The studies maintained that some of the problems faced by cities today, such as the decline of downtown retailing, the rise of suburban sprawl, unemployment, and the erosion of the tax base, are attributable to some extent to the disintegration of downtown business districts, which was partly brought about by the appearance of suburban shopping centers. (The authors made the somewhat unrealistic assertion, however, that while other factors, such as highway development and the widespread use of the automobile, contributed to the overall decline of downtown business districts, the downtowns nevertheless could have survived these incursions if zoning laws had restricted the location of suburban shopping centers.)

The authors indicated that as urban business areas decayed, governments at all levels were compelled to devote public funds to their restoration. The studies asserted that during the 1960s and the 1970s, for example, the programs funded by the federal government to revitalize decaying downtowns had been an "enormous" cost to taxpayers, and that the use of public funds to restore blighted downtown business districts was also taking place in small rural towns. The authors maintained that because tax dollars were being used in this manner, the impact of discount chains on the economies of rural communities was a matter of public concern.

The studies asserted that the refurbishing of decaying downtowns was not the only way in which discount chains influenced the allocation of public funds in rural areas. They maintained that the town fathers of many communities were so anxious to attract discount chains that they were willing to invest tax dollars to help finance their building costs, a practice that had led to open disputes in some communities, pitting downtown merchants against real estate developers, city officials, and even some citizens who were seeking an "improved shopping alternative." The authors concluded, however, that with regard to economic conditions in general and retailing in particular, the overall impact of retail chains on small rural communities was not detrimental. They asserted that, based on their findings, the fears of some that discount chains "may create economic hardships on the areas in which they locate" were unfounded, and pointed out that some segments of a local economy, such as service employees, undeniably enjoyed sizable gains, while those merchants who managed successfully to adapt to the changed retail environment also stood to derive "positive benefits" from the arrival of a discount chain in their community.[7]

When Wal-Mart announced that it would enter a town, generally consumers eagerly awaited the store's opening because of its discount prices, and the appeal of the firm's low prices was not limited to consumers of modest means. "Anybody will shop there," said Kenneth Stone, "if they know they'll save five or ten bucks." Although popular with consumers, small-town merchants found it difficult to compete with prices that sometimes were cheaper even than the wholesale prices they paid for their merchandise. The clerk in a local store in one Arkansas town, for example, stated that in 1988 Wal-Mart sold hand towels at two for $5 that the local retailer had purchased wholesale for $2.63 each.[8]

To ensure that Wal-Mart's prices remained below the local competition, the firm's personnel frequently checked prices in local stores. Merchants who attempted to compete in price with the discount chain found that they, too, had to monitor Wal-Mart's prices to keep their own prices viable. Checking prices in a Wal-Mart store, however, often proved challenging for local merchants, because the firm would evict anyone discovered in its stores with a notepad or a camera. Wal-Mart's practice of price comparison especially offended some local merchants. Both in its stores and in local newspapers, Wal-Mart would advertise that its prices were lower than the prices of local competitors by mentioning a local business by name and then comparing that business's higher prices on specific items with Wal-Mart's lower prices. Commenting on the tactic, one independent businessman said, "It was a strategy [that] I regarded as extremely underhanded."[9]

Despite Wal-Mart's price advantage, Kenneth Stone and others maintained that local merchants could survive against the discount chain through enhanced service, and trade journals such as *Hardware Age* offered advice on ways that its subscribers could adapt, recommending such things as changing a hardware store's product mix; broadening key departments, such as plumbing and electrical supplies; and carrying items that Wal-Mart did not carry. Some merchants capitalized on such advice and did well by sharpening their merchandising skills. For example, the local hardware store in Warsaw, Indiana, a town with a population of 11,240, thrived even after the arrival of Wal-Mart because of the specialized services it offered shoppers, such as cutting keys, repairing screens, and assisting customers in selecting their garden seeds.[10]

Many small-town businesspeople, however, disdained the idea that local merchants could save their businesses by offering greater service. In Pawhuska, Oklahoma, the local mom-and-pop pharmacy for years had offered its customers such amenities as credit and around-the-clock emergency service. After Wal-Mart arrived, however, and consumers discovered that its prices for such maintenance drugs as insulin, blood-pressure medicine, and ulcer remedies were as much as $10 below the local drugstore's prices, the owners saw their sales volume drop and predicted that the store "won't be here in another year." Some retailers maintained that consumers would even go so far as to shop at a local business merely to receive product information; then they would go to Wal-Mart to purchase the item. "All people pay attention to nowadays is price," said the owner of a hardware and building-supply firm that closed after 14 years in business, the victim of a Wal-Mart opening in Waverly, Iowa. "They want service, too, but they don't want to pay for it."[11]

Beyond its "everyday low prices," to attract customers Wal-Mart always advertised a few popular products, such as disposable diapers or sugar, at prices near or below cost. In the 1980s this loss-leader policy involved the firm in a dispute over the issue of resale price maintenance.

Although resale price maintenance had been illegal since 1976, Wal-Mart and other discount chains became alarmed by the position taken by President Ronald Reagan's Department of Justice during the early 1980s in support of resale price maintenance. Believing that suppliers should be allowed to set minimum retail prices for their products, the Justice Department urged manufacturers who had been charged with price-maintenance violations to apply to the department for assistance. In support of resale price maintenance, the justice department adopted the so-called free rider argument, which was based on the premise that consumer demand for a product was stimulated in part by the product services provided by full-service retailers, who had to charge higher retail prices to defray the expense of the services they offered. The Justice Department maintained that so long as suppliers were prohibited from controlling retail prices, certain types of retailers, namely discounters, would cut back on product services to attract customers who had received those services from another retailer. A spokesperson for the Justice Department maintained that such "free riding" ultimately would "decrease total services provided and thereby decrease total sales of the product."

A Wal-Mart executive voiced the firm's opinion on the matter, indicating that any effort to reinstate resale price maintenance would constitute a resurrection of the old fair-trade laws, since it would "keep discounters from selling certain items below cost." In a fuller explanation of Wal-Mart's position, Rob Walton stated that resale price maintenance posed a "great danger" because it threatened the firm's reason to exist: its capability of selling goods more cheaply than other retailers. He asserted that if manufacturers were allowed to set minimum retail prices for their products, Wal-Mart would be deprived of its "ability to compete in the sale of those goods." In response to the Justice Department's free rider objections, Walton denied that customers to any significant degree first shopped full-service retailers and then bought from Wal-Mart. He stated that only a "very small portion" of Wal-Mart's sales were made in that manner and that for "99%" of the merchandise sold by the firm, full product services were not needed by customers. Despite such protests, in 1988 in the case of *Business Electronics Corp. v. Sharp Electronics Corp.*, the Supreme Court reinstated resale price maintenance when it declared that manufacturers could terminate dealings with discounters who sold products below a specified retail price. In 1991, however, Congress passed a bill that once again made resale price maintenance illegal.[12]

Wal-Mart's loss-leader policy also embroiled the company in controversy at the local level. During the mid-1980s Wal-Mart was sued by five small-town drugstore owners in Oklahoma who opposed the policy. One of the plaintiffs, the owner of the drugstore in Hominy, Oklahoma, maintained that by offering loss-leader items "well below cost," Wal-Mart was engaging in "predatory pricing" that was deliberately designed to damage small-town competitors. In the suit the firm was charged with violating an obscure state law, passed in 1941, that had been enacted to protect small businesses by requiring merchants to sell products at least 6.75 percent above cost unless the store was having a sale or matching a competitor's price.[13]

Wal-Mart responded by spending an estimated $80,000 in a campaign to convince the Oklahoma state legislature to repeal the law. The firm sponsored a massive lobbying effort; along with other discount chains, it placed newspaper advertisements urging readers to "stop higher consumer prices" by writing to their state representatives; and it put petitions in its stores for customers to sign, calling for lower prices. Wal-Mart was unsuccessful in its attempts to get the law repealed, however, and the case went to trial in 1987. In its defense Wal-Mart maintained that it had established no special price structure in its Oklahoma units. The firm asserted that it observed a one-price policy in all of its stores and that its prices in Oklahoma were consistent with prices throughout the chain. An investigation undertaken by the plaintiffs, however, indicated that the firm charged prices in Texas that, according to one of the plaintiffs, were "uniformly higher than in Oklahoma." This evidence caused the court to dismiss Wal-Mart's argument and rule in favor of the independent businesses.[14]

During the 1980s, as the controversy mounted over Wal-Mart's impact on the economy of small towns, the firm found a staunch ally in the local chambers of commerce throughout its trade area. In 1989 the trade journal *Discount Merchandiser* surveyed more than 30 chambers of commerce in cities and towns where Wal-Mart had been in operation from one month to 10 years. The spokespeople for these chambers of commerce overwhelmingly endorsed Wal-Mart's presence in their towns, citing such benefits for consumers as low prices and the availability of a wider variety of goods and services, as well as increased employment opportunities for the citizens of the communities. Echoing the findings of some scholars, they conceded that the business environment in their towns had changed as a result of Wal-Mart's arrival, and they did not deny that at first local retailers might not have liked being forced to redefine their business methods. They contended, however, that those local merchants who had been willing to adapt ultimately had profited from the increased retail traffic that Wal-Mart brought to their towns. A member of the Clinton, Indiana, chamber of commerce explained, "We have some small downtown businesses that suffered at first, but now they have diversified into different specialty areas and seem to be doing real well. I think that everyone now shares in the wealth because a lot of people are coming to Clinton to shop." In fact, the chamber of commerce leaders overwhelmingly identified the increased number of shoppers drawn to their communities from surrounding areas as a leading benefit of Wal-Mart's presence.

The chamber of commerce officers also stressed the new business opportunities that had become available for local merchants as a result of Wal-Mart's arrival. They told of merchants who had successfully established new service businesses, such as restaurants and gas stations. The executive director of the chamber of commerce in Decatur, Alabama, stated that the "shopping center Wal-Mart moved into had virtually no other tenants until they came in. It has attracted a yogurt store, a couple of pizza places, and a dress store; I wouldn't hesitate to say that Wal-Mart and the increased traffic are directly responsible for that." Some spokespeople even went so far as to insist that local businesses had not suffered in the least and that no local merchants had been driven out of business by Wal-Mart. The mayor of Bradley, Illinois, for example, said, "To my knowledge Wal-Mart has not hurt any other business, in fact, shops near the store claim their business is up because of the increased traffic."

The chamber of commerce leaders not only credited Wal-Mart with attracting shoppers from neighboring towns, but they also were keenly aware of Wal-Mart's contribution toward keeping local shoppers spending their money at home, rather than leaving to shop in a larger nearby city. As an officer of the chamber of commerce in Sparta, Tennessee, observed, "Wal-Mart has had a very positive effect on our community. The store keeps people from going to shop in . . . other towns near us. If they [Wal-Mart] weren't here, those tax dollars would be leaving our city; so now, the sales tax goes to help our own school system." And another chamber of commerce spokesperson stated, "Wal-Mart has created a sense of belonging for our community. Many of us have talked about how we used to go to [another town] to do our shopping, but we don't have to do that any longer. We just buy what we need locally. And that is why we're so grateful to Wal-Mart."[15]

While various chambers of commerce praised Wal-Mart for its contributions to their local economies, the press sometimes told a different story. An article in *U.S. News and World Report* entitled "How Wal-Mart Hits Main St." stated that when Wal-Mart arrives in small towns, "downtown business districts begin to empty, leaving fewer sponsors for Little League teams and a smaller pool of advertisers for the high school yearbook." The article also stated that in a small prairie town in northeast Iowa, just the announcement that Wal-Mart intended to locate there had caused some local merchants to close their businesses. A front-page article in the *Wall Street Journal* entitled "Arrival of Discounter Tears the Fabric of Small-Town Life" reported on the devastation wrought by Wal-Mart on some local businesses in rural Oklahoma. The article depicted a unique merchant-customer relationship in small towns, where "drug-stores still deliver" and shopkeepers "support Future Farmers' pig sales, . . . offer charge accounts, and repair broken items." It described one occasion on a Sunday night in Pawhuska, Oklahoma, when the local druggist had stopped repairing a leaky faucet in his house to open his store for a customer. The druggist related that while filling the man's prescription, they "talked about his wife Pansy and the Shriners and the Blue and Gold Cub Scout banquet." The article indicated that the huge discounter and its low prices, while popular with consumers, had done irreparable damage to this once-harmonious relationship, and quoted businesspeople who blamed Wal-Mart for turning former customers and friends into hostile critics who now accused the local merchants of "rob-bing them."[16]

In describing Wal-Mart's effect on rural communities in the Midwest, an article in the *New York Times Magazine* featured Independence, Iowa, a small town 60 miles west of Dubuque. The article depict-ed Independence after the arrival of Wal-Mart as a ghost town, where "about a mile to the east [of the new Wal-Mart], stores stand empty on the two-block strip of Main Street that was once the commercial heart of Independence. 'For Sale' and 'For Rent' signs are taped to their dusty windows. Most of the surviving shops are struggling to stay alive."

The article stated that the economy of Independence, like that of so many other midwestern towns, had been damaged by the farm crisis of the 1980s. Many farms in the surrounding area had failed; because the demand for agricultural equipment had dropped, the John Deere facto-ry in a nearby town had laid off some ten thousand workers; young peo-ple left town after finishing high school; property values had declined; and the town budget had stagnated. Retail businesses in the area had also been hurt by the opening of a new portion of highway that allowed motorists to bypass Independence. To some, however, the worst blow was the arrival of Wal-Mart. According to the publisher of the local newspa-per and former president of the chamber of commerce, the suffering of independent merchants imposed by Wal-Mart caused a decline in news-paper advertising that forced the paper to lay off half of its 24 employees within two years. Bemoaning the decline of customer loyalty to the downtown merchants, the publisher stated, "People would support the local businessman all their lives. But people aren't motivated by that kind of sentiment anymore. Wal-Mart has replaced the need for Main Street."

The *New York Times Magazine* article went on to depict a climate of hostility that began to envelop the community almost from the moment it became known that Wal-Mart was coming. The article indicated that the manner in which Wal-Mart acquired the land on which its store would be built was consistent with its actions elsewhere. One resident related that Wal-Mart entered Independence "quietly. You might even say covertly." According to the article, the firm first recruited a prominent resident of the town to find a suitable store site and then to defend the company against the anticipated opposition of the local merchants. When Wal-Mart deemed the price of the chosen acreage on the outskirts of Independence too high, the firm threatened to locate in a neighboring town instead. The strategy worked, and a purchase price was agreed on. Wal-Mart, however, still would not exercise its option to purchase the land until the town agreed to certain stipulations, including rezoning the site from agricultural to commercial use, installing water and sewer lines, and providing the firm with a financial incentive of $1.3 million from revenue bonds floated by the town.

After Wal-Mart opened in 1984, approximately one dozen local businesses closed over the next four years, according to the article, including a variety store, a furniture store, a sporting goods store, and a men's clothing store that had been in operation for a century. The owner of another local dime store complained bitterly of her inability to compete against the "richest-man-in-the-world's prices" and indicated that her 50-year-old store probably would have to be closed. The owner of the local hardware store told of attempting to compete with the discount giant by diversifying his inventory and offering specialized services, such as performing repair work for customers. Despite these efforts, his business still declined. "The biggest difference now," he complained, "is that you've got to work so hard, so many hours, just to break even, to say nothing of making a buck."

Commenting on Wal-Mart's impact on Independence, Kenneth Stone reported that in its first full year in operation, Wal-Mart's sales volume was approximately $10 million. Since the town's total retail sales volume had increased only $2.1 million that year, Stone concluded that some businesses in Independence had suffered "substantial losses," while towns within a 20-mile radius of Independence had lost about 6 percent of their annual sales volume. Stone also pointed out that the 95 jobs generated by Wal-Mart approximately equaled the number of jobs that were lost on Main Street. He further indicated that about half of those employees were part-time workers who received wages only slightly higher than minimum wage.[17]

Wal-Mart received more unfavorable publicity as a result of its decision to close its store in Hearne, Texas, a town with a population of 5,600, located about 95 miles northeast of Austin. The store in Hearne was closed in December 1990 after being in operation for 10 years. A spokesman for Wal-Mart stated that the outlet had never been profitable and attributed its disappointing performance to its proximity to two other Wal-Mart stores in the area. Because the firm had closed only six stores in its history, the novelty of the store closing in Hearne became national news. In articles in such publications as the *New York Times* and *USA Today*, some residents of the town vented their frustration over the loss of the store in statements that did not portray the company in a flattering light. These citizens felt that in closing the store Wal-Mart had betrayed the community. Irate townspeople blamed Wal-Mart for depleting Hearne of shopping alternatives and then departing, leaving them no choice but to drive 26 miles to another town to shop. (According to the local chamber of commerce, five of eight major businesses in Hearne had closed since Wal-Mart's arrival.) One long-time resident of the community said, "They [Wal-Mart] don't care about what they've done to us. I don't drive. . . . Before they came there were other places to go, . . . but now there's nothing else." A minister and former resident of Hearne wrote to the *Dallas Morning News* also expressing bitterness toward Wal-Mart. He accused the discount chain of killing his hometown twice— once when it entered the town and damaged its local businesses, and a second time when it left. He indicated, however, that the citizens of Hearne also bore some measure of responsibility for their plight. "Wal-Mart leaves an empty building as testimony to the '80s greed," he wrote, "and it leaves a downtown of vacated shops as testimony to our rush to save a little money (maybe not a very different kind of greed)."[18]

As Wal-Mart grew, some of the firm's alleged business practices became the object of increasingly rigorous public scrutiny. The company was criticized for the aloof and secretive methods of its local store managers and for their lack of involvement in local public affairs; for an excessively harsh and combative attitude on the part of the company toward local merchants; and for its frequent demands for such concessions as new utility lines, revised zoning, tax breaks, and special financing, in exchange for its willingness to grace a town with its presence. Journalist Neal Peirce, for example, wrote in his syndicated newspaper column of the "heavy-handed tactics" used by the firm in its efforts to establish a store in Lincoln, Nebraska. Peirce reported that when Wal-Mart's initial choice of a store location was rebuffed by the city council, the firm, according to one council member, at first refused to consider other locations. When Wal-Mart subsequently returned to the city council with the idea of locating a store on the edge of downtown Lincoln, among the concessions demanded by the company were that the city raze 12 entire city blocks, including 15 historic buildings; compel 59 existing businesses to relocate; and move railroad tracks and an electrical substation. The total cost to the taxpayers of Lincoln would have been $18 million. The mayor of Lincoln told Peirce that he had rejected Wal-Mart's proposal because the firm's demands were so excessive. In his column Peirce staunchly upheld the right of discount chains such as Wal-Mart to compete across the nation and indicated that they should not be barred from entering a market. He questioned, however, the virtue of using public funds, including the taxes paid by the very stores that would be placed most at risk, to underwrite the chains' entry into local communities.[19]

Public opposition to Wal-Mart's entering a town has been rare. In at least two communities, however, there have been organized campaigns to keep the discount chain out. In 1989 Wal-Mart temporarily abandoned plans to build a store in Steamboat Springs, Colorado, after residents took their city council to court and won a referendum that prohibited the firm from building a store there. Later, however, Wal-Mart did open an outlet in Steamboat Springs. In that same year, when Wal-Mart announced that it intended to locate in Iowa City, Iowa, some residents of that town also resisted the discount chain's proposed entry into their community. The site of the University of Iowa, Iowa City had a population of 50,000 in 1989. When Wal-Mart announced its intention of building a store on the outskirts of the city, the local merchants, in league with sympathetic residents, objected. The residents who opposed Wal-Mart's coming feared that the discount chain would drive the independent merchants out of business. This, they believed, would cause the demise of the city's college-town atmosphere, which was in large measure a creation of its quaint downtown shopping district. One Wal-Mart critic said, "The small downtown is one of Iowa's most important traits. A Wal-Mart brings the possibility of urban blight." After the city council approved a rezoning measure that would have allowed Wal-Mart to build, angry opponents secured enough signatures on a petition to hold a referendum on the issue. Said one activist, "It's amazing how arrogant city councils get when they see a Wal-Mart coming." The opposition group also launched a campaign to defeat the mayor and members of the city council who voted in favor of the rezoning.

Wal-Mart's supporters in Iowa City charged the merchants and their allies with turning the dispute into an "emotional issue that essentially says we shouldn't build Wal-Marts because they're too good at what they do," and a spokesman for the firm insisted that the downtown shops would benefit from the additional traffic that Wal-Mart would supply, "provided they offer superior service and aren't gouging their customers." The campaign to keep Wal-Mart out failed, but only by a narrow margin, since 46 percent of the voters in the referendum opposed the firm's entry.[20]

Some analysts have predicted that these isolated instances of opposition to Wal-Mart will become more commonplace and that in the future the unbridled enthusiasm felt by the residents of most small towns for Wal-Mart will wane. They advance the theory that local merchants, who in the past have been the firm's most vociferous critics, may be joined by the inhabitants of neighboring towns, if those neighbors see their own tax base decline and find that the savings they enjoy from buying at the nearby Wal-Mart are absorbed by the higher taxes they must pay to shore up their own decaying communities.[21]

Recently there has emerged a growing chorus of journalists and others lamenting the decline of small-town America, with some writers conjuring up images of the nation's once-proud heartland transformed into a vast rural wasteland distinguished only by the ubiquitous presence of Wal-Mart stores as a traveler passes from one nondescript community to the next.[22] These commentators express genuine concerns, but the problem is not a new one. Country towns have been dying for decades, and the reasons are far more numerous and complex than the presence of Wal-Mart.

The decline of rural communities can be traced at least to the late nineteenth century, when the popularity with farmers of mail-order catalogs from such firms as Montgomery Ward and Sears hurt local economies. During the early twentieth century, small-town businesses were damaged further as the growing popularity of the automobile allowed rural consumers to journey to larger towns and cities to shop. The decline accelerated during the 1950s with the coming of school consolidation and the interstate highway system, which gave rural shoppers even greater mobility. In recent years, problems in agriculture and industry have eroded local economies and caused the rural population of many areas to stagnate, which, in turn, has hastened the decay of small-town business districts.[23]

Although larger economic forces have been behind the changing economic character of rural America, Wal-Mart's impact on small towns was nevertheless significant. It is undeniable that Wal-Mart dramatically reshaped the economic and social structures of rural communities, forcing some local firms out of business in the process. Wal-Mart executives acknowledged that the firm's entry into rural markets affected local economies, but they insisted that the benefits to these communities outweighed the disadvantages. The firm also denied that it was responsible for the demise of local businesses. To Sam Walton, the reason for the difficulty suffered by some proprietary enterprises was not competition from Wal-Mart but the outmoded business practices of Main Street merchants. He maintained that his company had been "invited" into small towns by mom-and-pop retailers who remained mired in the past by charging high prices, offering only a spotty selection of goods, and refusing to open on Sunday or during evening hours. Echoing the founder's sentiment, Wal-Mart chief executive officer David Glass maintained that local businesses could survive in competition against Wal-Mart, saying that those merchants who "don't do better or who do go out of business" do so because they are not willing to improve their business practices or "reposition themselves in the market."²⁴

In truth, however, the adversity suffered by some local retailers was not always due to an unwillingness to change, as Wal-Mart liked to suggest, but to an inability to change. Those local merchants did not necessarily engage in an inferior type of retailing, merely a different type of retailing—one that fell prey to Wal-Mart's size and efficiency. Wal-Mart touted its ability to buy goods more cheaply than other merchants and then pass the savings on to its customers, while at the same time it implied that local merchants somehow were remiss in their retail practices or their prices would be lower and their selection of goods more varied. But this was not necessarily the case. Oftentimes the price structures and inventory levels of local businesses were the inevitable results of their small size. They were unable to charge prices that were as low as Wal-Mart's for various reasons, not least of which was that they did not enjoy the lower wholesale prices made available to Wal-Mart because of its ability to buy in quantity.

It is indisputable that some independent businesses fail as a result of Wal-Mart's presence in their community and that the economies of neighboring towns, in particular, often suffer. On balance, however, Wal-Mart may serve the greater economic good. Its stores attract legions of customers, and local enterprises that do not compete directly with Wal-Mart seem to benefit. In addition, sales tax revenues increase when Wal-Mart arrives in a town. Most important, of course, is the firm's role as a discount merchandiser. As such, it makes accessible to numerous small-town consumers a wide variety of reasonably priced goods that otherwise would not be conveniently available to them.

8

Wal-Mart Becomes America's Leading Retail Firm

THE 1980s HAD BEEN a decade of tremendous success for Wal-Mart, and as the 1990s dawned the firm continued its precedent-setting pace of growth. In fiscal 1991 Wal-Mart enlarged its trade territory to 34 states by entering 6 new states, opening 10 stores in California, 3 in Nevada, 5 in North Dakota, 3 in Pennsylvania, 7 in South Dakota, and 5 in Utah. This growth fulfilled the company's aim of expanding to the West Coast and the Northeast.

Wal-Mart arrived on the West Coast in August 1990, when it opened a store in Lancaster, California, a high desert community with a population of 44,000, located approximately 65 miles north of Los Angeles. At 116,000 square feet, the store's size was typical of the urban units being built by the firm during the early 1990s. The store's opening was conducted in the traditional Wal-Mart fashion. Very little advertising was done other than a special grand-opening wrapper that was placed around the normal monthly circular. The store did receive heavy local and regional press coverage, however. Additionally the firm counted on favorable word-of-mouth publicity and familiarity with Wal-Mart among some residents to stimulate business. The company planned to open a distribution center the following year in the town of Porterville, located in the central part of the San Joaquin Valley.

Wal-Mart entered the Northeast in 1989 when it opened a Sam's Club in Delran Township, New Jersey, part of the greater-Philadelphia market area. The firm selected York, Pennsylvania, located about 35 miles southwest of Philadelphia and some 40 miles northwest of Atlantic City, as the site of its first discount store in the region. Opened in October 1990, it was, at 130,000 square feet, the largest discount store in the chain. Wal-Mart's strategy in Pennsylvania was to avoid the two major cities, Pittsburgh and Philadelphia, and open units in small cities in the central part of the state. Beyond establishing additional stores in New Jersey and Pennsylvania, Wal-Mart planned to saturate the Northeast during the early 1990s by opening several more Sam's Clubs and Wal-Mart stores in Maryland, New York, New Hampshire, Delaware, and Maine. Wal-Mart was also shopping for a site for a distribution center somewhere in New England to support its outlets.

While expansion to both coasts at last made Wal-Mart a national chain, these new regions presented special challenges for the firm. In the West Wal-Mart was entering a market dominated by a strong competitor, Dayton Hudson's successful Target discount chain. In the Northeast Wal-Mart faced higher real estate costs and a more competitive market, as well as the task of finding employees who exhibited as high a degree of dedication as those in the small towns of the South. The firm also confronted the prospect of a stronger union presence, which could create problems for Wal-Mart similar to the union-related difficulties encountered by the struggling Carrefour hypermarket in Philadelphia. The company believed a stronger union environment could threaten the familial relationship between corporate management and hourly associates that had characterized the company throughout its first 20 years of growth. Indeed, the overall appeal of Wal-Mart's homespun image, which had done so much to ingratiate the firm with shoppers throughout its original market area, was uncertain with the Northeast's more sophisticated consumers.[1]

Wal-Mart opened 3 new distribution centers in fiscal 1991, bringing its total number to 16. Each distribution center served an average of 98 stores, significantly fewer in number than Wal-Mart's competitors' distribution facilities. Covering in excess of 1 million square feet each, the new distribution centers were located in Seymour, Indiana; Searcy, Arkansas; and Loveland, Colorado. With the opening of these facilities Wal-Mart's square footage of distribution capacity grew from 11.8 to 14.6 million square feet, an increase of 23.7 percent. The firm closed out this remarkable year of expansion by opening a record-breaking 36 stores on a single day, 30 January 1991. Wal-Mart's additions brought the total number of discount stores to 1,573, and they encompassed 111 million square feet of retail space, an increase of 19 percent over the preceding year. The stores continued to grow not only in number but also in size. By fiscal 1991 standard store sizes ranged from 30,000 to more than 110,000 square feet; 65,000 square feet was the average. During the same year, the firm embarked on another retail experiment by converting four surplus buildings into stores it called Bud's Warehouse Outlet. These 40,000-square-foot stores sold mainly closed out and refurbished goods, few of which came from Wal-Mart's discount stores.[2]

On 6 July 1990 Wal-Mart securities experienced the ninth two-for-one split since their first public offering 20 years earlier. As a result, for example, 100 of the original shares of Wal-Mart stock, which had sold for $1,650 in 1970, had grown to 51,200 shares, and at the market price of nearly $33 each a few days after the split, they were worth approximately $1.7 million. During fiscal 1991 Wal-Mart not only was the nation's fastest-growing retailer, but it was also the nation's most profitable. It had a net income of $1.3 billion on net sales of $32.6 billion, an increase over the previous year's net income of 20 percent and over the previous year's net sales of 26 percent overall and 10 percent for existing stores. Comparable gross sales per square foot in all retail divisions grew to $263, up from $250 the preceding year. This record of performance caused Wal-Mart to pass K mart in November 1990 to become the nation's second largest retailer. Then, in early 1991, the long-anticipated moment arrived: Wal-Mart overtook Sears to become the nation's largest retailer. Behind Wal-Mart, K mart occupied the second spot with an increase in sales of 8.5 percent to $32.1 billion in its fiscal year, while Sears slipped to number three with an increase in sales of only 1.2 percent to $31.9 billion for calendar year 1990. Wal-Mart had been steadily gaining on Sears throughout the 1980s. Just 10 years earlier, Wal-Mart's net sales of $2.4 billion had been less than 12 percent of Sears's, but by the end of the decade Sears's North American sales (including those from 131 stores in Canada and Mexico) had increased from $28 billion in 1988 to $31.9 billion in 1990, a growth rate of only 14 percent. During the same period, Wal-Mart's sales had more than doubled, from $16 billion to $32.6 billion.[3]

A number of factors contributed to Wal-Mart's triumph over Sears and K mart. One key element was the firm's small-town origins. By locating stores on the outskirts of small communities where local merchants were its only rivals, Wal-Mart absorbed business for miles around. Unfettered by competition from major retail chains, Wal-Mart refined the fundamental business practices that ultimately would enable it to reach the pinnacle of retail success. Wal-Mart's rural locations had compelled the firm to invest in its own inventory-replenishment system, which had evolved into an intricate network of distribution centers, an extensive fleet of trucks, and state-of-the-art computer and communications systems that enabled the firm to function with great efficiency.

K mart, on the other hand, was slow to adopt a distribution and communications network as efficient as Wal-Mart's, in part because of the immense expenditures involved. While Wal-Mart expanded its truck fleet, for example, K mart elected to curtail ownership of its trucks, because it considered subcontracted trucking cheaper. Because of its failure to keep pace in distribution and marketing technology, K mart was plagued by an inability to replenish inventory in a timely manner. As recently as 1991 in some of K mart's stores, hundreds of merchandise pegs were empty, and basic items, such as men's black socks, were missing. As part of the remodeling program that K mart chief executive officer Joseph Antonini had launched in the late 1980s, the chain had belatedly moved to improve its inventory-control system by installing checkout scanning in all stores and consolidating its merchandising operations at central locations. While these improvements made K mart more efficient, they did not give the chain a competitive advantage over Wal-Mart or Target, since those firms already had sophisticated inventory-control systems in operation.[4]

In addition to efficient inventory replenishment, Wal-Mart's intricate distribution and technology systems contributed to the firm's low cost of sales. During fiscal 1991, for example, the company's overhead expenses of 15 percent of sales were significantly below K mart's 23 percent and Sears's 29 percent. Wal-Mart's ability to surpass Sears was due in part to these lower overhead expenses. Years of top-heavy bureaucratic management had caused Sears's operating costs to spiral. In 1990, for example, Sears's headquarters staff consisted of 6,000 employees, compared with Wal-Mart's 2,500. Sears, moreover, had proved unable to get its swollen expenses under control, despite cutbacks in its unwieldy catalog offerings and painful reductions in personnel.

Wal-Mart's lower overhead expenses allowed the company to maintain one of its greatest advantages over its rivals—prices that were uniformly and consistently attractive to consumers. The overwhelming appeal of Wal-Mart's prices generated a burgeoning sales volume that stimulated further economies for the firm, which, in turn, made Wal-Mart even more efficient than its competitors. In fiscal 1990, for example, Wal-Mart's sales per square foot of $250 were significantly better than K mart's $150. The productivity level of Wal-Mart's personnel also was superior to that of its competitors. In fiscal 1991, for example, Wal-Mart's 328,000 associates, whose ranks had grown from 41,000 in fiscal

1982, generated an average of more than $95,000 in sales per employee, compared with approximately $85,000 for Sears employees.[5]
Wal-Mart's ability to keep its stores well stocked and its prices low were complemented by another asset, the high quality of its products. Beginning in the mid-1970s, the priorities of American consumers changed dramatically. Shoppers increasingly resented the business methods of traditional retailers, including declining customer service, too-frequent sales promotions, and higher markups, which translated into higher prices. At the same time consumers found their disposable income squeezed by such factors as inflation, recession, and the widening gap between rich and poor in America that was caused in part by declining union influence, increasingly rigorous education requirements for better-paying jobs, and the rise in the divorce rate. As a result, dollar-conscious consumers demanded greater value in their retail purchases—and to shoppers value meant paying affordable prices for nationally advertised, brand-name goods, because brand names implied higher quality and status. At one time both Sears, with its private-brand merchandise at moderate prices, and K mart, with its brand-name products at discount prices, had been perceived by the buying public as representing quality. But Sears's higher prices and K mart's shift away from brand-name products in favor of private-brand goods had overlooked the growing demand on the part of consumers for brand-name merchandise at low prices. Wal-Mart, in contrast, was committed to offering its small-town customers brand-name products at reasonable prices, and by expanding its emphasis on brand names as it grew, while at the same time keeping its prices low, Wal-Mart had acquired the image of offering greater value than its competitors.[6]

Sears's preeminence as America's leading retailer had been built by selling its own nationally branded products at prices that were within the reach of middle-class consumers, but Sears's focus on the traditional, home-owning, middle-America family had failed to keep pace with changing demographics. Income had shifted away from the middle class and reduced the purchasing power of those shoppers to such an extent that one economist concluded, "The buying power of the middle class isn't there." As its business had eroded over the years, Sears had repeatedly attempted to revitalize its image with consumers, but even the tardy strategies adopted during the late 1980s—carrying brand-name products and more-fashionable apparel—had failed to produce the desired results. The company was particularly disappointed when its highly publicized shift to lower prices did not improve profits; instead, the policy served only to alienate further many customers, who complained that they often could not find promised bargains on brand-name goods. The failure of the low-price strategy was due in large measure to Sears's inability to contain its bloated overhead expenses, while Wal-Mart's high sales per square foot, low expense ratio, and high profit margin allowed it to sell brand-name goods at prices that Sears could not match. "Most of the changes [Sears has] been trying to make, like the low pricing, are just poor imitations of what companies like Wal-Mart have already been doing," observed one analyst. "By the time they get up to speed, the rest of the world has moved ahead, and Sears is in the position of being a Johnny-come-lately with the need to change again." After Sears ceased to be the nation's leading retailer, its ongoing inability to adapt caused sales and profits, as well as the price of its stock, to continue to drop.[7]

By the early 1990s Joseph Antonini's revitalization program had wrought significant changes at K mart. Because the firm had been stigmatized to a great degree by its women's apparel, which had been almost exclusively private label, had too often lacked style, and had been poorly constructed, Antonini had incorporated higher-priced fashion goods in K mart's apparel offerings. He had also revamped K mart's inventory by eliminating 30 percent of the 110,000 items it once had stocked. As a result of his commitment to carrying more brand-name goods, trendy products such as Bugle Boy jeans, Seiko watches, and Sony electronics had begun to appear in the stores in increased numbers. And K mart's everyday-low-price strategy had caused the firm to drop prices on more than 8,000 of its more popular offerings. While Antonini's modifications enhanced the chain's sales performance, K mart, like Sears, found it difficult to rebuild its image with consumers, who remained unconvinced that K mart's products could match Wal-Mart's, either in quality or price.[8]

Still another way in which Wal-Mart surpassed its rivals was in its ability to create an appealing retail environment. Surveys indicated, for example, that K mart trailed Wal-Mart in customer satisfaction. Beyond the obvious advantage of price, consumers who frequented Wal-Mart indicated that they found it a comfortable place to shop—clean, well organized, and friendly. Customers at K mart, on the other hand, often expressed frustration at the dingy atmosphere and poor service they encountered there. The more appealing ambience of Wal-Mart's stores was attributable in part to the wide disparity between the age of Wal-Mart's and K mart's outlets. During the years that Wal-Mart had opened new stores rapidly, as well as remodeled vigorously to keep old stores fresh, K mart's management had neglected its outlets. As a result Wal-Mart's stores were significantly newer than K mart's. *Discount Store News* estimated that in 1990, 45 and 40 percent, respectively, of Wal-Mart's and Target's stores were three years old or less, while only 10 percent of K mart's stores were that new and 85 percent of K mart's stores were antiquated, having been in operation eight years or more. By the early 1990s, however, as a result of Antonini's $3 billion renovation program, many of K mart's outlets were larger and featured wide aisles, bright track lighting, better merchandise display, eye-catching graphics, and an updated logo. Nevertheless, while Antonini's modernization program had greatly improved the appearance of the chain, some analysts doubted that he could duplicate one of Wal-Mart's greatest assets, its bedrock commitment to customer service. Unlike Walton, who constantly hammered the importance of meeting the needs of customers, K mart's executives had never embraced the idea with equal enthusiasm. But Antonini began appearing with regularity on K mart's nationwide telecommunication system, exhorting K mart personnel to improve their efforts to serve customers.[9]

At Sears, as well, customer service had declined and stores looked dull and dated. In an effort to replace the bulky, outdated appearance of Sears's outlets with a more vibrant shopping environment, Sears chief executive officer Edward Brennan not only refurbished the stores but also reorganized some of them by introducing so-called power formats, which were boutique-like areas where shoppers could buy brand-name items in settings resembling specialty shops. Sears's most successful power format was its Brand Central showrooms for appliances and electronics. While Brennan's efforts to rejuvenate Sears were an improvement, the greatest impediment to their efficient execution companywide was Sears's cumbersome organizational structure. Noting the problem, a high-ranking source at Sears commented, "We arrive at a strategy, but not everyone in the organization adheres to it. They hedge. . . . A lot of the new stores look disjointed. They tend to become confusing places to shop. The bureaucratic culture is an enormous part of the problem."[10]

Wal-Mart's leadership proved more astute than K mart's or Sears's in the matter of diversification. While Wal-Mart diversified during the mid-1980s into the lucrative membership-warehouse business, both K mart and Sears diverted vital cash flow from their respective financial bases of retailing and discounting to pursue less successful ventures. About the same time that Wal-Mart established its Sam's Clubs, Bernard Fauber, then K mart's chief executive officer, wrongly assumed that the chain's markets were becoming saturated and rejected the opportunity to enter the warehouse-club business, instead choosing to diversify into specialty retailing. Only belatedly did K mart enter the warehouse-club business by purchasing Pace Membership Warehouse, Inc., in 1989. While Sam's Clubs contributed significantly to Wal-Mart's corporate sales and profits, K mart's specialty businesses did not. In 1990, for example, K mart's four specialty chains, Business Square, Sports Authority, Pay Less Drug Stores, and Waldenbooks, accounted for 22 percent of the firm's sales but contributed only 11 percent to operating income. As for Sears's diversification, some analysts believe that Sears placed too much emphasis on nonretailing pursuits following its restructuring in 1980, and they partly attribute the decline in Sears's share of general-merchandise sales from 41 percent in 1980 to 13 percent 10 years later to the firm's preoccupation during those years with its real estate and financial services subsidiaries.[11]

One of Wal-Mart's most unique advantages over its rivals was the dedication of its workforce. Reflecting the conservative, deeply religious examples of Sam and Helen Walton, Wal-Mart's employees readily exhibited the small-town virtues of hard work and friendliness, tempered with a certain vague suspicion of anyone not steeped in the firm's value system. Many of Wal-Mart's associates were not college graduates, which did not alarm the firm's senior executives, who stated flatly that they were not very interested in individuals who possessed a master of business administration or a similar advanced degree, since such specialists tended to devote more attention to "numbers" than to "people." Instead, the firm seemed to prefer high school graduates, whose ideals it could mold into utter loyalty to the company, primarily through intensive training seminars at Bentonville. One manifestation of the company's apparent perception of higher education as an impediment to the absorption of the Wal-Mart way of doing things was the firm's commitment to promoting mostly from within the company.

Nowhere was the high level of enthusiasm exhibited by Wal-Mart's employees more evident than at the general headquarters in Bentonville. Throughout the bustling facility employees were uniformly pleasant and at the same time highly protective of Wal-Mart's image. Their manner was one of crisp efficiency coupled with guarded courtesy. When asked about the cheerful industry that pervaded the facility, company spokespeople maintained that it was inspired largely by the self-effacing example of Sam Walton himself. Significant too, of course, was the handsome benefits package for employees, built around an enviable stock-option program and generous incentives for early retirement; this undoubtedly played no small role in the manifest goodwill that emanated from Bentonville. But whatever its source, a peculiarly religious atmosphere seemed to pervade Wal-Mart's headquarters. In fact, employee allegiance to the company's corporate culture, that almost mystical formula of success based on the zeal of Wal-Mart's associates and the company's willingness to treat them as partners and listen to their ideas, at times seemed to take on nearly cultlike proportions.

Undeniably, the prevailing reason for Wal-Mart's triumph over its competitors was Sam Walton. Having provided his firm with stable guidance for 30 years, Walton manifested a steadfast commitment to the business fundamentals of price, quality, efficiency, and customer service that stood in stark contrast to Sears and K mart, where changes in leadership sometimes took those firms in desultory directions, causing them to stray from the precepts on which their success had been built. Beyond his remarkable managerial skills, Walton possessed other talents that were invaluable to Wal-Mart's rise to retail preeminence. The quintessential merchant, he had the ability to anticipate what his customers would buy and to recognize and capitalize on nascent retail trends. His engaging personality, moreover, had a significant impact on Wal-Mart's growth, giving the company an image that was unique among retail firms. His charisma inspired a remarkable degree of loyalty and admiration from both his personnel and his customers. With regard to the special affection that Wal-Mart shoppers manifested toward Walton, one analyst said, "Some [customers] say he is the richest man in America. Yet there is no cynicism or resentment of his wealth, because consumers feel it has been earned." Commenting on the all-encompassing role Walton played in the success of his firm, the analyst concluded, "Wal-Mart is out front because of the distinctive leadership and controls established by its founder. If Wal-Mart is going to be derailed, it will more likely come from the inside than from the outside as the succession of leadership is completed during the next few years."[12]

Wal-Mart's growth did not abate after it passed K mart and Sears to become the nation's leading retailer. In fiscal 1992 Wal-Mart's net sales increased 35 percent to $43.9 billion, and net income increased 25 percent to $1.6 billion. There were 1,720 Wal-Mart stores in operation in 39 states and 208 Sam's Clubs in 37 states. Comparable sales per gross square foot of total discount-store and warehouse-club space grew to $279 and $522, respectively. Operating expenses fell to 15.3 percent of sales, the lowest ever for Wal-Mart and far below comparable efficiency rates for K mart and Sears, while Wal-Mart's sales per employee rose. Also in fiscal 1992 Wal-Mart introduced a private brand name, Sam's American Choice, for certain products that were made in America, such as soft drinks, and while the firm reaffirmed its commitment to offering brand-name merchandise, it indicated that the private brand might be extended to other products. In July 1991 Wal-Mart and Cifra, S.A., Mexico's largest retailer, which had $2.2 billion in sales in 1990, announced the formation of two joint ventures: one to build wholesale clubs in Mexico and another to create an import-export company that would give Cifra's Mexican suppliers access to Wal-Mart's outlets in the

United States. Late in the year Wal-Mart and Cifra opened two wholesale clubs in Mexico City. Patterned after the Sam's Clubs, the stores, called Club Aurrera, were the first of several planned by the two companies (see Table 8-1).[13] Investor confidence in Wal-Mart stock remained strong during the early 1990s. It sold at approximately $40 a share in the spring of 1991, and its price-earnings ratio climbed to 35. At the same time, in comparison, K mart stock was trading at $42 and had a price-earnings ratio of 11, which was below the market average of 17.6, while Target's parent company, Dayton Hudson, was trading at $74 with a price-earnings ratio of 14, reflecting the high debt levels it had incurred as a result of recent acquisitions. Wal-Mart stock reached an all-time high of $59.875 a share in January 1992. Although Wal-Mart's shares of stock were even more expensive, at 38 times earnings and twice the level of the Standard & Poor's 500 index, Wall Street analysts believed that the growth potential of the stock remained excellent. Some asserted that Wal-Mart, with a stock market value of $66 billion in 1992, might even surpass Exxon's $79 billion to become the company with the highest stock market value in the nation.[14]

As the 1990s began, Wal-Mart's management was keenly aware that the decade would be characterized by intensive competition. In 1989 David Glass had caused a sensation when he forecast that 50 percent of the nation's existing retail operations would be out of business by the year 2000 (he later added that this projected rate of failure was too low). Analysts predicted that the heightened competition of the 1990s would be caused by such factors as a slow growth in the number of consumers, a reduction in disposable income, a saturated marketplace, and a demand

TABLE 8-1. Growth of Wal-Mart Stores, Inc., Fiscal 1991–1992

	1991	1992
Stores in operation	1,573	1,720
Sam's Clubs	148	208
Net sales	$32,601,594	$43,886,902
Total revenue	32,863,408	44,289,423
Costs and expenses	30,820,648	41,736,286
Income before taxes	2,042,760	2,553,137
Net income	1,291,024	1,608,476

Note: Amounts shown are in thousands of dollars.

Source: Annual reports of Wal-Mart Stores, Inc.

for convenience, due to the continued decrease in the amount of time consumers would have to shop. Wal-Mart's executives realized, moreover, that since its inception, discount merchandising in particular had been a highly competitive industry. For example, of the top ten discounters in 1962—the year that Wal-Mart, K mart, and Target had been founded— not one was still in business 30 years later.[15]

During the early years of the decade, America's three leading discount firms, Wal-Mart, K mart, and Target (who collectively controlled 70 percent of the discount market in 1991) already were girding themselves for the competitive struggles that lay ahead. One way that Wal-Mart hoped to perpetuate its remarkable record of growth in this competitive environment was by enlarging its commitment to the $300 billion-a-year supermarket business through the expansion of its Supercenters. The firm operated 12 Supercenters in August 1992, and some analysts predicted that there would be 400 Supercenters by 1996. Another path of growth for the company was through the expansion of its Sam's Clubs, whose sales in fiscal 1992 rose 30 percent to $9.4 billion. Wal-Mart also hoped to maintain its rapid growth by expanding more deeply into the Northeast, California, and Mexico. In the pursuit of these goals, however, Wal-Mart would face aggressive competition from a revitalized K mart and an expanding Target, as well as from efficient category killers such as Toys "R" Us and Home Depot.[16]

Analysts predicted that K mart would benefit more and more from Joseph Antonini's massive remodeling program, and pointed out that K mart could take comfort in two encouraging trends. First, its prime urban locations meant that numerous shoppers had better access to K mart than to Wal-Mart, and, second, in 1990 K mart's biggest sales gains had been in the South, where it competed more directly with Wal-Mart than in any other region. The only other discounter strong enough to compete with Wal-Mart and K mart was Target, which during the early 1990s consisted of 420 stores and enjoyed sales in excess of $8 billion. Located primarily in the Midwest, California, and Texas, Target—an upscale discounter that sold better-quality, higher-priced apparel to a more select customer and yet matched or came close to other discounters on such everyday items as cleaning supplies and food—was eager to compete with Wal-Mart and K mart and had plans to enter the Southeast, Wal-Mart's territory. While these three leading discounters most likely would accelerate their advances into one another's domains as the decade progressed, direct competition would not be the only avenue of growth available to them. They also could take market shares away from weaker retail operations, such as Sears, J. C. Penney, and other national department stores; specialty chains; and ailing regional discount chains like Ames Department Stores.[17]

Wal-Mart's greatest challenge in the years ahead would lie not in its ability to compete with rival retail organizations but in its capacity to overcome irreplaceable loss. As his discount empire continued to grow, Sam Walton's physical strength ebbed. Early in 1990 Walton was diagnosed as having a form of bone cancer known as multiple myeloma. In the months that followed, declining health compelled him to diminish his involvement in corporate affairs, and he busied himself with writing his autobiography, *Sam Walton: Made in America, My Story*. In March 1992 President George Bush flew to Bentonville to present the Medal of Freedom, the nation's highest civilian honor, to a frail and wheelchair-bound Walton. Soon thereafter, on 5 April 1992, Sam Walton died at the age of 74. Following his father's death, Rob Walton took his place as chairman of Wal-Mart, and David Glass, as president and chief executive officer, continued to direct the company.[18]

Sam Walton, one of the nation's leading twentieth-century entrepreneurs, built a business that transformed mass merchandising in America. Wal-Mart significantly altered the relationship between manufacturer and merchant by expanding the power and influence of the retailer in the marketing and distribution of products. By consistently offering consumers brand-name goods at discount prices, Wal-Mart imposed rigorous price and quality standards on the retail industry as a whole and revolutionized the shopping habits and expectations of a generation of consumers. Yet Walton's accomplishments transcended the world of commerce. As he neared the end of his life his popularity grew, and the public lavished on him a measure of affection rarely accorded a businessman. Although widely respected and admired for his success, many Americans simply liked Sam Walton as a person, possibly because they looked beyond the magnate of wealth and achievement and found in the man a refreshing devotion to hard work, modesty, and simplicity that was worthy of acclaim.

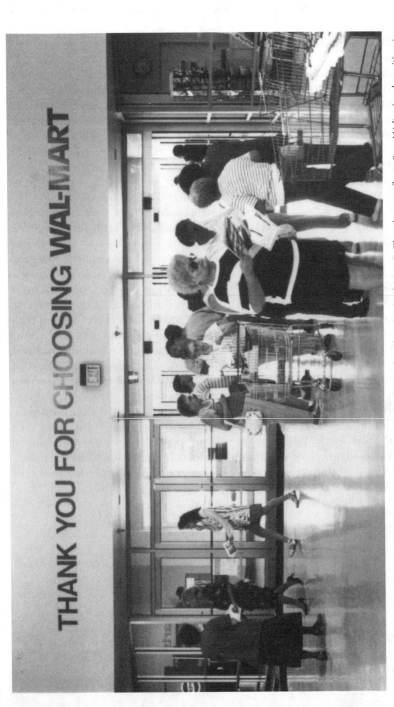

Emblazoned over the exits of Wal-Mart stores is the slogan "Thank You for Choosing Wal-Mart." The phrase reflects Sam Walton's admonition to his personnel that the needs of customers must be satisfied because they "do not have to shop at Wal-Mart." *Courtesy of Mass Market Retailers*

CHRONOLOGY

1918	Samuel Moore Walton is born 29 March to Thomas Gibson and Nancy Lee Walton, a young farm couple living near Kingfisher, Oklahoma.
1921	James L. (Bud) Walton is born.
1936	Sam Walton graduates from Hickman High School in Columbia, Missouri.
1940	Sam Walton graduates from the University of Missouri with a B.A. degree in economics.
1940	Sam Walton begins his career in retailing on 3 June by going to work for J. C. Penney in Des Moines, Iowa.
1942–1945	Sam Walton serves in the U. S. Army, achieving the rank of captain.
1943	Sam Walton marries Helen Robson of Claremore, Oklahoma, on 14 February.
1944	Sam and Helen Walton's first child, Samuel Robson (Rob), is born.
1945	Sam Walton opens a Ben Franklin variety store in Newport, Arkansas.
1946	Sam and Helen Walton's second child, John Thomas, is born.
1948	Sam and Helen Walton's third child, James Carr (Jim), is born.
1949	Sam and Helen Walton's fourth child, Alice, is born.
1950	Unable to renew the lease of his Newport variety store, Sam Walton buys another store in the Ben Franklin chain, Harrison's variety store, which he renames Walton's 5 & 10, in Bentonville, Arkansas.

1952   Sam Walton opens a second variety store, also named Walton's 5 & 10, with self-service, in Fayetteville, Arkansas.

1953   Sam Walton inaugurates self-service in Walton's 5 & 10 in Bentonville.

1954   Sam and Bud Walton open a Ben Franklin variety store in a shopping center in Ruskin Heights, Missouri, a suburb of Kansas City.

1962   Sam Walton opens his first large variety store, named Walton's Family Center, in St. Robert, Missouri. The size of Sam Walton's variety-store chain peaks at 16 units. City Products Corporation, the parent company of the Ben Franklin chain of variety stores, rejects Sam Walton's franchise proposal for a discount store in Arkansas. In March the S. S. Kresge Company opens its first K mart discount store in Garden City, Michigan, a Detroit suburb; in May the Dayton Corporation opens its first Target discount store in Roseville, Minnesota, a suburb of St. Paul. In July Sam Walton opens the first Wal-Mart Discount City in Rogers, Arkansas.

1969   Sam Walton's firm incorporates as Wal-Mart, Inc., on 31 October. Wal-Mart opens a general headquarters and distribution facility in Bentonville.

by 1970   Wal-Mart has a total of 32 outlets (18 Wal-Mart Discount City and 14 variety stores) in operation in four states and net sales of $31 million.

1970   The firm changes its name to Wal-Mart Stores, Inc., on 2 January. The first public sale of Wal-Mart Stores securities occurs on 1 October.

1972   Wal-Mart Stores is listed on the New York Stock Exchange.

1974   Sam Walton relinquishes his leadership of Wal-Mart Stores to Ronald M. Mayer.

1976   Sam Walton reclaims the leadership of Wal-Mart Stores and Mayer resigns.

1977   Sam Walton closes the Walton's Family Center store in Waynesville, Missouri, his last remaining variety store. Wal-Mart Stores purchases 16 Mohr Value Discount Department stores.

by 1980   Wal-Mart Stores, with 276 outlets in 11 states and net sales of more than $1 billion, becomes the youngest retail firm in the United States and the only regional retailer ever to reach that volume.

1981   Wal-Mart Stores purchases the 106-unit Kuhn's Big K Stores Corporation.

1983   Wal-Mart Stores opens its first Sam's Wholesale Club in Oklahoma City and its first dot Discount Drugs in Des Moines, Iowa.

1984   Sam Walton dances the hula on Wall Street. Wal-Mart Stores opens it first Helen's Arts and Crafts store in Springfield, Missouri.

1985   Wal-Mart Stores inaugurates its Buy American program. With a fortune of $2.8 billion, Sam Walton is named the richest man in the United States by *Forbes* magazine.

1987   Wal-Mart Stores launches its own satellite communications network. Wal-Mart Stores opens its pilot Hypermart USA in Garland, Texas, a suburb of Dallas.

1988   Sam Walton relinquishes the job of chief executive officer of Wal-Mart Stores to David D. Glass, while retaining the title of chairman of the board. Wal-Mart Stores opens its first Wal-Mart Supercenter in Washington, Missouri. Wal-Mart Stores sells its Helen's Arts and Crafts stores.

by 1990   Wal-Mart Stores operates a total of 1,531 stores in twenty-nine states and has net sales of $25.8 billion.

1990   Sam Walton is diagnosed as having a form of bone cancer known as multiple myeloma. Wal-Mart Stores sells its dot Discount Drugs chain. The ninth two-for-one split of Wal-Mart Stores securities occurs. Wal-Mart Stores changes the name of its Sam's Wholesale Clubs to Sam's Clubs. Wal-Mart Stores passes K mart to become the nation's second-largest retailer.

1991   Wal-Mart Stores overtakes Sears to become the nation's largest retailer.

1992   President George Bush presents the Medal of Freedom to Sam Walton.

1992   Sam Walton dies on 5 April at the age of 74.

NOTES AND REFERENCES

CHAPTER 1

1. Sam Walton with John Huey, *Sam Walton: Made in America, My Story* (New York: Doubleday, 1992), 3–5 (quotation on 5), 11–13; Wal-Mart Stores, Inc., *Making the Difference: The Story of Wal-Mart* (Bentonville, Ark.: Wal-Mart Stores, 1990), 4; and *Discount Store News* 28 (18 December 1989): 88. A journalistic biography of Walton that contains information on his family history may be found in Vance H. Trimble, *Sam Walton: The Inside Story of America's Richest Man* (New York: Dutton, 1990), 10–28.

2. Walton with Huey, *Made in America*, 13–14; and *The Cresset, 1935* (Hickman High School yearbook), 33, 48, 52, 56; *The Cresset, 1936*, n.p.

3. Walton with Huey, *Made in America*, 14–16 (quotation on 15); Wal-Mart Stores, Inc., *Making the Difference*, 6; *Financial World* 155 (15 April 1986): 28; Trimble, *Walton*, 29–34; *The Savitar, 1940* (University of Missouri yearbook), 74, 124, 126, 129; Columbia (Mo.) *Tribune*, 15 March 1965, 5; Columbia (Mo.) *Missourian*, 17 March 1965, 4; and *Missouri Alumnus* 28 (June 1940): 11.

4. Walton with Huey, *Made in America*, 17–21 (first and second quotations on 18); *Financial World* 155 (15 April 1986): 29; *Discount Store News* 28 (18 December 1989): 88; Wal-Mart Stores, Inc., *Making the Difference*, 6; *Fortune* 124 (23 September 1991): 50 (third quotation); and Trimble, *Walton*, 44, 47.

5. U.S. Department of Commerce, *Survey of Current Business: Annual Supplement* (Washington, D.C.: U.S. Government Printing Office, 1931), 160–61; *Printers' Ink* 145 (20 December 1928): 25; and *Business Week*, 6 August 1930, 14. For a discussion of Butler Brothers and the Ben Franklin variety-store chain, see Sandra S. Vance and Roy V. Scott, "Butler Brothers and the Rise and Decline of the Ben Franklin Variety

Stores: A Study in Franchise Retailing," *Essays in Economic and Business History* 11 (1993): 258–71. For a discussion of some facets of chain-store operation during the 1920s, see *Nation's Business* 13 (February 1925): 44–46. The standard account of chain stores is Godfrey M. Lebhar, *Chain Stores in America, 1859–1962* (New York: Chain Store Publishing Corporation, 1963).

6. Harry Kursh, *The Franchise Boom* (Englewood Cliffs, N.J.: Prentice-Hall, 1968), 4; Mansel G. Blackford and K. Austin Kerr, *Business Enterprise in American History* (Boston: Houghton Mifflin Company, 1990), 370–71; William P. Hall, "Franchising—New Scope for an Old Technique," *Harvard Business Review* 42 (January–February 1964): 62–65; and Douglas J. Dalrymple and Donald L. Thompson, *Retailing: An Economic View* (New York: Free Press, 1969), 73–75. For information on the origins and the development of franchising, see Carl M. Larson, Robert E. Weigand, and John S. Wright, *Basic Retailing* (Englewood Cliffs, N.J.: Prentice-Hall, 1982), 49–51; and Donald W. Hackett, *Franchising: The State of the Art* (Chicago: American Marketing Association, 1977), 4–5. For a recent study of franchising in specific industries, see Thomas S. Dicke, *Franchising in America: The Development of a Business Method, 1840–1980* (Chapel Hill: University of North Carolina Press, 1992). The author examines franchising by the McCormick Harvesting Machine Company, the I. M. Singer Company, the Ford Motor Company, the Sun Oil Company, and Domino's Pizza. See also Charles L. Vaughn, *Franchising: Its Nature, Scope, Advantages, and Development* (Lexington, Mass.: D. C. Heath and Company, 1974).

7. *Moody's Manual of Investments, 1946*, 1506; Butler Brothers, *Annual Report, 1936*, n.p. (second quotation); *Annual Report, 1938*, n.p. (first quotation); Hall, "Franchising," 65; and Paul D. Converse and Harvey W. Huegy, *The Elements of Marketing* (New York: Prentice-Hall, 1940), 403–4.

8. Writers' Program of the Work Projects Administration in the State of Arkansas, *Arkansas: A Guide to the State* (New York: Hastings House, 1941), 206–7, 307–9; and Trimble, *Walton*, 45.

9. Butler Brothers, *Annual Report, 1936*, n.p.; *Annual Report, 1938*, n.p.; Converse and Huegy, *Elements of Marketing*, 404; and *Printers' Ink* 145 (20 December 1928): 28.

10. *Printers' Ink* 183 (12 May 1938): 63. For information on the life and work of retail saleswomen, see Frances R. Donovan, *The Saleslady* (Chicago: University of Chicago Press, 1929); and Susan P. Benson, *Counter Cultures: Saleswomen, Managers, and Customers in American Department Stores, 1890–1940* (Urbana: University of Illinois Press, 1986). For a detailed description of a typical variety store during the

1930s, see Nelson A. Miller, *Establishing and Operating a Variety and General Merchandise Store* (Washington: U.S. Government Printing Office, 1946).

11. Fred M. Jones, *Principles of Retailing* (New York: Pitman Publishing Corporation, 1949), 74, 176.

12. William T. Kelley, "Small-Town Monopoly: A Case Study," *Journal of Retailing* 31 (Summer 1955): 63–66, 101–2.

13. Newport (Ark.) *Weekly Independent*, 15 March 1946, 17 June 1949, 20 May 1949, 17 August 1949; and Trimble, *Walton*, 53.

14. Walton with Huey, *Walton*, 21–31 (quotation on 30); Wal-Mart Stores, Inc., *Making the Difference*, 9; *Discount Store News* 28 (18 December 1989): 90; and Trimble, *Walton*, 54–56, 64.

15. Walton with Huey, *Made in America*, 31–32; Little Rock *Arkansas Gazette*, 23 April 1972, C3; and *Discount Store News* 28 (18 December 1989): 90 (quotation). In addition to hunting quail, Walton was an avid tennis player. For an account of Walton's quail hunting and comments on his personality, see *Southpoint* 20 (February 1990): 58–61.

16. Work Projects Administration, *Arkansas*, 206–7, 307–9; Milton D. Rafferty, *The Ozarks: Land and Life* (Norman: University of Oklahoma Press, 1980), 3–14, 271–72; David M. Tucker, *Arkansas: A People and Their Reputation* (Memphis: Memphis State University Press, 1985), chap. 11; and Walton with Huey, *Made in America*, 32. A readable history of Arkansas may be found in Harry S. Ashmore, *Arkansas: A History* (New York: W. W. Norton & Company, 1984).

17. Walton with Huey, *Made in America*, 32–33; Little Rock *Arkansas Gazette*, 6 May 1990, F1; Bentonville (Ark.) *Benton County Democrat*, 27 July 1950; Wal-Mart Stores, Inc., *Making the Difference*, 9; *Discount Store News* 28 (18 December 1989): 90; and Trimble, *Walton*, 61–64 (quotation on 64). Forty years after the Bentonville store opened, the structure became a visitors center and company museum. See Springdale (Ark.) *Morning News*, 13 May 1990.

18. Bentonville (Ark.) *Benton County Democrat*, 7 August 1952, 20 August 1953.

19. Ibid., 23 October 1952, 13 November 1952, 4 December 1952, 5 March 1953, 16 July 1953, 5 October 1953, 3 December 1953, 6 May 1954, 13 May 1954, 20 May 1954, 10 June 1954, 17 June 1954, 1 July 1954, 29 July 1954, 16 September 1954; and Trimble, *Walton*, 68, 89.

20. Bentonville (Ark.) *Benton County Democrat*, 30 October 1952; Walton with Huey, *Made in America*, 33, 34, 35–36 (quotation on 35); and Trimble, *Walton*, 72–73.

21. Bentonville (Ark.) *Benton County Democrat*, 2 April 1953, 20 August 1953 (quotations).

22. Walton with Huey, *Made in America*, 35–36; *Financial World* 158 (4 April 1989): 60; Bentonville (Ark.) *Benton County Democrat*, 30 October 1952; *Discount Store News* 28 (18 December 1989): 90; Little Rock *Arkansas Gazette*, 6 May 1990, F1; *Arkansas Times* 10 (February 1984): 105; and Trimble, *Walton*, 73.

23. Walton with Huey, *Made in America*, 37–38 (quotations on 37); Wal-Mart Stores, Inc., Annual 10–K Report to the U.S. Securities and Exchange Commission (hereafter Annual 10–K Report), 1990, 3; Wal-Mart Stores, Inc., *Making the Difference*, 6; and Trimble, *Walton*, 73.

24. Walton with Huey, *Made in America*, 38–41 (quotation on 38); and Trimble, *Walton*, 73–76, 82–83.

25. Walton with Huey, *Made in America*, 36, 41; and Trimble, *Walton*, 78 (quotation).

26. Walton with Huey, *Made in America*, 41–42; Trimble, *Walton*, 83; *Financial World* 158 (4 April 1989): 60; Wal-Mart Stores, Inc. *Making the Difference*, 9; and *Discount Store News* 28 (18 December 1989): 90.

27. *Moody's Industrial Manual, 1959*, 658.

CHAPTER 2

1. Lewis Atherton, *The Pioneer Merchant in Mid-America* (Columbia: University of Missouri Press, 1939), 90–102; and Benjamin C. Butcher, "The Development of Large-Scale Retail Price-Cutting Institutions in the United States since 1870" (Ph.D. diss., University of Illinois, 1965), 7, 12. For additional information on some of America's early retail forms, see J. R. Dolan, *The Yankee Peddlers of Early America* (New York: Clarkson N. Potter, 1964); Richardson Wright, *Hawkers and Walkers in Early America: Strolling Peddlers . . . and Others from the Beginning to the Civil War* (New York: Frederick Ungar Publishing Company, 1927); and Elliott Ashkenazi, *The Business of Jews in Louisiana, 1840–1875* (Tuscaloosa: University of Alabama Press, 1988).

2. Alfred D. Chandler, Jr., *The Visible Hand: The Managerial Revolution in American Business* (Cambridge, Mass.: Harvard University Press, 1977), 207–24.

3. Butcher, "Large-Scale Retail Price-Cutting Institutions," 13–14, 18, 27–28, 36, 38, 51; Harold Barger, *Distribution's Place in the American Economy since 1869* (Princeton, N.J.: Princeton University Press, 1955), 30; and Chandler, *Visible Hand*, 225–27. See also John W. Ferry, *A History of the Department Store* (New York: Macmillan Company, 1960). For a list of "notable department stores," see Robert Hendrickson, *The Grand Emporiums: The Illustrated History of America's Great Department Stores* (New York: Stein and Day, 1979), 468–83. The standard account of Macy's is Ralph M. Hower, *History of Macy's of New York, 1858–1919* (Cambridge, Mass.: Harvard University Press, 1943).

4. Penrose Scull with Prescott C. Fuller, *From Peddlers to Merchant Princes: A History of Selling in America* (Chicago: Follett Publishing Company, 1967), 159, 162. The history of chain stores can be followed in Godfrey M. Lebhar, *Chain Stores in America, 1859–1962* (New York: Chain Store Publishing Corporation, 1963). See also Theodore N. Beckman and Herman C. Nolen, *The Chain Store Problem: A Critical Analysis* (New York: McGraw-Hill Book Company, 1938). For J. C. Penney, see Norman Beasley, *Main Street Merchant: The Story of the J. C. Penney Company* (New York: Whittlesey House, 1948).

5. Hendrickson, *Grand Emporiums*, 115–23; Preston J. Beil, ed., *Variety Store Retailing* (New York: Variety Store Merchandiser Publications, 1956), 12–15; *Moody's Industrial Manual, 1987*, 3597; and Gary Hoover, Alta Campbell, and Patrick J. Spain, eds., *Hoover's Handbook: Profiles of over 500 Major Corporations, 1991* (Austin, Tex.: Reference Press, 1990), 592. See also John K. Winkler, *Five and Ten: The Fabulous Life of F. W. Woolworth* (New York: Robert M. McBride & Company, 1940); and James Brough, *The Woolworths* (New York: McGraw-Hill Book Company, 1982).

6. Beil, *Variety Store Retailing*, 15–17; and Robert Drew-Bear, *Mass Merchandising: Revolution and Evolution* (New York: Fairchild Publications, 1970), 210.

7. Malcolm P. McNair and Eleanor G. May, *The Evolution of Retail Institutions in the United States* (Cambridge, Mass.: Marketing Science Institute, 1976), 16; Hendrickson, *Grand Emporiums*, 207–10, 220–26; Hoover et al., eds., *Hoover's Handbook*, 385; and Thomas A. Woods, *Knights of the Plow: Oliver H. Kelley and the Origins of the Grange in Republican Ideology* (Ames: Iowa State University Press, 1991), 161.

8. Hendrickson, *Grand Emporiums*, 236–43; and Hoover et al., eds., *Hoover's Handbook*, 492. See also Gordon L. Weil, *Sears, Roebuck, U.S.A.: The Great American Catalog Store and How It Grew* (Briarcliff Manor, N.Y.: Stein and Day, 1977); and Boris Emmet and John E. Jeuck, *Catalogues and Counters: A History of Sears, Roebuck and Company* (Chicago: University of Chicago Press, 1950).

9. Hendrickson, *Grand Emporiums*, 235–36; and Butcher, "Large-Scale Retail Price-Cutting Institutions," 70. See also Orange A. Smalley and Frederick D. Sturdivant, *The Credit Merchants: A History of Spiegel, Inc.* (Carbondale: Southern Illinois University Press, 1973).

10. Butcher, "Large-Scale Retail Price-Cutting Institutions," 98.

11. Hendrickson, *Grand Emporiums*, 228–29; Butcher, "Large-Scale Retail Price-Cutting Institutions," 79–80; James C. Worthy, *Shaping an American Institution: Robert E. Wood and Sears, Roebuck* (Urbana: University of Illinois Press, 1984); and Frank B. Latham, *1872–1972, A Century of Serving Consumers: The Story of Montgomery Ward* (Chicago: Montgomery Ward & Company, 1972), 70–72.

12. Drew-Bear, *Mass Merchandising*, 24–26; Butcher, "Large-Scale Retail Price-Cutting Institutions," 104, 130–32, 147–48; and McNair and May, *Retail Institutions in the United States*, 27–30.

13. *Barron's* 48 (22 April 1968): 11; Beil, *Variety Store Retailing*, 17–19; and McNair and May, *Retail Institutions in the United States*, 35–36.

14. Milton P. Brown, William Applebaum, and Walter J. Salmon, *Strategy Problems of Mass Retailers and Wholesalers* (Homewood, Ill.: Richard D. Irwin, 1970), 7–8; and *Stores* 42 (November 1960): 6–8, 12, 14, 16–18, 20–21.

15. John R. Darling, "Retailing in the American Economy, 1948–1962" (Ph.D. diss., University of Illinois, 1967), 1–2, 64–75, 79, 85; and James R. Lowry, *The Retailing Revolution Revisited* (Muncie, Ind.: Ball State University, 1969), 2.

16. Lowry, *Retailing Revolution Revisited*, 1; *Fortune* 65 (April 1962): 100; *U.S. News and World Report* 53 (21 May 1962): 46–50; *Commercial and Financial Chronicle* 176 (16 October 1952): 4–5; Brown, Applebaum, and Salmon, *Strategy Problems of Mass Retailers*, 9, 11–12; McNair and May, *Retail Institutions in the United States*, 43–45, 48–49; Beil, *Variety Store Retailing*, 20–21; *Barron's* 37 (28 October 1957): 5–6; ibid. 48 (22 April 1968): 11; *Business Week*, 20 July 1946, 78–79; ibid., 8 November 1952, 54–56, 58, 60; *Sales Management* 62 (1 April 1949): 37–40; ibid. 72 (1 February 1954): 80, 82, 84–85; ibid. 86 (7 April 1961): 82–84, 87–90; Darling, "Retailing in the American Economy," 143; *Financial World* 110 (29 October 1958): 14, 16; and *Magazine of Wall Street* 105 (12 March 1960): 678.

17. William H. Bolen, *Contemporary Retailing* (Englewood Cliffs, N.J.: Prentice-Hall, 1978), 14; *Time* 116 (21 October 1980): 51, 54; Darling, "Retailing in the American Economy," 140–41, 143; Frances M. Lehman, "The Discount House," *Journal of Retailing* 19 (February 1943): 19–22, 24–25; *Barron's* 38 (17 November 1958): 3; and Delbert J. Duncan and Stanley C. Hollander, *Modern Retailing Management: Basic Concepts and Practices* (Homewood, Ill.: Richard D. Irwin, 1977), 22.

18. John W. Wingate and Arnold Corbin, *Changing Patterns in Retailing: Readings on Current Trends* (Homewood, Ill.: Richard D. Irwin, 1956), 111; *Printers' Ink* 247 (30 April 1954): 31–33; and Danny N. Bellenger and Jac L. Goldstucker, *Retailing Basics* (Homewood, Ill.: Richard D. Irwin, 1983), 23–24.

19. F. W. Gilchrist, "The Discount House," *Journal of Marketing* 17 (January 1953): 267–72; Stanley C. Hollander, "The Discount House," *Journal of Marketing* 18 (July 1953): 57–59; Richard E. Westervelt, "The Discount House Problem," *Journal of Retailing* 30 (Summer 1954): 69–70, 89–90; and Ralph S. Alexander and Richard M. Hill, "What to Do About

the Discount House," *Harvard Business Review* 33 (January–February 1955): 56–58. A 1954 doctoral dissertation on the topic, now published, is Stanley C. Hollander, *Discount Retailing, 1900–1952: An Examination of Some Divergences from the One-Price System in American Retailing* (New York: Garland Publishing, 1986).

20. Butcher, "Large-Scale Retail Price-Cutting Institutions," 158–60. For detailed figures by different types of stores on margins since 1869, see Barger, *Distribution's Place in the American Economy*, 81.

21. J. Barry Mason and Morris L. Mayer, *Modern Retailing: Theory and Practice* (Dallas: Business Publications, 1978), 236–37; Douglas J. Dalrymple and Donald L. Thompson, *Retailing: An Economic View* (New York: Free Press, 1969), 221–22, 224; Butcher, "Large-Scale Retail Price-Cutting Institutions," 106–12, 123–27, 150; Marshall C. Howard, *Legal Aspects of Marketing* (New York: McGraw-Hill Book Company, 1964), 39–40; *Consumer Bulletin* 40 (October 1957): 15–17; and Jack G. Kaikati, "Don't Discount Off-Price Retailers," *Harvard Business Review* 63 (May–June 1985): 88.

22. Dalrymple and Thompson, *Retailing*, 222–24; and *Editor and Publisher* 87 (6 February 1954): 16; ibid. (30 October 1954): 15, 30 (quotations).

23. *Fortune* 45 (June 1952): 210; *Barron's* 38 (17 November 1958): 3; *Printers' Ink* 262 (14 March 1958): 24, 27; *Business Week*, 18 July 1964, 126; and *Discount Merchandiser* 6 (June 1966): 63.

24. Drew-Bear, *Mass Merchandising*, 111–15; *Barron's* 41 (18 September 1961): 29, 31, 34; ibid. 46 (7 March 1966): 26; and *Discount Merchandiser* 6 (June 1966): 63.

25. *Business Week*, 2 June 1962, 34; *Printers' Ink* 275 (14 April 1961): 41–42; *Barron's* 36 (16 January 1956): 5–6; Butcher, "Large-Scale Retail Price-Cutting Institutions," 135; and *Tide* 32 (October 1958): 39.

26. *Fortune* 54 (November 1956): 122–34, 259–60, 262, 264; *Barron's* 39 (2 December 1959): 29–30; *Electrical Merchandising Week* 91 (30 November 1959): 31–33; *Business Week*, 17 September 1966, 50; and Drew-Bear, *Mass Merchandising*, 119, 135–36.

27. Duncan and Hollander, *Modern Retailing Management*, 22; Scull with Fuller, *From Peddlers to Merchant Princes*, 253; Drew-Bear, *Mass Merchandising*, 74–81; *Barron's* 54 (15 July 1974): 11; and *Discount Merchandiser* 20 (June 1980): 76.

28. *Sales Management* 85 (19 August 1960): 46–48, 50; *Dun's Review and Modern Industry* 76 (November 1960): 151, 153–54, 156; *Barron's* 41 (27 February 1961): 11–12; ibid. 40 (25 July 1960): 20–21; Drew-Bear, *Mass Merchandising*, 251–71; and Lowry, *Retailing Revolution Revisited*, 7–8.

29. Lowry, *Retailing Revolution Revisited*, 6–7; James R. Lowry and William R. Davidson, *Leased Departments in Discount Merchandising* (Columbus: Bureau of Business Research of Ohio State University, 1967), 11–27; *Business Week*, 15 October 1960, 59–60; and Drew-Bear, *Mass Merchandising*, 272–76.

30. Drew–Bear, *Mass Merchandising*, 217; *Discount Merchandiser* 8 (January 1968): 105–7; *Commercial and Financial Chronicle* 200 (20 August 1964): 669; *Business Week*, 29 January 1966, 126–28, 130, 132, 134; *Stores* 51 (July 1969): 51–52, 54; *Discount Merchandiser* 4 (October 1964): 44–45; and *Barron's* 49 (21 July 1969): 3.

31. *Financial World* 116 (25 October 1961): 11; *Fortune* 49 (April 1954): 150; *Business Week*, 14 November 1964, 58, 60, 65, 67; Drew-Bear, *Mass Merchandising*, 228–34; and Brough, *The Woolworths*, 209–10.

32. Brown, Applebaum, and Salmon, *Strategy Problems of Mass Retailers*, 720–27; *Stores* 51 (July 1969): 54–55; and Hendrickson, *Grand Emporiums*, 128, 430–31.

33. Drew-Bear, *Mass Merchandising*, 170; and *Discount Merchandiser* 4 (December 1964): 19.

34. *Discount Merchandiser* 5 (June 1965): 12; and *Barron's* 43 (18 December 1963): 3, 8, 10, 12–13; ibid. 41 (30 October 1961): 18.

35. *Business Week*, 13 March 1948, 70, 72, 74, 76, 78–79; ibid., 3 October 1964, 90, 94 (quotation), 96; and *Discount Merchandiser* 5 (August 1965): 68–69.

36. *Discount Merchandiser* 5 (January 1965): 21–22; Drew-Bear, *Mass Merchandising*, 233; Lowry, *Retailing Revolution Revisited*, 8; and *Barron's* 44 (14 September 1964): 3, 16–17 (quotation on 16).

37. James U. McNeal, "Reactions of a Small Town to a Rumored Discount House," *Journal of Retailing* 41 (Winter 1965–66): 1–9 (quotation on 3), 62; and *Discount Merchandiser* 6 (May 1966): 56, 58.

38. *Fortune* 65 (April 1962): 100–102; and Butcher, "Large-Scale Retail Price-Cutting Institutions," 162–64.

39. Lowry, *Retailing Revolution Revisited*, 4–6; *Barron's* 45 (31 May 1965): 16; ibid. 43 (17 June 1963): 3; *Dun's Review and Modern Industry* 78 (16 October 1961): 98; and *Business Week*, 18 August 1962, 109; ibid., 1 December 1962, 78, 80, 85, 86; ibid., 18 July 1964, 126.

40. Brown, Applebaum, and Salmon, *Strategy Problems of Mass Retailers and Wholesalers*, 740–43, 745, 748.

41. M. S. Moyer, "The Roots of Large-Scale Retailing," *Journal of Marketing* 26 (October 1962): 55–56.

CHAPTER 3

1. *Arkansas Times* 10 (February 1984): 56 (quotation).

2. *Discount Store News* 28 (18 December 1989): 90 (quotation); Sam Walton with John Huey, *Sam Walton: Made in America, My Story* (New York: Doubleday, 1992), 42, 79, 81; and Vance H. Trimble, *Sam Walton: The Inside Story of America's Richest Man* (New York: Dutton, 1990), 91–92.

3. Walton with Huey, *Made in America*, 42; *Business Week*, 20 March 1971, 60–61, 64; Robert Drew-Bear, *Mass Merchandising: Revolution and Evolution* (New York: Fairchild Publications, 1970), 344–50 (first quotation on 349); Walton with Huey, *Made in America*, 42 (second quotation); Trimble, *Walton*, 99–100; *Discount Merchandiser* 9 (June 1969): 40; ibid. 10 (October 1970): 84; ibid. 12 (June 1972): 38TL; ibid. 16 (July 1976): 74; *Barron's* 49 (28 July 1969): 31; ibid. 51 (18 January 1971): 3; *Advertising Age* 38 (27 November 1967): 6; and *Chain Store Age Executive* 54 (August 1978): 94; ibid. 55 (August 1979): 97.

4. Wal-Mart Stores, Inc., *Making the Difference*, 9; *Financial World* 155 (15 April 1986): 30; ibid. 158 (4 April 1989): 60; *Arkansas Times* 10 (February 1984): 56; *Forbes* 120 (1 December 1977): 48; and *Business Week*, 5 November 1979, 145 (quotation).

5. Walton with Huey, *Made in America*, 42–43; and Trimble, *Walton*, 98.

6. City Products Corporation, *Annual Report, 1959*, 2–3, 5–9; *Annual Report, 1949*, n.p.; *Moody's Industrial Manual, 1965*, cxxv, 1224–25; *Magazine of Wall Street* 105 (12 March 1960): 692, 694; *Financial World* 114 (10 August 1960): 13; and Edwin H. Lewis and Robert S. Hancock, *The Franchise System of Distribution* (Minneapolis: University of Minnesota, 1963), 52, 54–55, 69.

7. Trimble, *Walton*, 97 (first quotation), 99 (second quotation).

8. Ibid., 100; Walton with Huey, *Made in America*, 43, 48; *Arkansas Times* 10 (February 1984): 57; and *Financial World* 158 (4 April 1989): 60–61.

9. Walton with Huey, *Made in America*, 43 (quotations), 47; *Financial World* 158 (4 April 1989): 61; Trimble, *Walton*, 101; Wal-Mart Stores, Inc. *Making the Difference*, 10; and Wal-Mart Stores, Inc., *Annual Report, 1975*, 4.

10. Walton with Huey, *Made in America*, 44, 80; *Discount Store News* 28 (18 December 1989): 97; and Trimble, *Walton*, 101–2.

11. Rogers (Ark.) *Daily News*, 30 June 1962, n.p., 1 (quotations).

12. Ibid., 12 July 1962, 8; ibid., 19 July 1962, 12; Wal-Mart Stores, Inc., *Making the Difference*, 10; and Trimble, *Walton*, 102–3.

13. Rogers (Ark.) *Daily News*, 30 June 1962, 2 (first quotation); Walton with Huey, *Made in America*, 43, 51–52, 55 (second quotation on 52); and Trimble, *Walton*, 103.

14. Rogers (Ark.) *Daily News*, 12 July 1962, 8 (quotation); Wal-Mart Stores, Inc., *Making the Difference*, 10; *Discount Store News* 28 (18

December 1989): 97; Trimble, *Walton*, 103; and Wal-Mart Stores, Inc., Preliminary Prospectus, filed with the U.S. Securities and Exchange Commission 30 March 1970, 8.

15. Walton with Huey, *Made in America*, 80–81 (quotation).

16. Ibid., 45–46 (quotation); and Trimble, *Walton*, 104, 105, 106.

17. Walton with Huey, *Made in America*, 46; and *Discount Store News* 28 (18 December 1989): 97 (quotation).

18. Walton with Huey, *Made in America*, 46; Wal-Mart Stores, Inc., *Making the Difference*, 13; *Discount Store News* 28 (18 December 1989): 97; and Wal-Mart Stores, Inc., Preliminary Prospectus (30 March 1970), 8.

19. James R. Lowry, *The Retailing Revolution Revisited* (Muncie, Ind.: Ball State University, 1969), 1; and *Barron's* 51 (18 January 1971): 3.

20. Walton with Huey, *Made in America*, 50–51 (quotation on 51), 56, 81, 83, 93, 190; Trimble, *Walton*, 93, 103, 122, 124, 125; Wal-Mart Stores, Inc., Prospectus, filed with the U.S. Securities and Exchange Commission 26 April 1972, 14; and Wal-Mart Stores, Inc., Preliminary Prospectus (30 March 1970), 7, 8.

21. Wal-Mart Stores, Inc., Preliminary Prospectus (30 March 1970), 3, 7, 8, 9 (quotations), 10.

22. Ibid., 9 (first quotation); Walton with Huey, *Made in America*, 87; *Discount Store News* 28 (18 December 1989): 97, 199; and *Arkansas Times* 10 (February 1984): 107 (second quotation).

23. Wal-Mart Stores, Inc., Preliminary Prospectus (30 March 1970), 9; Wal-Mart Stores, Inc., *Annual Report, 1976*, 9; *Forbes* 130 (16 August 1982): 43 (quotation); Trimble, *Walton*, 119, 120; and *Stores* 70 (January 1988): 130.

24. Walton with Huey, *Made in America*, 87, 89, 90, 91; and Trimble, *Walton*, 112, 122, 139, 160.

25. Columbia (Mo.) *Tribune*, 15 March 1965, 5; ibid., 16 March 1965, 4; Columbia (Mo.) *Missourian*, 17 March 1965, 4; and *Moody's Bank and Finance Manual, 1974*, 2361.

26. Wal-Mart Stores, Inc., Preliminary Prospectus (30 March 1970), 7, 10–11; City Products Corporation, Ben Franklin Franchise Agreement between City Products Corporation and Walco Stores, Inc., filed with the U.S. Securities and Exchange Commission 17 March 1969; and City Products Corporation, Supplemental Franchise Contract for Chain Stores between City Products Corporation and Wal-Mart Stores, Inc., filed with the U.S. Securities and Exchange Commission 8 April 1970.

27. Wal-Mart Stores, Inc., Preliminary Prospectus (30 March 1970), 7, 10–11.

28. Walton with Huey, *Made in America*, 88, 89, 91; Wal-Mart Stores, Inc., *Making the Difference*, 13, 15; Trimble, *Walton*, 130–32; Wal-Mart, Inc., Certificate of Incorporation, filed with the Delaware Division of

Corporations, Dover, 31 October 1969; and Wal-Mart, Inc., Amendment to Certificate of Incorporation, filed with the Delaware Division of Corporations, Dover, 2 January 1970.

29. Wal-Mart Stores, Inc., Preliminary Prospectus (30 March 1970), 3, 14–15; Wal-Mart Stores, Inc., Prospectus, filed with the U.S. Securities and Exchange Commission 1 October 1970, 3, 15–16; and Wal-Mart Stores, Inc., Certificates of Ownership and Merger, filed with the Delaware Division of Corporations, Dover, 20 and 29 March 1972.

30. Wal-Mart Stores, Inc., Preliminary Prospectus (30 March 1970), 13; Walton with Huey, *Made in America*, 53; and Trimble, *Walton*, 115, 116, 132.

31. Walton with Huey, *Made in America*, 93–98; Wal-Mart Stores, Inc., *Making the Difference*, 13, 15; Trimble, *Walton*, 127, 132–37; *SEC News Digest*, 7 April 1970, 4; *Wall Street Transcript* 28 (30 April 1970): 20324; Wal-Mart Stores, Inc., Prospectus (1 October 1970), 1, 3–4, 18; and *Moody's OTC Industrial Manual, 1971*, 419, 1124–25; ibid., *1973*, 601.

CHAPTER 4

1. *Marketing and Media Decisions* 22 (March 1987): 25 (quotation).

2. Wal-Mart Stores, Inc., Prospectus, filed with the U.S. Securities and Exchange Commission 26 April 1972, 6, 8; and *Discount Merchandiser* 11 (June 1971): 43–44.

3. Wal-Mart Stores, Inc., *Annual Report, 1972*, 2, 3, 4, 5; *Annual Report, 1973*, 2; *Annual Report, 1974*, 1, 2; *Annual Report, 1976*, 16; Wal-Mart Stores, Inc., Prospectus (26 April 1972), 8; and *Wall Street Transcript* 33 (13 September 1971): 25433; ibid. 40 (9 April 1973): 32539.

4. Wal-Mart Stores, Inc., Prospectus (26 April 1972), 3, 12; and Wal-Mart Stores, Inc., *Annual Report, 1973*, 1; *Annual Report, 1974*, 1.

5. *Financial World* 133 (6 May 1970): 10; *Barron's* 54 (15 July 1974): 11; *Business Week*, 10 February 1973, 87; and *Fortune* 104 (21 September 1981): 75.

6. *Fortune* 92 (July 1975): 122; *Dun's Review* 106 (October 1975): 82; *Wall Street Transcript* 48 (3 June 1975): 40697; ibid. 77 (23 June 1980): 58321; and *Wall Street Journal*, 21 July 1980, 21 (quotations).

7. Wal-Mart Stores, Inc., Annual 10–K Report, 1977, Item 10(a), 8; Wal-Mart Stores, Inc., *Annual Report, 1976*, 17; and *Wall Street Journal*, 16 January 1975, 9.

8. Wal-Mart Stores, Inc., *Annual Report, 1974*, 3; *Annual Report, 1975*, 1, 4; *Discount Merchandiser* 14 (July 1974): 94; and Wal-Mart Stores, Inc., Annual 10–K Report, 1974, 5, 6. In 1981 Household Finance Corporation would become a wholly owned subsidiary of Household International, Inc., a newly formed holding company. Another subsidiary, Household

Merchandising, Inc., would assume the responsibility of managing the retailing activities of the old Household Finance Corporation, including the Ben Franklin chain of franchised variety stores. In January 1986 Household International, Inc., would sell Household Merchandising, Inc., including the Ben Franklin chain, to FoxMeyer Drug Company. The nation's third largest drug wholesaler, FoxMeyer was a subsidiary of National Intergroup, Inc. By 1989 there were still 1,300 Ben Franklin stores in operation in 49 states; they were located mainly in rural towns. *Chain Store Age* 48 (November 1972): E32; ibid. 49 (November 1973): E45; ibid. 53 (November 1977): 30–31; *Chain Store Age Executive* 50 (November 1974): 20; ibid. 54 (November 1978): 53; ibid. 62 (November 1986): 111–12; *Moody's Bank and Finance Manual, 1983,* 5488; ibid., *1986,* 5411; *Moody's Industrial Manual, 1990,* 5992–93; and *Wall Street Journal,* 12 September 1989, C25.

9. *Chain Store Age Executive* 52 (April 1976): 15; ibid. 55 (August 1979): 81; Sam Walton with John Huey, *Sam Walton: Made in America, My Story* (New York: Doubleday, 1992), 195; *Fortune* 104 (21 September 1981): 75, 84; *Business Week,* 16 February 1981, 52, 53, 54; Henry H. Beam, "Strategic Discontinuities: When Being Good May Not Be Enough," *Business Horizons* 33 (July–August 1990): 11; *Forbes* 126 (21 July 1980): 37, 38; *Chain Store Age Executive* 55 (August 1979): 81; and Richard S. Tedlow, *New and Improved: The Story of Mass Marketing in America* (New York: Basic Books, 1990), 338–39. A journalistic account of the problems experienced by Sears from 1973 through the mid-1980s may be found in Donald R. Katz, *The Big Store: Inside the Crisis and Revolution at Sears* (New York: Viking, 1987).

10. *Forbes* 147 (27 May 1991): 86, 90; ibid. 127 (27 April 1981): 189; Walton with Huey, *Made in America,* 81 (quotation), 190, 191; Vance H. Trimble, *Sam Walton: The Inside Story of America's Richest Man* (New York: Dutton, 1990), 92; Beam, "Strategic Discontinuities," 11–12; *Financial World* 148 (1 March 1979): 32, 33; ibid. 152 (31 March 1983): 51; *Stores* 51 (July 1969): 54; *Fortune* 104 (21 September 1981): 74–75; and *Chain Store Age Executive* 55 (September 1979): 46.

11. *Fortune* 104 (21 September 1981): 75; and Wal-Mart Stores, Inc., *Annual Report, 1976,* 1, 15.

12. Walton with Huey, *Made in America,* 196; Little Rock *Arkansas Gazette,* 1 February 1975, A12; *Discount Merchandiser* 17 (August 1977): 16; *Wall Street Transcript* 58 (12 September 1977): 48175; and Wal-Mart Stores, Inc., *Annual Report, 1978,* 2–3, 4.

13. Wal-Mart Stores, Inc., *Annual Report, 1980,* 2, 3; Wal-Mart Stores, Inc., Annual 10–K Report, 1974, 5; *Wall Street Transcript* 55 (21 February 1977): 46292; Arthur A. Thompson, Jr., and A. J. Strickland III, *Strategic*

Management: Concepts and Cases (Homewood, Ill.: BPI, Irwin, 1990), 911; and *Chain Store Age Executive* 55 (August 1979): 97.

14. Wal-Mart Stores, Inc., *Annual Report, 1980*, 2, 5, 7.

15. Wal-Mart Stores, Inc., *Annual Report, 1980*, 5; *Annual Report, 1973*, 4; *Annual Report, 1975*, 5; *Annual Report, 1976*, 6; New Orleans *Times Picayune/States Item*, 9 June 1979, sec. 3, p. 9; *Discount Merchandiser* 13 (January 1973): 40, 43; ibid. 17 (June 1977): 34; and *Business Week*, 5 November 1979, 146.

16. Little Rock *Arkansas Gazette*, 6 March 1983, B1; and *Arkansas Times* 10 (February 1984): 110.

17. Wal-Mart Stores, Inc., *Annual Report, 1976*, 7; *Annual Report, 1974*, 6; *Annual Report, 1975*, 1, 2, 8, 20; *Annual Report, 1973*, 12; *Annual Report, 1974*, 16; *Discount Merchandiser* 13 (January 1973): 43; *Business Week*, 5 November 1979, 146; Thompson and Strickland, *Strategic Management*, 903, 916; and Pankaj Ghemawat, "Wal-Mart Stores' Discount Operations," Harvard Business School Case No. 9-387-018 (Boston: Harvard Business School Publishing Division, 1986), 6, 7.

18. Wal-Mart Stores, Inc., *Annual Report, 1972*, 5; *Annual Report, 1976*, 6; *Business Week*, 5 November 1979, 145; *Chain Store Age* 46 (July 1970): E40–E45; and *Wall Street Transcript* 56 (11 April 1977): 46771.

19. Wal-Mart Stores, Inc., *Annual Report, 1978*, 5 (quotation); *Annual Report, 1980*, 5.

20. Wal-Mart Stores, Inc., *Annual Report, 1975*, 4–5; *Wall Street Transcript* 31 (22 March 1971): 23601; ibid. 33 (13 September 1971): 25433; ibid. 48 (30 June 1975): 40697; *Arkansas Times* 10 (February 1984): 56 (quotation); *Business Week*, 5 November 1979, 145, 146; and *Discount Merchandiser* 13 (January 1973): 40.

21. Wal-Mart Stores, Inc., *Annual Report, 1972*, 5; *Business Week*, 5 November 1979, 146 (first quotation); and *Financial World* 150 (1 November 1981): 24 (second quotation).

22. Wal-Mart Stores, Inc., *Annual Report, 1975*, 6 (first quotation); *Annual Report, 1976*, 6; *Annual Report, 1972*, 5; *Annual Report, 1978*, 5; and *Financial World* 145 (15 August 1976): 28 (second quotation).

23. *Fortune* 119 (30 January 1989): 53; *Financial World* 158 (4 April 1989): 61; *Discount Store News* 28 (18 December 1989): 109 (first quotation); and *Arkansas Times* 10 (February 1984): 55 (second quotation).

24. *Wall Street Transcript* 56 (11 April 1977): 46771; *Discount Store News* 28 (18 December 1989): 97; and Wal-Mart Stores, Inc., *Annual Report, 1972*, 4; *Annual Report, 1973*, 2; *Annual Report, 1976*, 6.

25. *Discount Merchandiser* 13 (January 1973): 42.

26. Wal-Mart Stores, Inc., *Annual Report, 1975*, 1, 10, 11; *Annual Report, 1976*, 6; *Annual Report, 1978*, 10; and George Stalk, Philip Evans,

and Lawrence E. Shulman, "Competing on Capabilities: The New Rules of Corporate Strategy," *Harvard Business Review* 70 (March–April 1992): 58.

27. Wal-Mart Stores, Inc., *Annual Report, 1978,* 3; *Annual Report, 1980,* 2, 3.

28. Wal-Mart Stores, Inc., *Annual Report, 1976,* 6; *Annual Report, 1974,* 6; *Annual Report, 1978,* 10.

29. Wal-Mart Stores, Inc., *Annual Report, 1974,* 5; *Annual Report, 1976,* 7; *Annual Report, 1978,* 11; *Antitrust Law and Economics Review* 14 (1982): 87; *Discount Merchandiser* 13 (January 1973): 41; and Ghemawat, "Wal-Mart Stores' Discount Operations," 5.

30. Walton with Huey, *Made in America,* 86; Wal-Mart Stores, Inc., Preliminary Prospectus (30 March 1970), 9; Wal-Mart Stores, Inc., *Annual Report, 1976,* 6–7; *Annual Report, 1978,* 9; *Annual Report, 1980,* 2, 10; *Discount Store News* 28 (18 December 1989): 203; and *Fortune* 119 (30 January 1989): 55 (quotation).

31. Wal-Mart Stores, Inc., *Making the Difference,* 15; and Wal-Mart Stores, Inc., *Annual Report, 1978,* 3 (quotation).

32. Wal-Mart Stores, Inc., *Annual Report, 1973,* 3; Wal-Mart Stores, Inc., *Making the Difference,* 16; Walton with Huey, *Made in America,* 126, 131–32; *Fortune* 119 (30 January 1989): 55; *Business Week,* 5 November 1979, 146; and *Discount Merchandiser* 13 (January 1973): 43.

33. Wal-Mart Stores, Inc., *Annual Report, 1980,* 9; Little Rock *Arkansas Gazette,* 12 January 1986, B7; *Fortune* 119 (30 January 1989): 52; Memphis *Commercial Appeal,* 2 June 1990, B3; and Walton with Huey, *Made in America,* 229–30.

34. Wal-Mart Stores, Inc., *Annual Report, 1976,* 8 (quotations).

35. Wal-Mart Stores, Inc., *Annual Report, 1972,* 4; *Annual Report, 1989,* 7; *Annual Report, 1987,* 11; *Annual Report, 1976,* 7; *Annual Report, 1984,* 10; *Discount Merchandiser* 13 (January 1973): 44; ibid. 28 (January 1988): 49; Wal-Mart Stores, Inc., Notice of Annual Meeting of Shareholders, 2 May 1991, 4; *Arkansas Times* 10 (February 1984): 108; and *Maclean's* 100 (7 December 1987): 34. For the story of one associate who began as a stock boy in St. Joseph, Missouri, and retired 20 years later with a "six figure income," see Little Rock *Arkansas Gazette,* 24 August 1986, D1, D2. Similar accounts can be found in Walton with Huey, *Made in America,* 132–34.

36. *Wall Street Transcript* 56 (16 May 1977): 47055; and Walton with Huey, *Made in America,* 128–29.

37. Wal-Mart Stores, Inc., *Annual Report, 1976,* 7, 10; *Annual Report, 1980,* 8–9; *Annual Report, 1974,* 4; *Annual Report, 1978,* 7. For descriptions of the management-training program as it existed in the 1970s and

the 1980s, respectively, see *Discount Merchandiser* 13 (January 1973): 44; and Thompson and Strickland, *Strategic Management*, 916–17.

38. Wal-Mart Stores, Inc., *Annual Report, 1980*, 12; and *Arkansas Times* 10 (February 1984): 106–7 (quotation on 107).

39. Wal-Mart Stores, Inc., *Annual Report, 1975*, 6 (first and third quotations); *Annual Report, 1976*, 6 (second quotation); *Discount Merchandiser* 14 (July 1974): 94; and *Antitrust Law and Economics Review* 14 (1982): 85.

40. Walton with Huey, *Made in America*, 149–53 (first quotation on 150); Trimble, *Walton*, 160–64; Wal-Mart Stores, Inc., *Making the Difference*, 19; *Wall Street Journal*, 27 November 1974, 30; ibid., 29 June 1976, 15 (second and third quotations); and *Financial World* 145 (15 August 1976): 28. See also *New York Times*, 29 June 1976, 41.

41. *Wall Street Journal*, 28 August 1978, 23; Wal-Mart Stores, Inc., Annual 10–K Report, 1974, 13; Annual 10–K Report, 1975, 12; Annual 10–K Report, 1976, 14; Annual 10–K Report, 1977, 14–15; Annual 10–K Report, 1979, 15; Annual 10–K Report, 1980, 15; and Wal-Mart Stores, Inc., *Annual Report, 1978*, 24; *Annual Report, 1980*, 26.

42. *Arkansas Times* 10 (February 1984): 105 (quotations); and Trimble, *Walton*, 77.

43. *Arkansas Times* 10 (February 1984): 105 (quotations).

44. *Forbes* 120 (1 December 1977): 46 (quotation).

45. *Maclean's* 100 (7 December 1987): 34; and *Discount Store News* 28 (18 December 1989): 235. For a discussion of the management style at Wal-Mart, see Thomas J. Peters and Robert H. Waterman, Jr., *In Search of Excellence: Lessons from America's Best-Run Companies* (New York: Harper and Row, 1982), 246–47, 311–12.

46. Austin Teutsch, *The Sam Walton Story: An Inside Look at the Man and His Empire* (New York: Berkeley Books, 1992), 38–39 (quotation).

47. Little Rock *Arkansas Gazette*, 6 May 1979, F1, F17; and *Arkansas Times* 10 (February 1984): 106.

48. Wal-Mart Stores, Inc., *Annual Report, 1978*, 1, 2; *Annual Report, 1980*, 7; and *Arkansas Times* 10 (February 1984): 110.

49. Wal-Mart Stores, Inc., *Annual Report, 1980*, 2, 7.

CHAPTER 5

1. *Fortune* 104 (13 July 1981): 122; and *Chain Store Age Executive* 57 (August 1981): 51.

2. Wal-Mart Stores, Inc., *Annual Report, 1982*, 8; *Wall Street Journal*, 10 December 1980, 37; ibid., 29 July 1981, 34; ibid., 9 March 1982, 36; Sam Walton with John Huey, *Sam Walton: Made in America, My Story* (New York: Doubleday, 1992), 196–98; Vance H. Trimble, *Sam Walton: The Inside Story of America's Richest Man* (New York: Dutton, 1990), 195;

Mergers and Acquisitions 16 (Winter 1982): R33; *Arkansas Times* 10 (February 1984): 109; *Wall Street Transcript* 76 (10 May 1982): 65700; and *Discount Merchandiser* 21 (January 1981): 28 (quotation).

3. *Fortune* 104 (21 September 1981): 85; *Chain Store Age Executive* 57 (July 1981): 37, 39; ibid. 58 (January 1982): 90; ibid. 59 (August 1983): 52; *Forbes* 129 (4 January 1982): 226, 227; and *Financial World* 152 (31 March 1983): 50.

4. *Chain Store Age Executive* 59 (August 1983): 52, 54; Wal-Mart Stores, Inc., *Annual Report, 1982*, 1–2; *Annual Report, 1983*, 9, 10–12; *Discount Merchandiser* 23 (September 1983): 16 (first and second quotations); *Wall Street Transcript* 78 (13 December 1982): 68025; and *Time* 125 (23 May 1983): 43 (third quotation).

5. Wal-Mart Stores, Inc., *Annual Report, 1984*, 1–4; *Annual Report, 1985*, 1–3.

6. Pankaj Ghemawat, "Wal-Mart Stores' Discount Operations," Harvard Business School Case No. 9-387-018 (Boston: Harvard Business School Publishing Division, 1986), 2, 3; Wal-Mart Stores, Inc., *Annual Report, 1985*, 3; *Wall Street Transcript* 100 (9 May 1988): 89369; *Financial World* 153 (4–17 April 1984): 92; *Discount Merchandiser* 24 (November 1984): 54 (quotation); ibid. 25 (August 1985): 12; and Walton with Huey, *Made in America*, 110.

7. *Chain Store Age Executive* 62 (August 1986): 16; ibid. 61 (November 1985): 46; Wal-Mart Stores, Inc., Annual 10–K Report, 1986, 1, 6; and Ghemawat, "Wal-Mart Stores' Discount Operations," 1.

8. *Wall Street Journal*, 29 June 1982, 20; and *Chain Store Age Executive* 61 (November 1985): 46. The company's site-selection process remained virtually unchanged. The firm would first make an extensive market survey, then perform a demographic study, and, as a final step, gather detailed information concerning the site. *Wall Street Transcript* 78 (4 October 1982): 67333.

9. *Fortune* 115 (8 June 1987): 210; *Marketing and Media Decisions* 22 (March 1987): 79; and Wal-Mart Stores, Inc., *Annual Report, 1987*, 1, 3, 9, 14–15.

10. Wal-Mart Stores, Inc., *Annual Report, 1988*, 2; and *Discount Merchandiser* 28 (May 1988): 38 (quotation).

11. Wal-Mart Stores, Inc., *Annual Report, 1988*, 2.

12. Wal-Mart Stores, Inc., *Annual Report, 1989*, 2, 14–15; *Annual Report, 1988*, 2, 12–13; *Annual Report, 1990*, 4, 6, 8; Wal-Mart Stores, Inc., Annual 10–K Report, 1989, 5; *Wall Street Transcript* 100 (20 June 1988): 89930; and *Fortune* 119 (5 June 1989): 378.

13. *Business Week*, 26 November 1990, 135; *Fortune* 123 (6 May 1991): 50; *Chain Store Age Executive* 64 (November 1988): 64, 65, 66; and *Forbes* 129 (7 June 1982): 128, 130.

14. *Forbes* 126 (21 July 1980): 37; ibid. 147 (27 May 1991): 90; *Business Week*, 16 February 1981, 53; Wal-Mart Stores, Inc., *Annual Report, 1987*, 16, 17; and K mart Corporation, *Annual Report, 1984*, n.p.

15. *Chain Store Age Executive* 64 (November 1988): 69; *Business Week*, 12 November 1990, 66, 68; *Advertising Age* 60 (23 January 1989): 1; *Forbes* 143 (20 February 1989): 124; *U.S. News and World Report* 107 (11 December 1989): 53; and Henry H. Beam, "Strategic Discontinuities: When Being Good May Not Be Enough," *Business Horizons* 33 (July–August 1990): 11.

16. *Forbes* 137 (5 May 1986): 128; ibid. 147 (27 May 1991): 90, 92; *Fortune* 119 (2 January 1989): 41; and K Mart Corporation, *Annual Report, 1988*, 3.

17. Wal-Mart Stores, Inc., *Annual Report, 1982*, 12; *Annual Report, 1990*, 2; Trimble, *Walton*, 300–301; Memphis *Commercial Appeal*, 4 April 1990, B4; *New York Times*, 10 June 1987, sec. 4, p. 10; ibid., 24 December 1987, sec. 4, p. 4; *Wall Street Transcript* 88 (20 May 1985): 77909; and *Wall Street Journal* (SW ed.), 3 October 1990, C2 (quotations).

18. *Business Week*, 22 February 1988, 146; and *Wall Street Transcript* 98 (9 November 1987): 87393; ibid. 102 (31 October 1988): 91467.

19. Wal-Mart Stores, Inc., *Annual Report, 1982*, 10; *Annual Report, 1983*, 10; *Annual Report, 1984*, 2; *Annual Report, 1985*, 2; *Annual Report, 1987*, 3; *Annual Report, 1988*, 16; *Annual Report, 1989*, 18; *Annual Report, 1990*, 8; *Discount Store News* 28 (18 December 1989): 29, 79; and *New York Times*, 1 July 1991, C2.

20. Wal-Mart Stores, Inc., *Annual Report, 1989*, 11; *Annual Report, 1991*, 2; *Discount Store News* 28 (18 December 1989): 199–201; George Stalk, Philip Evans, and Lawrence E. Shulman, "Competing on Capabilities: The New Rules of Corporate Strategy," *Harvard Business Review* 70 (March–April 1992): 58; and *Fortune* 119 (30 January 1989): 54 (quotation).

21. Stalk, Evans, and Shulman, "Competing on Capabilities," 58; Wal-Mart Stores Inc., *Annual Report, 1982*, 3; *Annual Report, 1984*, 3; *Annual Report, 1985*, 4, 7, 8; *Annual Report, 1987*, 9–10; *Annual Report, 1991*, 3; *Business Month* 132 (December 1988): 42; *Chain Store Age Executive* 61 (September 1985): 49–50; *Computerworld* 24 (9 July 1990): 1, 8; *Discount Store News* 28 (18 December 1989): 203; *New York Times*, 1 July 1991, C1, C2; and D. P. Diffine, *Always a Winner* (Searcy, Ark.: Harding University, 1989), 42. For further information regarding the EDI and Quick Response systems, see *Women's Wear Daily* 159 (1 March 1990): 4; ibid. (3 May 1990): 13–16; ibid. 160 (6 September 1990): 15–18; ibid. (4 October 1990): 7–11; ibid. (6 December 1990): 38, 40.

22. Wal-Mart Stores, Inc., *Annual Report, 1988*, 2; *Fortune* 119 (30 January 1989): 54; and Little Rock *Arkansas Gazette*, 4 February 1990, F1,

F5; ibid., 3 June 1989, C1 (quotation). See also *Aviation Week and Space Technology* 122 (11 March 1985): 75.

23. *Discount Store News* 28 (18 December 1989): 171, 172, 179, 181, 186, 189, 234.

24. *Financial World* 158 (4 April 1989): 60; and *Discount Store News* 28 (18 December 1989): 235.

25. *New York Times*, 24 January 1988, sec. 3, p. 7; *Discount Store News* 28 (18 December 1989); Little Rock *Arkansas Gazette*, 29 December 1989, C2; and *Fortune* 119 (30 January 1989): 69; ibid. 123 (11 February 1991): 52, 57. See also Trimble, *Walton*, 244–47.

26. *Forbes* 136 (28 October 1985): 114; ibid. 144 (23 October 1989): 146, 147, 150, 162, 164; ibid. 146 (22 October 1990): 124; *New York Times*, 10 April 1985, sec. 4, p. 1; and Little Rock *Arkansas Gazette*, 20 October 1987, A1 (quotation).

27. Wal-Mart Stores, Inc., *Annual Report, 1982*, 25; *Annual Report, 1987*, 31; *New York Times*, 21 August 1984, sec. 4, p. 2; ibid., 18 November 1986, sec. 4, p. 2; *Fortune* 119 (30 January 1989): 58; *Maclean's* 100 (7 December 1987): 34; Ghemawat, "Wal-Mart Stores' Discount Operations," 7; *Business Week*, 15 February 1988, 29; *Discount Merchandiser* 24 (August 1984): 10; *Marketing and Media Decisions* 22 (March 1987): 80, 82; and Little Rock *Arkansas Gazette*, 2 February 1988, A1. Shewmaker, a millionaire with extensive real estate interests and a cattle-breeding operation, would remain on Wal-Mart's board of directors for five years and serve as a corporate consultant for $100,000 a year. He also became a $5,000-a-day retailing consultant. *Wall Street Journal*, 2 February 1988, 43; and *Nation's Business* 76 (November 1988): 20.

28. *Wall Street Transcript* 78 (4 October 1982): 67335; *Business Month* 132 (December 1988): 42; *Springfield!* 7 (December 1985): 30–31; *Wall Street Journal*, 2 February 1988, 43; *Discount Store News* 28 (18 December 1989): 83; *Fortune* 119 (30 January 1989): 55; and *Business Week*, 15 February 1988, 29.

29. *Arkansas Times* 10 (February 1984): 57; and *Financial World* 153 (4–17 April 1984): 92.

30. *Discount Store News* 28 (18 December 1989): 79, 97, 104; and *Fortune* 121 (29 January 1990): 46.

31. Walton and Huey, *Made in America*, 224, 225; Ghemawat, "Wal-Mart Stores' Discount Operations," 6–7; *U.S. News and World Report* 91 (20 July 1981): 73; ibid. 99 (2 December 1985): 62; *Wall Street Transcript* 77 (12 July 1982): 66449; and *Marketing and Media Decisions* 22 (March 1987): 80.

32. *Fortune* 119 (30 January 1989): 53.

33. *Maclean's* 100 (7 December 1987): 34; *Discount Store News* 28 (18 December 1989): 104; and *Business Week*, 27 March 1989, 90 (quotation).
34. *Maclean's* 100 (7 December 1987): 34; and *Arkansas Times* 10 (February 1984): 105.
35. Wal-Mart Stores, Inc., *Annual Report, 1991*, 20, 21; and *Discount Store News* 28 (18 December 1989): 104.
36. *Discount Merchandiser* 22 (December 1982): 8 (first quotation); *Building Supply Home Centers* 154 (February 1988): 100; Wal-Mart Stores, Inc., *Annual Report, 1984*, 10; *Annual Report, 1987*, 11–13; *Annual Report, 1988*, 8 (second quotation); *Annual Report, 1990*, 3; and Jackson (Miss.) *Clarion-Ledger*, 5 January 1991, B7 (third quotation).
37. *Marketing and Media Decisions* 22 (March 1987): 80; Wal-Mart Stores, Inc., *Annual Report, 1985*, 6, 10; and *Arkansas Times* 10 (February 1984): 57 (quotation).
38. Wal-Mart Stores, Inc., *Annual Report, 1988*, 8 (first and second quotations); *Arkansas Times* 10 (February 1984), 57, 105; and *Marketing and Media Decisions* 22 (March 1987): 82 (third quotation).
39. Walton with Huey, *Made in America*, 227; *Business Month* 132 (December 1988): 42; Wal-Mart Stores, Inc., *Annual Report, 1987*, 12; *Annual Report, 1988*, 2; *Annual Report, 1989*, 3; *Fortune* 121 (29 January 1990): 46; *Management Solutions* 32 (October 1987): 19; and *Discount Merchandiser* 28 (January 1988): 49.
40. *Fortune* 121 (29 January 1990): 46 (first quotation); and *Financial World* 158 (4 April 1989): 62 (second and third quotations). See also Wal-Mart Stores, Inc., *Annual Report, 1989*, 7; and *Discount Store News* 28 (18 December 1989): 79.
41. Wal-Mart Stores, Inc., *Annual Report, 1988*, 4, 6; and Wal-Mart Stores, Inc., *Wal-Mart: Corporate and Public Affairs*, 1990, 3. See also Walton with Huey, *Made in America*, 235–40. In 1987 out of a total of $6.1 million in charitable contributions raised between the foundation and individual stores, the foundation contributed $4.3 million, which equalled 0.41 percent of Wal-Mart's pretax earnings of $1.07 billion. In comparison, K mart contributed $17.4 million in 1987, or 1.49 percent of its pretax earnings of $1.17 billion. That year the average contribution for some 228 corporations was 1.05 percent. *Marketing and Media Decisions* 22 (March 1987): 82; *Building Supply Home Centers* 154 (February 1988): 100; and *Discount Store News* 28 (18 December 1989): 221, 222, 225.
42. *Building Supply Home Centers* 154 (February 1988): 100; *Arkansas Times* 10 (February 1984): 114; and *Discount Store News* 28 (18 December 1989): 221, 226 (quotations), 228.

43. *Business Week*, 15 February 1988, 29; and *Discount Store News* 28 (18 December 1989): 101, 104.

44. *New York Times*, 16 March 1984, sec. 2, p. 3; and Wal-Mart Stores, Inc., *Making the Difference*, 21. For an account of Walton's purported chagrin over dancing the hula on Wall Street, see Trimble, *Walton*, 147–48.

45. *Fortune* 119 (30 January 1989): 58 (quotations). See also Walton with Huey, *Made in America*, 223. Walton's often-repeated motto was "The customer is the boss." To Walton this meant, "The customer can fire everybody in the company from the chairman down." Wal-Mart Stores, Inc., *Annual Report, 1989*, 5 (first quotation); and *Discount Store News* 28 (18 December 1989): 104 (second quotation).

46. Jackson (Miss.) *Clarion-Ledger*, 5 January 1991, B7 (quotation); and Monroeville (Ala.) *Monroe Journal*, 16 May 1991, B2.

47. *Arkansas Times* 10 (February 1984): 108. When asked at the meeting why workers at distribution centers in Texas made $1.50 more per hour than those in Searcy, Walton bluntly responded that he could hire workers in Arkansas for lower wages than in Texas.

48. Little Rock *Arkansas Gazette*, 3 September 1988, B1 (quotation); ibid., 15 September 1988, B1.

49. New Orleans *Times Picayune/States Item*, 13 July 1986, A14; *Maclean's* 100 (7 December 1987): 34; *Rolling Stone*, 11 September 1986, 15 (quotation); and *Discount Store News* 28 (18 December 1989): 235. Wal-Mart, as well as some other chains, such as Kroger, also removed from its racks several women's magazines that contained an advertisement for a moisturizing lotion that featured a nude woman.

50. *Marketing and Media Decisions* 22 (March 1987): 80, 82; *Sales and Marketing Management* 138 (March 1987): 41–43; and *Wall Street Journal*, 11 December 1986, 29. See also Little Rock *Arkansas Gazette*, 17 December 1986, C3.

51. *Fortune* 119 (30 January 1989): 58 (first quotation); and Wal-Mart Stores, Inc., *Annual Report, 1991*, 3 (second quotation). See also Walton with Huey, *Made in America*, 186–87.

52. *Advertising Age* 60 (13 March 1989): 66; *Wall Street Journal*, 14 July 1989, B4; *Discount Store News* 28 (18 December 1989): 109, 112; ibid. 29 (12 February 1990): 1; and *Housewares*, 21 May 1990, 6.

53. *New York Times*, 1 July 1991, C1, C2 (quotation).

54. Little Rock *Arkansas Gazette*, 11 April 1985, C1; Wal-Mart Stores, Inc., *Annual Report, 1985*, 9; *Building Supply Home Centers* 154 (February 1988): 100–101; *Nation's Business* 76 (April 1988): 24, 26; and Walton with Huey, *Made in America*, 241–43.

55. Wal-Mart Stores, Inc., *Annual Report, 1990*, 2; *Advertising Age* 60 (21 August 1989): 1, 66; *Fortune* 121 (12 February 1990): 50; *Stores* 72 (October 1990): 69; and *New York Times*, 1 July 1991, C2.

56. *Discount Store News* 28 (18 December 1989): 235; and *Sam's Buy-Line* 4 (Fall 1990): 3 (quotation). See also *Fortune* 121 (12 February 1990): 50.

57. *Wall Street Journal*, 22 September 1989, n.p.

CHAPTER 6

1. *Progressive Grocer*, June 1990, 95; *Stores* 67 (March 1985): 22. For a discussion of Wal-Mart's deep-discounting ventures of the 1980s, see Sandra S. Vance and Roy V. Scott, "Wal-Mart Stores in the 1980s: Innovative Formats for Modern Retailing," *Essays in Economic and Business History* 10 (1992): 298–309.

2. Wal-Mart Stores, Inc., *Annual Report, 1984*, 2; *Annual Report, 1985*, 1–3; *Wall Street Transcript* 88 (24 June 1985): 78372; and *Chain Store Age Executive* 59 (December 1983): 16.

3. *Discount Store News* 29 (12 February 1990): 2; *Drug Store News*, 9 April 1990, 53; *Chain Drug Review*, 26 February 1990, 26; Vance H. Trimble, *Sam Walton: The Inside Story of America's Richest Man* (New York: Dutton, 1990), 292; *Wall Street Journal*, 3 May 1988, 51; Wal-Mart Stores, Inc., Annual 10–K Report, 1989, 3; Annual 10–K Report, 1990, 3; and *Discount Store News* 28 (18 December 1989): 171, 196, 234; ibid. 29 (16 July 1990): 7. In 1990 Wal-Mart integrated eyecare centers, known as Vision Centers, into its operation when it opened two centers in Wal-Mart stores in Greenwood and Plainfield, Indiana, followed by a third in a Sam's Wholesale Club in Chicago. Although other discount chains had struggled with the format, Wal-Mart expected to do well with it.

4. Wal-Mart Stores, Inc., *Annual Report, 1984*, 11; *Stores* 71 (July 1989): 41; and *Chain Store Age Executive* 62 (November 1986): 73.

5. *Discount Merchandiser* 24 (April 1984): 9; *Dun's Business Month* 125 (April 1985): 76–78; Walter J. Salmon, "Wholesale Club Industry," Harvard Business School Case No. 9-586-021 (Boston: Harvard Business School Publishing Division, 1990), 1–4, 7, 22; Wal-Mart Stores, Inc., *Annual Report, 1989*, 13; Wal-Mart Stores, Inc., Annual 10–K Report, 1990, 5; Sam's Wholesale Club, Advantage Card membership application form; Pankaj Ghemawat, "Wal-Mart Stores' Discount Operations," Harvard Business School Case No. 9-387-018 (Boston: Harvard Business School Publishing Division, 1986), 7; *Business Week*, 28 May 1990, 48; *Chain Store Age Executive* 62 (November 1986): 70, 73; and *Stores* 71 (July 1989): 42.

6. Salmon, "Wholesale Club Industry," 7–14, 22; *Dun's Business Month* 125 (April 1985): 76; *Discount Store News* 29 (16 July 1990): 87; K mart Corporation, *Annual Report, 1989*, 4; and *Wall Street Journal* (SW ed.), 7 November 1990, B1.

7. *Barron's* 63 (5 September 1983): 13; Salmon, "Wholesale Club Industry," 7–8, 22; *Discount Store News* 29 (16 July 1990): 84; and *Dun's Business Month* 125 (April 1985): 78 (quotation).

8. Salmon, "Wholesale Club Industry," 9; *Discount Store News* 29 (26 November 1990): 3; ibid. 28 (18 December 1989): 43; *Discount Merchandiser* 27 (November 1987): 26; Ghemawat, "Wal-Mart Stores' Discount Operations," 8; and *Dun's Business Month* 125 (April 1985): 78 (quotation).

9. Salmon, "Wholesale Club Industry," 2, 22; *Financial World* 158 (4 April 1989): 62; *Women's Wear Daily* 160 (17 August 1990): 10; *Discount Merchandiser* 24 (April 1984): 9; and *Stores* 70 (March 1988): 56; ibid. 71 (July 1989): 41 (quotation).

10. *Dun's Business Month* 125 (April 1985): 76; Wal-Mart Stores, Inc., Audiovisual program presented at the Wal-Mart Visitors Center, Bentonville, Arkansas; *Stores* 70 (March 1988): 56; ibid. 71 (July 1979): 41; *Chain Store Age Executive* 64 (December 1988): 19; ibid. 62 (November 1986): 73; and *Wall Street Transcript* 80 (16 May 1983): 69794.

11. Wal-Mart Stores, Inc., *Annual Report, 1984*, 2; *Annual Report, 1985*, 1; *Annual Report, 1987*, 1; *Annual Report, 1988*, 3; *Annual Report, 1989*, 13; *Annual Report, 1990*, 1; Little Rock *Arkansas Gazette*, 30 May 1987, A1; and *Discount Store News* 29 (16 July 1990): 85.

12. Wal-Mart Stores, Inc., *Annual Report, 1984*, 3; *Annual Report, 1990*, 8; *Discount Store News* 28 (18 December 1989): 43; ibid. 29 (16 July 1990): 85; and Little Rock *Arkansas Gazette*, 14 June 1989, C1.

13. *Discount Store News* 28 (18 December 1989): 43; ibid. 29 (16 July 1990): 84, 87; *Fortune* 120 (Fall 1989): 154; Salmon, "Wholesale Club Industry," 8, 22; Wal-Mart Stores, Inc., *Annual Report, 1989*, 3; and *Discount Merchandiser* 29 (July 1989): 12.

14. *Chain Store Age Executive* 62 (November 1986): 69–70; and *Dun's Business Month* 125 (April 1985): 78 (quotation).

15. *Wall Street Journal* (SW ed.), 7 November 1990, B1; Wal-Mart Stores, Inc., *Annual Report, 1989*, 13; *Annual Report, 1990*, 5; and *USA Today*, 7 November 1990, B1 (quotation).

16. Wal-Mart Stores, Inc., *Annual Report, 1991*, 5; *Women's Wear Daily* 160 (17 August 1990): 10; and *Discount Store News* 29 (16 July 1990): 85.

17. *New York Times*, 1 April 1990, F11; *Chain Store Age Executive* 64 (December 1988): 19; ibid. (January 1988): 18; *Stores* 70 (March 1988): 61; *Fortune* 118 (24 October 1988): 152; and *Business Week*, 28 May 1990, 48.

18. *Chain Store Age Executive* 64 (January 1988): 15; and *New York Times*, 1 April 1990, F11 (quotations).

19. *Stores* 70 (March 1988): 55, 59; ibid. 71 (July 1989):42; *Chain Store Age Executive* 51 (March 1975): 27, 28; ibid. 64 (January 1988): 18; *Business Week*, 26 November 1990, 135; and *Discount Store News* 29 (16 July 1990): 1. See also *Fortune* 118 (24 October 1988): 148.

20. *Stores* 70 (March 1988): 55, 60; *Chain Store Age Executive* 61 (September 1985): 25, 26; *New York Times*, 1 April 1990, F11; and *Hardware Age* 226 (February 1989): 48. Rounding out the French presence in the United States was the 230,000-square-foot Auchan hypermarket, operated by a firm of the same name and opened in Houston in 1988, and a third Bigg's with 235,000 square feet, which opened in the Denver area in 1989. *Business Week*, 28 May 1990, 48, 52.

21. *Stores* 70 (March 1988): 54; *Chain Store Age Executive* 64 (January 1988): 15; and *Business Week*, 28 May 1990, 48 (quotation).

22. *New York Times*, 1 April 1990, F11 (first quotation); and Jackson (Miss.) *Clarion-Ledger*, 17 August 1990, B6 (second and third quotations).

23. *Stores* 71 (July 1989): 42.

24. K mart Corporation, *Annual Report, 1988*, 4; *Annual Report, 1989*, 5; Little Rock *Arkansas Gazette*, 17 January 1989, C1; Atlanta *Constitution*, 28 January 1989, E1; *Advertising Age* 60 (23 January 1989): 1; *Chain Store Age Executive* 65 (March 1989): 16, 17; and Jackson (Miss.) *Clarion-Ledger*, 17 August 1990, B6 (first and second quotations); ibid., 15 July 1990, G1 (third quotation); ibid., 12 June 1992, B5.

25. K mart Corporation, *Annual Report, 1989*, 5; *New York Times*, 1 April 1990, F11; *Chain Store Age Executive* 65 (March 1989): 17; Jackson (Miss.) *Clarion Ledger*, 15 July 1990, G1; ibid., 17 August 1990, B6; and *Fortune* 118 (24 October 1988): 148.

26. *Stores* 70 (March 1988): 59; ibid. 71 (July 1989): 42; *Advertising Age* 59 (9 May 1988): S–26; and *New York Times*, 4 February 1988, sec. 4, p. 2.

27. *Stores* 70 (March 1988): 58, 59; ibid. 71 (July 1989): 41; *New York Times*, 4 February 1988, sec. 4, p. 1; Little Rock *Arkansas Gazette*, 7 September 1989, C2; Wal-Mart Stores, Inc., *Annual Report, 1988*, 3; *Chain Store Age Executive* 64 (January 1988): 15, 17; *Time* 131 (8 February 1988): 50; and *Fortune* 118 (24 October 1988): 149.

28. *Advertising Age* 59 (9 May 1988): S–26; *Time* 131 (8 February 1988): 50; and *National Petroleum News* 80 (April 1988): 15 (quotations). Terming the Wal-Mart Super USA Convenience Stores an "experiment," Wal-Mart opened nine units. In January 1991 the firm sold all of its convenience stores to Conoco, a Houston-based division of Du Pont and a major convenience-store operator. Little Rock *Arkansas Gazette*, 18 November 1989, C1, F2; and *Supermarket News*, 28 January 1991, 6.

29. *Stores* 70 (March 1988): 58.

30. *New York Times*, 4 February 1988, sec. 3, p. 7; Little Rock *Arkansas Gazette*, 23 January 1988, C1; ibid., 7 September 1989, C1; Wal-Mart Stores, Inc., *Annual Report, 1989*, 2; *Discount Merchandiser* 28 (May 1988): 18; and *Advertising Age* 59 (9 May 1988): S–26.

31. *Discount Store News* 28 (18 December 1989): 47; Little Rock *Arkansas Gazette*, 1 March 1990, C1; and *Business Week*, 28 May 1990, 48 (quotation).

32. *Business Week*, 28 May 1990, 48 (quotation); and *Discount Store News* 28 (18 December 1989): 47, 50.

33. *Business Week*, 22 August 1988, 61; *Discount Store News* 28 (18 December 1989): 47; *Advertising Age* 59 (9 May 1988): S–26; *Chain Store Age Executive* 64 (December 1988): 19; and *Discount Merchandiser* 28 (May 1988): 26 (quotations).

34. *Discount Merchandiser* 28 (May 1988): 26 (first quotation), 30 (second quotation). In 1990 Wal-Mart opened 186,000-square-foot Supercenters in Jefferson City and Poplar Bluff, Missouri, and a 147,000-square-foot Supercenter in Mount Pleasant, Texas. *Discount Store News* 28 (18 December 1989): 47.

35. Wal-Mart Inc., *Annual Report, 1989*, 2–3; *Business Week*, 28 May 1990, 48; *Chain Store Age Executive* 64 (December 1988): 18; *Advertising Age* 59 (9 May 1988): S–26; and *Discount Merchandiser* 28 (May 1988): 26, 32, 37 (quotation).

36. *Chain Store Age Executive* 64 (December 1988): 19 (quotation); ibid. 65 (December 1989): 28, 30, 34 (24–44 contain a summary of the Supercenter's overall impact on the business community of Washington).

37. Wal-Mart Stores, Inc., *Annual Report, 1989*, 2, 3; *Chain Store Age Executive* 64 (December 1988): 18, 19; and *Discount Merchandiser* 28 (May 1988): 26 (second quotation), 38 (first quotation).

38. Wal-Mart Stores, Inc., *Annual Report, 1991*, 2; *Discount Store News* 29 (15 October 1990): 3; and *Supermarket News*, 8 October 1990, 1, 2.

CHAPTER 7

1. Jackson (Miss.) *Clarion-Ledger*, 3 June 1990, G5 (first quotation); ibid., 29 July 1990, H3; and Little Rock *Arkansas Gazette*, 3 September 1989, A14 (second and third quotations). For a discussion of some aspects of Wal-Mart's growth, including the firm's impact on small towns in the South, see Sandra S. Vance and Roy V. Scott, "Sam Walton and Wal-Mart Stores, Inc.: A Study in Modern Southern Entrepreneurship," *Journal of Southern History* 58 (May 1992): 231–52.

2. Little Rock *Arkansas Gazette*, 15 March 1988, C1 (quotations).

3. Jackson (Miss.) *Clarion-Ledger*, 3 June 1990, G5 (quotation).

4. Kenneth E. Stone, *The Impact of Wal-Mart Stores on Other Businesses in Iowa*, report issued by Iowa State University, 1989. The quoted word is on 3 and 15. See also *American Demographics* 12 (June 1990): 59; and *U.S. News and World Report* 106 (13 March 1989): 54.

5. *Mississippi Business Journal* 12 (8 October 1990): 1, 8, 9; Jackson (Miss.) *Clarion-Ledger*, 3 June 1990, G5 (sixth quotation); ibid., 18 September 1990, B6; ibid., 20 September 1990, B6; Stone, *Impact of Wal-Mart Stores*, 13 (second quotation), 14–15 (first, third, fourth, fifth, seventh, and eighth quotations on 15); and *Newsweek* 114 (13 November 1989): 65.

6. Thomas Keon, Edward Robb, and Lori Franz, *Effect of Wal-Mart Stores on the Economic Environment of Rural Communities*, report issued by the Business and Public Administration Research Center and College of Business and Public Administration at the University of Missouri at Columbia, [1989] (first through seventh quotations on 1; succeeding quotations on 18, 20, 2, and 9, respectively); *Missouri Alumnus* 80 (Spring 1992): 31; and Little Rock *Arkansas Gazette*, 1 November 1989, C1. See also *Discount Store News* 28 (18 December 1989): 216, 218, 237.

7. John Ozment and Michael A. Jones, "Changing Economic Conditions of Small Rural Trade Areas: Some Notes on the Presence of Discount Retail Chains," in B. J. Dunlap, ed., *Proceedings of the Thirteenth Annual Conference of the Academy of Marketing Science*, New Orleans, April 1990, 451–56 (ninth quotation on 456); John Ozment and Greg Martin, "Changes in the Competitive Environments of Rural Trade Areas: Effects of Discount Retail Chains," *Journal of Business Research* 21 (November 1990): 277–87 (first quotation on 285; second quotation on 280; third and seventh quotations on 278; tenth quotation on 286); and John Ozment and Michael A. Jones, "Growth of Discount Retail Chains in Rural Communities: An Analysis of Issues," in Robert L. King, ed., *Retailing: Theory and Practice for the Twenty-first Century* (Charleston, S.C.: Academy of Marketing Science, 1985), 11–15 (fourth, fifth, and sixth quotations on 11; eighth quotation on 14).

8. *Discount Merchandiser* 29 (November 1989): 54; *New York Times Magazine*, Part 2: *Business World*, 2 April 1989, 29 (quotation), 30; *U.S. News and World Report* 106 (13 March 1989): 53; and Little Rock *Arkansas Gazette*, 4 September 1989, C2.

9. *Hardware Age* 225 (February 1988): 36, 39, 42; and *Chain Store Age Executive* 65 (December 1989): 30 (quotation).

10. *Hardware Age* 225 (February 1988): 36; and *American Demographics* 12 (June 1990): 59.

11. *Wall Street Journal*, 14 April 1987, 1 (first quotation), 23; and *U.S. News and World Report* 106 (13 March 1989): 54 (second quotation).

12. *Wall Street Journal*, 14 April 1987, 23; *Chain Store Age Executive* 58 (March 1982): 55 (first quotation), 72 (second quotation); Lester Telser, "Why Should Manufacturers Want Fair Trade?" *Journal of Law and Economics* 3 (October 1960): 86–105; J. Barry Mason and Morris L. Mayer, *Modern Retailing: Theory and Practice* (Dallas: Business Publication, 1978), 237; Patrick J. Kaufmann, "Dealer Termination Agreements and Resale Price Maintenance: Implications of the *Business Electronics* Case and the Proposed Amendment to the Sherman Act," *Journal of Retailing* 64 (Summer 1988): 114–19; Mary E. Allender, "Why Did Manufacturers Want Fair Trade?" *Essays in Economic and Business History* 11 (1993): 221–22, 226–28; *Antitrust Law and Economics Review* 14 (1982): 82 (third and fourth quotations), 90 (fifth and sixth quotations); and Robert J. Aalberts and Ellen Day, "Is Discounting Destined for Difficult Times?" *Business* 39 (January–March 1989): 27, 29–31.

13. *American Druggist* 196 (December 1987): 39–40 (second quotation on 39; first quotation on 40); and *Wall Street Journal*, 14 April 1987, 1, 23.

14. *Wall Street Journal*, 14 April 1987, 1, 23 (first quotation); and *American Druggist* 196 (December 1987): 40 (second quotation).

15. *Discount Merchandiser* 29 (November 1989): 56–57, 58 (third quotation on 56; first quotation on 56–67; second quotation on 57; fourth and fifth quotations on 58).

16. *U.S. News and World Report* 106 (13 March 1989): 53 (first quotation); and *Wall Street Journal*, 14 April 1987, 1 (second, third, fourth, and fifth quotations), 23.

17. *New York Times Magazine*, Part 2: *Business World*, 2 April 1989, 28 (first quotation), 29 (second quotation), 30 (third and fourth quotations), 66–67 (fifth quotation on 66; sixth quotation on 67), 68. The mayor of Independence said that after the publication of the article, he received several telephone calls from other small-town officials asking, "How can *we* keep Wal-Mart out? I asked them why they would *want* to keep them out." *Discount Store News* 28 (18 December 1989): 218.

18. *New York Times*, 14 December 1990, A12 (first quotation; in microfilm editions, this is on A18); *USA Today*, 11 October 1990, A3; and Dallas *Morning News*, 26 January 1992, J4 (second quotation). See also *Time* 139 (20 April 1992): 52.

19. *Time* 139 (20 April 1992): 52; and Jackson (Miss.) *Clarion-Ledger*, 15 October 1990, A7 (quotation).

20. *Newsweek* 114 (13 November 1989): 65 (quotations); and Ozment and Martin, "Changes in the Competitive Environments of Rural Trade Areas," 278.

21. *Time* 139 (20 April 1992): 52.

22. See, for example, *Time* 139 (20 April 1992): 50–52. For a nostalgic account by journalist Hugh Sidey of the decline of small towns and rural culture in the prairie and plains states, see *Time* 134 (9 October 1989): 30–36.

23. *U.S. News and World Report* 112 (20 April 1992): 8; ibid. 106 (13 March 1989): 54; and William P. Hall, "Franchising—New Scope for an Old Technique," *Harvard Business Review* 42 (January–February 1964): 71.

24. Ozment and Martin, "Changes in the Competitive Environments of Rural Trade Areas," 278 (second quotation); and *Hardware Age* 225 (February 1988): 32 (first quotation).

CHAPTER 8

1. Wal-Mart Stores, Inc., *Annual Report, 1991*, 2; *Discount Store News* 28 (18 December 1989): 232; ibid. 29 (20 August 1990): 1, 2; ibid. (15 October 1990): 3; ibid. (1 October 1990): 1; ibid. (17 December 1990): 6; *Drug Store News*, 18 June 1990, 4; and Memphis *Commercial Appeal*, 16 March 1990, B5.

2. Wal-Mart Stores, Inc., *Annual Report, 1991*, 1, 2; *Discount Store News* 30 (4 February 1991): 2; Wal-Mart Stores, Inc., *Facts About Wal-Mart Stores, Inc.*, 1990, 2; and *Housewares*, 21 October 1990, 3.

3. Wal-Mart Stores, Inc., *Annual Report, 1982*, n.p.; *Annual Report, 1991*, 1, 2; Sam Walton with John Huey, *Sam Walton: Made in America, My Story* (New York: Doubleday, 1992), 98; *New York Times*, 10 July 1990, D18; ibid., 1 March 1991, C4; *Fortune* 123 (3 June 1991): 274; and Jackson (Miss.) *Clarion-Ledger*, 22 February 1991, B7.

4. George Stalk, Philip Evans, and Lawrence E. Shulman, "Competing on Capabilities: The New Rules of Corporate Strategy," *Harvard Business Review* 70 (March–April 1992): 58, 59; *Forbes* 145 (8 January 1990): 194; ibid. 149 (6 January 1992): 168, 170; and *Fortune* 123 (6 May 1991): 54, 58.

5. *Time* 137 (25 February 1991): 62; *U.S. News and World Report* 110 (13 May 1991): 55, 56; *Business Week*, 27 August 1990, 34; *Fortune* 123 (6 May 1991): 54, 58; and *Forbes* 147 (27 May 1991): 92–93.

6. Jack G. Kaikati, "Don't Discount Off-Price Retailers," *Harvard Business Review* 63 (May–June 1985): 88; and *Business Week*, 8 October 1990, 62.

7. *Time* 137 (25 February 1991): 63; *Chain Store Age Executive* 64 (November 1988): 69; *Business Week*, 26 November 1990, 137 (first quotation); ibid., 27 August 1990, 34; and Jackson (Miss.) *Clarion-Ledger*, 28 October 1990, G5 (second quotation).

8. *Discount Store News* 29 (16 July 1990): 73; *Fortune* 123 (6 May 1991): 52; Jackson (Miss.) *Clarion-Ledger*, 26 August 1990, G1; and *New York Times*, 9 August 1992, sec. 3, p. 5.

9. *Discount Store News* 28 (18 December 1989): 161–62; *Forbes* 145 (8 January 1990): 194; ibid. 147 (27 May 1991): 92; *Fortune* 123 (6 May 1991): 52, 54, 58; and *New York Times*, 9 August 1992, sec. 3, p. 5. See also Vance H. Trimble, *Sam Walton: The Inside Story of America's Richest Man* (New York: Dutton, 1990), 267–68.

10. *Time* 137 (25 February 1991): 63 (quotation); *U.S. News and World Report* 110 (13 May 1991): 55, 56; *Newsweek* 116 (3 September 1990): 52; and Jackson (Miss.) *Clarion-Ledger*, 28 October 1990, G5.

11. *Chain Store Age Executive* 64 (November 1988): 65; *Forbes* 147 (27 May 1991): 90, 93, 95; *Women's Wear Daily* 164 (9 December 1992): 18; and Jackson (Miss.) *Clarion-Ledger*, 28 October 1990, G5.

12. *Discount Store News* 28 (18 December 1989): 169 (quotations).

13. Wal-Mart Stores, Inc., *Annual Report, 1992*, 2, 3, 5; *New York Times*, 9 August 1992, sec. 3, p. 5; and *Forbes* 148 (5 August 1991): 80, 81.

14. *Fortune* 123 (6 May 1991): 51; and *New York Times*, 9 August 1992, sec. 3, p. 5.

15. *Fortune* 123 (6 May 1991): 50, 59; and *Retail Control* 58 (February 1990): 8–13.

16. *Fortune* 123 (6 May 1991): 51; *New York Times*, 9 August 1992, sec. 3, p. 5; and Wal-Mart Stores, Inc., *Annual Report, 1992*, 8.

17. *New York Times*, 9 August 1992, sec. 3, p. 5; *Business Week*, 7 October 1991, 120; *Fortune* 123 (6 May 1991): 52, 54; *Forbes* 147 (27 May 1991): 96; and *Women's Wear Daily* 164 (9 December 1992): 18.

18. *Wall Street Journal* (SW ed.), 6 April 1992, A1; *Sam's Buy-Line* 6 (Summer 1992): 3; and *Newsweek* 119 (25 May 1992): 67.

BIBLIOGRAPHY

Corporate Documents

Butler Brothers. *Annual Report*, 1936–56.
———. *Success in Retailing: The Variety Business.* New York: Butler Brothers, 1920.
———. *The Butler Way System Book.* New York: Butler Brothers, 1920.
City Products Corporation. *Annual Report*, 1949–59.
———. Ben Franklin Franchise Agreement between City Products Corporation and Walco Stores, Inc., filed with the U.S. Securities and Exchange Commission 17 March 1969.
———. Supplemental Franchise Contract for Chain Stores between City Products Corporation and Wal-Mart Stores, Inc., filed with the U.S. Securities and Exchange Commission 8 April 1970.
Dayton Hudson Corporation. *Annual Report*, 1980–91.
K mart Corporation. *Annual Report*, 1978–91.
Southard, C. D. "What's Happening to Butler Brothers: Year End Conference Talk." Presented at Butler Brothers annual meeting, Chicago, 1954.
Wal-Mart, Inc. Amendment to Certificate of Incorporation, filed with the Delaware Division of Corporations, Dover, 2 January 1970; 3 May 1971.
———. Certificate of Incorporation filed with the Delaware Division of Corporations, Dover, 31 October 1969.
Wal-Mart Stores, Inc. Advantage Card membership application form for Sam's Wholesale Club.
———. *Annual Report*, 1972–92.
———. Annual 10-K Report to the U.S. Securities and Exchange Commission, 1972–92.

————. Certificate of Amendment to Certificate of Incorporation, filed with the Delaware Division of Corporations, Dover, 22 March 1972; 18 August 1975; 14 November 1980; 4 June 1982; 3 June 1983; 19 February 1988.

————. Certificate of Designation, Preferences, Rights, and Limitations . . . of Preferred Stock, . . . filed with the Delaware Division of Corporations, Dover, 11 August 1982.

————. Certificate of Ownership and Merger, filed with the Delaware Division of Corporations, Dover, 20 and 29 March 1972; 25 January 1991.

————. Listing Application to the New York Stock Exchange, 21 June 1972.

————.*Making the Difference: The Story of Wal-Mart*. Bentonville, Ark.: Wal-Mart Stores, 1990.

————. Notice of Annual Meeting of Shareholders, 2 May 1991.

————. Preliminary Prospectus, filed with the U.S. Securities and Exchange Commission 30 March 1970.

————. Prospectus, filed with the U.S. Securities and Exchange Commission 1 October 1970; 26 April 1972.

————. Restated Certificate of Incorporation, filed with the Delaware Division of Corporations, Dover, 25 October 1988.

F. W. Woolworth Company. *Annual Report*, 1975–90.

Periodicals and Newspapers

Advertising Age
American Business
American Demographics
American Druggist
Antitrust Law and Economics Review
Arkansas Times
Atlanta *Constitution*
Aviation Week and Space Technology
Barron's
Bentonville (Ark.) *Benton County Democrat*
Building Supply Home Centers
Business Month
Business Week
Business World
Chain Drug Review
Chain Store Age
Chain Store Age Executive
Columbia (Mo.) *Missourian*

Columbia (Mo.) *Tribune*
Commercial and Financial Chronicle
Computerworld
Consumer Bulletin
Consumer Research Bulletin
Dallas *Morning News*
Discount Merchandiser
Discount Store News
Drug Store News
Dun's
Dun's Business Month
Dun's Review
Dun's Review and Modern Industry
Economist
Editor and Publisher
Electrical Merchandising Week
Engineering News-Record
Financial World
Forbes
Fortune
Hardware Age
Housewares
Jackson (Miss.) *Clarion-Ledger*
Little Rock *Arkansas Gazette*
Maclean's
Magazine of Wall Street
Management Solutions
Marketing and Media Decisions
Memphis *Commercial Appeal*
Mergers and Acquisitions
Mississippi Business Journal
Missouri Alumnus
Modern Packaging
Monroeville (Ala.) *Monroe Journal*
National Petroleum News
Nation's Business
New Orleans *Times Picayune/States Item*
Newport (Ark.) *Weekly Independent*
Newsweek
New York Times
New York Times Magazine
Printers' Ink

Progressive Grocer
Publishers' Weekly
Retail Control
Rogers (Ark.) *Daily News*
Rolling Stone
St. Louis *Post-Dispatch*
Sales and Marketing Management
Sales Management
Sam's Buy-Line
SEC News Digest
Southpoint
Springdale (Ark.) *Morning News*
Springfield!
Stores
Supermarket News
Tide
Time
USA Today
U.S. News and World Report
Wall Street Journal
Wall Street Transcript
Women's Wear Daily

Books and Articles

Aalberts, Robert J., and Ellen Day. "Is Discounting Destined for Difficult Times?" *Business* 39 (January–March 1989): 27–31.

Alexander, Ralph S., and Richard M. Hill. "What to Do About the Discount House." *Harvard Business Review* 33 (January–February 1955): 53–65.

Allender, Mary E. "Why Did Manufacturers Want Fair Trade?" *Essays in Economic and Business History* 11 (1993): 218–30.

Ashkenazi, Elliott. *The Business of Jews in Louisiana, 1840–1875.* Tuscaloosa: University of Alabama Press, 1988.

Ashmore, Harry S. *Arkansas: A History.* New York: W. W. Norton & Company, 1984.

Astor, Saul D. "The Inventory Shortage—Enigma of the Discount Industry." *Journal of Retailing* 40 (Summer 1964): 31–42.

Atherton, Lewis E. *Main Street on the Middle Border.* Bloomington: Indiana University Press, 1954.

———. *The Pioneer Merchant in Mid-America.* Columbia: University of Missouri Press, 1939.

————. *The Southern Country Store, 1800–1860*. Baton Rouge: Louisiana State University Press, 1949.

Backman, Jules. "Economic Characteristics of Retail Trade: Size and Volume." *Journal of Retailing* 32 (Fall 1956): 113–20, 154.

————. "The Local Nature of Chain-Store Operations." *Journal of Retailing* 32 (Winter 1956–57): 175–84.

Barger, Harold. *Distribution's Place in the American Economy since 1869*. Princeton, N.J.: Princeton University Press, 1955.

Barmash, Isadore. *More Than They Bargained For: The Rise and Fall of Korvettes*. New York: Lebhar-Friedman Books, 1981.

Bates, Albert D. "Warehouse Retailing: A Revolutionary Force in Distribution?" *California Management Review* 20 (Winter 1977): 74–80.

Beam, Henry H. "Strategic Discontinuities: When Being Good May Not Be Enough." *Business Horizons* 33 (July–August 1990): 10–14.

Beasley, Norman. *Main Street Merchant: The Story of the J. C. Penney Company*. New York: Whittlesay House, 1948.

Beckman, Theodore N., and Nathanael H. Engle. *Wholesaling: Principles and Practice*. New York: Ronald Press Company, 1949.

Beckman, Theodore N., and Herman C. Nolen. *The Chain Store Problem: A Critical Analysis*. New York: McGraw-Hill Book Company, 1938.

Beil, Preston J., ed. *Variety Store Retailing*. New York: Variety Store Merchandiser Publications, 1956.

Bellenger, Danny N., and Jac L. Goldstucker. *Retailing Basics*. Homewood, Ill.: Richard D. Irwin, 1983.

Benson, Susan P. *Counter Cultures: Saleswomen, Managers, and Customers in American Department Stores, 1890–1940*. Urbana: University of Illinois Press, 1986.

Bernstein, Louis M. "Does Franchising Create a Secure Outlet for the Small Aspiring Entrepreneur?" *Journal of Retailing* 44 (Winter 1968–69): 21–38.

Blackford, Mansel G., and K. Austin Kerr. *Business Enterprise in American History*. Boston: Houghton Mifflin Company, 1990.

Bogart, Leo. "Thinking Ahead: The Future of Retailing." *Harvard Business Review* 51 (November–December 1973): 16–18, 20, 25, 26, 28, 32, 176.

Bolen, William H. *Contemporary Retailing*. Englewood Cliffs, N.J.: Prentice-Hall, 1978.

Breth, Robert D. "The Challenge of Charge Accounts to Discount Merchants." *Journal of Retailing* 40 (Winter 1964–65): 11–16, 58.

Brough, James. *The Woolworths*. New York: McGraw-Hill, 1982.

Brown, Earl, and Robert Day. *Operating Results of Self-Service Discount Department Stores, 1968–1969*. Ithaca, N.Y.: Cornell University, [1969].

Brown, Milton P., William Applebaum, and Walter J. Salmon. *Strategy Problems of Mass Retailers and Wholesalers*. Homewood, Ill: Richard D. Irwin, 1970.

Bryant, Keith L., Jr., and Henry C. Dethloff. *A History of American Business*. Englewood Cliffs, N.J.: Prentice-Hall, 1990.

Cameron, Jan. *The Franchise Handbook: A Complete Guide to Selecting, Buying, and Operating*. New York: Crown Publishers, 1970.

Candilis, Wray O. "The Growth of Franchising." *Business Economics* 13 (March 1978): 15–19.

Chandler, Alfred D., Jr. "Business History: What Is It About?" *Journal of Contemporary Business* 10 (1981): 47–66.

———. *The Visible Hand: The Managerial Revolution in American Business*. Cambridge, Mass.: Harvard University Press, 1977.

Chute, A. Hamilton, comp. *A Selected and Annotated Bibliography of Retailing*. Austin: University of Texas Bureau of Business Research, 1964.

Clark, Thomas D. *Pills, Petticoats, and Plows: The Southern Country Store*. Indianapolis: Bobbs-Merrill Company, 1944.

Converse, Paul D., and Harvey W. Huegy. *The Elements of Marketing*. New York: Prentice-Hall, 1940.

The Cresset, 1935, 1936. Hickman High School, Columbia, Missouri.

Crutchfield, James A. "Income and Retail Expenditures in Small Areas." *Land Economics* 32 (August 1956): 285–88.

Dalrymple, Douglas J., and Donald L. Thompson. *Retailing: An Economic View*. New York: Free Press, 1969.

Dardis, Rachel, and Marie Sandler. "Shopping Behavior of Discount Store Customers in a Small City." *Journal of Retailing* 47 (Summer 1971): 60–72, 91.

Dardis, Rachel, and Louise Skow. "Price Variations for Soft Goods in Discount and Department Stores." *Journal of Marketing* 33 (April 1969): 45–50.

Davidson, William R., and Alton F. Doody. "The Future of Discounting." *Journal of Marketing* 27 (January 1963): 36–39.

Davidson, William R., Alton F. Doody, and James R. Lowry. "Leased Departments as a Major Force in the Growth of Discount Store Retailing." *Journal of Marketing* 34 (January 1970): 39–46.

Davidson, William R., et al. "The Retailing Life Cycle." *Harvard Business Review* 54 (November–December 1976): 89–96.

Dicke, Thomas S. *Franchising in America: The Development of a Business Method, 1840–1980*. Chapel Hill: University of North Carolina Press, 1992.

Diffine, D. P. *Always a Winner*. Searcy, Ark.: Harding University, 1989.

Dobson, John M. *A History of American Enterprise*. Englewood Cliffs, N.J.: Prentice-Hall, 1988.

Dodge, Robert E. "Discount Selling by the 'Legitimate' Retailers." *Journal of Retailing* 33 (Winter 1957–58): 182–83, 207.

———. "How Discount-House Selling Has Influenced Department Stores." *Journal of Retailing* 36 (Summer 1960): 97–101, 126.

Dolan, J. R. *The Yankee Peddlers of Early America*. New York: Clarkson N. Potter, 1964.

Donovan, Frances R. *The Saleslady*. Chicago: University of Chicago Press, 1929.

Drew-Bear, Robert. *Mass Merchandising: Revolution and Evolution*. New York: Fairchild Publications, 1970.

Duncan, Delbert J., and Stanley C. Hollander. *Modern Retailing Management: Basic Concepts and Practices*. Homewood, Ill.: Richard D. Irwin, 1977.

Editors of *Discount Merchandiser*. *Discount Retailing in the United States: A Detailed Marketing Study of a Dynamic New Force, the Discount Store*. New York: Super Market Publishing Company, 1963.

Edwards, Charles M., Jr., et al., comps. *A Bibliography for Students of Retailing*. New York: B. Earl Puckett Fund for Retail Education, 1966.

Ellsworth, T. D., and Katherine Mitchell. "Retail Trade in 1955." *Journal of Retailing* 32 (Summer 1956): 95–100.

Emmet, Boris, and John E. Jeuck. *Catalogues and Counters: A History of Sears, Roebuck and Company*. Chicago: University of Chicago Press, 1950.

Ettenson, Richard, Gary Gaeth, and Janet Wagner. "Evaluating the Effect of Country of Origin and the 'Made in the USA' Campaign: A Conjoint Approach." *Journal of Retailing* 64 (Spring 1988): 85–100.

Fenner, Phyllis. "Grandfather's Country Store." *American Mercury* 61 (December 1945): 672–77.

Ferry, John W. *A History of the Department Store*. New York: Macmillan Company, 1960.

Ghosh, Avijit, and Sara L. McLafferty. *Location Strategies for Retail and Service Firms*. Lexington, Mass.: D. C. Heath and Company, 1987.

Gilchrist, F. W. "The Discount House." *Journal of Marketing* 17 (January 1953): 267–72.

Goeldner, Charles R. "Automation: Evolution in Retailing." *Business Horizons* 5 (Summer 1962): 89–98.

Goldman, Arieh. "The Role of Trading Up in the Development of the Retailing System." *Journal of Marketing* 39 (January 1975): 54–62.

Goodrich, Jonathan N., and Jo Ann Hoffman. "Warehouse Retailing: The Trend of the Future?" *Business Horizons* 22 (April 1979): 45–50.

Gross, Claire M. "Services Offered by Discount Houses in Metropolitan New York." *Journal of Retailing* 32 (Spring 1956): 1–13, 47–48.

Gross, Walter L. "Strategies Used by Major Department Stores to Compete with Low-Margin Retailers." In *Retailing: Concepts, Institutions, and Management*, edited by Rom J. Markin, Jr. New York: Macmillan Company, 1971.

Hackett, Donald W. *Franchising: The State of the Art*. Chicago: American Marketing Association, 1977.

Hall, William P. "Franchising—New Scope for an Old Technique." *Harvard Business Review* 42 (January–February 1964): 60–72.

Harrison, Gilbert H. "Retail Mergers." *Mergers and Acquisitions* 17 (Winter 1983): 40–50.

Harwell, Edward M. *Management Development for Discount Stores*. New York: Lebhar-Friedman Books, 1982.

Hayes, Robert E., Jr. "The Business Economist at Work: K mart Corporation." *Business Economics* 24 (April 1989): 48–50.

Hendrickson, Robert. *The Grand Emporiums: The Illustrated History of America's Great Department Stores*. New York: Stein and Day, 1979.

Hidy, Ralph W. "Business History: A Bibliographical Essay." In *Recent Developments in the Study of Business and Economic History: Essays in Memory of Herman E. Krooss*, edited by Robert E. Gallman. Greenwich, Conn.: JAI Press, 1977.

———. "Business History: Present Status and Future Needs." *Business History Review* 44 (Winter 1970): 483–97.

Hollander, Stanley C. "The Discount House." *Journal of Marketing* 18 (July 1953): 57–59.

———. *Discount Retailing, 1900–1952: An Examination of Some Divergences from the One-Price System in American Retailing*. New York: Garland Publishing, 1986.

———. *Explorations in Retailing*. East Lansing: Bureau of Business and Economic Research of Michigan State University, 1969.

———. "The Wheel of Retailing." In *Retailing: Concepts, Institutions, and Management*, edited by Rom J. Markin, Jr. New York: Macmillan Company, 1971.

Hoover, Gary, Alta Campbell, and Patrick J. Spain, eds. *Hoover's Handbook: Profiles of over 500 Major Corporations, 1991*. Austin, Tex.: Reference Press, 1990.

Howard, Marshall C. *Legal Aspects of Marketing*. New York: McGraw-Hill Book Company, 1964.

Hower, Ralph M. *History of Macy's of New York, 1858–1919*. Cambridge, Mass.: Harvard University Press, 1943.

Hunt, Shelby F. "Franchising: Promises, Problems, Prospects." *Journal of Retailing* 53 (Fall 1977): 71–84.

Johnson, Kenneth M. "Rural Retailing Reborn." *American Demographics* 4 (September 1982): 22–25, 41–42.

Jones, Fred M. *Principles of Retailing*. New York: Pitman Publishing Corporation, 1949.

Jung, Allen F. "Price Variations among Discount Houses and Other Retailers: A Reappraisal." *Journal of Retailing* 37 (Spring 1961): 13–16, 51–52.

Kaikati, Jack G. "The Boom in Warehouse Clubs." *Business Horizons* 30 (March–April 1987): 68–73.

———. "Don't Discount Off-Price Retailers." *Harvard Business Review* 63 (May–June 1985): 85–92.

Katz, Donald R. *The Big Store: Inside the Crisis and Revolution at Sears*. New York: Viking, 1987.

Kaufmann, Patrick J. "Dealer Termination Agreements and Resale Price Maintenance: Implications of the *Business Electronics* Case and the Proposed Amendment to the Sherman Act." *Journal of Retailing* 64 (Summer 1988): 113–24.

Kelley, William T. "The Franchise System in Cooperative Drugstores." *Journal of Retailing* 33 (Winter 1957–58): 184–91.

———. "Small-Town Monopoly: A Case Study." *Journal of Retailing* 31 (Summer 1955): 63–66, 101–2.

Keon, Thomas, Edward Robb, and Lori Franz. *Effect of Wal-Mart Stores on Economic Environment of Rural Communities*. Issued by the Business and Public Administration Research Center and College of Business and Public Administration at the University of Missouri at Columbia, [1989].

Kerin, Roger A., and Nikhil Varaiya. "Mergers and Acquisitions in Retailing: A Review and Critical Analysis." *Journal of Retailing* 61 (Spring 1985): 9–34.

Kibarian, Barkev. "Why Department Stores Can Meet Discount House Competition." *Journal of Retailing* 36 (Winter 1960–61): 201–6, 224.

Konopa, Leonard J. "What Is Meant by Franchise Selling?" *Journal of Marketing* 27 (April 1963): 35–37.

Krugman, Herbert E. "Just Like Running Your Own Little Store. . . ." *Personnel* 34 (July–August 1957): 46–50.

Kursh, Harry. *The Franchise Boom*. Englewood Cliffs, N.J.: Prentice-Hall, 1968.

Larson, Carl M., Robert E. Weigand, and John S. Wright. *Basic Retailing*. Englewood Cliffs, N.J.: Prentice-Hall, 1982.

Latham, Frank B. *1872–1972, A Century of Serving Consumers: The Story of Montgomery Ward*. Chicago: Montgomery Ward & Company, 1972.

Lebhar, Godfrey M. *Chain Stores in America, 1859–1962*. New York: Chain Store Publishing Corporation, 1963.

Lebow, Victor. "The Crisis in Retailing." *Journal of Retailing* 33 (Spring 1957): 17–26, 55.

———. "Long-Term Trends in Retailing." *Journal of Retailing* 34 (Winter 1958–59): 211–215, 242–43.

Lee, Stewart M. "The Impact of Fair-Trade Laws on Retailing: A Comparison of Fair-Trade and Non–Fair-Trade Areas, 1933–1958." *Journal of Retailing* 41 (Spring 1965): 1–6.

Lehman, Frances M. "The Discount House." *Journal of Retailing* 19 (February 1943): 19–26.

Lewis, Edwin H., and Robert S. Hancock. *The Franchise System of Distribution*. Minneapolis: University of Minnesota, 1963.

Livesay, Harold C. "Entrepreneurial Dominance in Businesses Large and Small, Past and Present." *Business History Review* 63 (Spring 1989): 1–21.

Lowry, James R. *The Retailing Revolution Revisited*. Muncie, Ind.: Ball State University, 1969.

———. "Trends and Developments in Discount Merchandising." In *Retailing: Concepts, Institutions, and Management*, edited by Rom J. Markin, Jr. New York: Macmillan Company, 1971.

Lowry, James R., and William R. Davidson. *Leased Departments in Discount Merchandising*. Columbus: Bureau of Business Research of Ohio State University, 1967.

Luxenberg, Stan. *Roadside Empires: How the Chains Franchised America*. New York: Viking Penguin, 1985.

Mack, James S. "The Variety Store Looks Ahead." In *Marketing in Action: Readings*, edited by William J. Shultz and Edward M. Mazze. Belmont, Calif.: Wadsworth Publishing Company, 1963.

McNair, Malcolm P. "Significant Trends and Developments in the Postwar Period." In *Competitive Distribution in a Free High-Level Economy and Its Implications for the University*, edited by Albert B. Smith. Pittsburgh, Pa.: University of Pittsburgh Press, 1958.

McNair, Malcolm P., and Eleanor G. May. *The American Department Store, 1920–1960*. Boston: Graduate School of Business Administration of Harvard University, 1963.

———. *The Evolution of Retail Institutions in the United States*. Cambridge, Mass.: Marketing Science Institute, 1976.

McNeal, James U. "Reactions of a Small Town to a Rumored Discount House." *Journal of Retailing* 41 (Winter 1965–66): 1–9, 62.

Markin, Rom J., Jr., ed. *Retailing: Concepts, Institutions, and Management*. New York: Macmillan Company, 1971.

Mason, J. Barry, and Morris L. Mayer. *Modern Retailing: Theory and Practice*. Dallas: Business Publication, 1978.

Matthews, Norman. "The Department Store versus the Discount Store: A Practitioner's View." In *Competitive Structure in Retail Markets: The Department Store Perspective*, edited by Ronald W. Stampfl and Elizabeth C. Hirschman. Chicago: American Marketing Association, 1980.

Michman, Ronald D. "Changing Patterns in Retailing." *Business Horizons* 22 (October 1979): 33–38.

Miller, Nelson A. *Establishing and Operating a Variety and General Merchandise Store*. Washington: U.S. Government Printing Office, 1946.

Moody's Bank and Finance Manual, 1974, 1983.

Moody's Industrial Manual, 1959, 1965, 1987, 1990.

Moody's Manual of Investments, 1946.

Moody's OTC Industrial Manual, 1971.

Moyer, M. S. "The Roots of Large-Scale Retailing." *Journal of Marketing* 26 (October 1962): 55–59.

Nasrallah, Wahib, comp. *United States Corporation Histories: A Bibliography, 1965–1985*. New York: Garland Publishing, 1987.

Nelson, Walter H. *The Great Discount Delusion*. New York: David McCay Company, 1965.

Oxenfeldt, Alfred R. "The Retailing Revolution: Why and Whither?" *Journal of Retailing* 36 (Fall 1960): 157–62.

Ozment, John, and Michael A. Jones. "Changing Economic Conditions of Small Rural Trade Areas: Some Notes on the Presence of Discount Retail Chains." In *Proceedings of the Thirteenth Annual Conference of the Academy of Marketing Science*, edited by B. J. Dunlap. New Orleans, April 1990.

———. "Growth of Discount Retail Chains in Rural Communities: An Analysis of Issues." In *Retailing: Theory and Practice for the Twenty-First Century*, edited by Robert L. King. Charleston, S.C.: Academy of Marketing Science, 1985.

Ozment, John, and Greg Martin. "Changes in the Competitive Environments of Rural Trade Areas: Effects of Discount Retail Chains." *Journal of Business Research* 21 (November 1990): 277–87.

Peters, Thomas J., and Robert H. Waterman, Jr. *In Search of Excellence: Lessons from America's Best-Run Companies*. New York: Harper & Row, 1982.

Pfouts, Ralph W. "Retail Trade Patterns: The U.S. and the South, 1929–1958." *Southern Economic Journal* 29 (July 1962): 44–46.

Rafferty, Milton D. *The Ozarks: Land and Life.* Norman: University of Oklahoma Press, 1980.

Robichaud, Robert J. "Retail Profit Rise—What Does It Mean?" *Journal of Retailing* 42 (Fall 1966): 52–67.

Rosenberg, Leon J. *Dillard's: The First Fifty Years.* Fayetteville: University of Arkansas Press, 1988.

———. *Sangers': Pioneer Texas Merchants.* Austin: Texas State Historical Association, 1978.

Rosenbloom, Bert. "The Department Store and the Mass Merchandiser: Marketing Challenges and Strategic Responses." In *Competitive Structure in Retail Markets: The Department Store Perspective*, edited by Ronald W. Stampfl and Elizabeth C. Hirschman. Chicago: American Marketing Association, 1980.

———. "Strategic Planning in Retailing: Prospects and Problems." *Journal of Retailing* 56 (Spring 1980): 107–20.

Samson, Peter. "The Department Store, Its Past and Its Future: A Review Article." *Business History Review* 55 (Spring 1981): 26–34.

The Savitar, 1940. University of Missouri at Columbia.

Scull, Penrose, with Prescott C. Fuller. *From Peddlers to Merchant Princes: A History of Selling in America.* Chicago: Follett Publishing Company, 1967.

Smalley, Orange A., and Frederick D. Sturdivant. *The Credit Merchants: A History of Spiegel, Inc.* Carbondale: Southern Illinois University Press, 1973.

Stalk, George, Philip Evans, and Lawrence E. Shulman. "Competing on Capabilities: The New Rules of Corporate Strategy." *Harvard Business Review* 70 (March–April 1992): 57–69.

Stampfl, Ronald W., and Elizabeth C. Hirschman, eds. *Competitive Structure in Retail Markets: The Department Store Perspective.* Chicago: American Marketing Association, 1980.

Stone, Kenneth E. "The Impact of Wal-Mart Stores on Other Businesses in Iowa." Report issued by Iowa State University, 1989.

Tedlow, Richard S. *New and Improved: The Story of Mass Marketing in America.* New York: Basic Books, 1990.

Telser, Lester. "Why Should Manufacturers Want Fair Trade?" *Journal of Law and Economics* 3 (October 1960): 86–105.

Teutsch, Austin. *The Sam Walton Story: An Inside Look at the Man and His Empire.* New York: Berkley Books, 1992.

Thompson, Arthur A., Jr., and A. J. Strickland III. *Strategic Management: Concepts and Cases.* Homewood, Ill.: BPI, Irwin, 1990.

Thompson, Donald N. *Franchise Operations and Antitrust.* Lexington, Mass.: D. C. Heath and Company, 1971.

Trimble, Vance H. *Sam Walton: The Inside Story of America's Richest Man.* New York: Dutton, 1990.

Tucker, David M. *Arkansas: A People and Their Reputation.* Memphis: Memphis State University Press, 1985.

U.S. Bureau of Domestic Commerce. *Franchise Opportunities Handbook.* Washington: U.S. Government Printing Office, 1972.

Vance, Sandra S., and Roy V. Scott. "Butler Brothers and the Rise and Decline of the Ben Franklin Variety Stores: A Study in Franchise Retailing." *Essays in Economic and Business History* 11 (1993): 258–71.

———. "Sam Walton and Wal-Mart Stores, Inc.: A Study in Modern Southern Entrepreneurship." *Journal of Southern History* 58 (May 1992): 231–52.

———. "Wal-Mart Stores in the 1980s: Innovative Formats for Modern Retailing." *Essays in Economic and Business History* 10 (1992): 298–309.

Vaughn, Charles L. *Franchising: Its Nature, Scope, Advantages, and Development.* Lexington, Mass.: D. C. Heath and Company, 1974.

Walker, Q. Forrest. "Some Principles of Department Store Pricing." *Journal of Marketing* 14 (January 1950): 529–37.

Walton, Sam, with John Huey. *Sam Walton, Made in America: My Story.* New York: Doubleday, 1992.

Walton, S. Robson. "Antitrust, RPM, and the Big Brands: Discounting in Small-Town America." Part I. *Antitrust Law and Economics Review* 14 (1982): 81–90.

———. "Antitrust, RPM, and the Big Brands: Discounting in Small-Town America." Part II. *Antitrust Law and Economics Review* 15 (1983): 11–26.

Weil, Gordon L. *Sears, Roebuck, U.S.A.: The Great American Catalog Store and How It Grew.* Briarcliff Manor, N.Y.: Stein and Day, 1977.

Westervelt, Richard E. "The Discount House Problem." *Journal of Retailing* 30 (Summer 1954): 69–70, 89–90.

Wingate, John W. "Retail Merchandising as a Career." *Journal of Retailing* 20 (February 1944): 25–28, 32.

Wingate, John W., and Arnold Corbin. *Changing Patterns in Retailing: Readings on Current Trends.* Homewood, Ill.: Richard D. Irwin, 1956.

Winkler, John K. *Five and Ten: The Fabulous Life of F. W. Woolworth.* New York: Robert M. McBride & Company, 1940.

Woll, Milton. "Sources of Revenue to the Franchisor and Their Strategic Implications." *Journal of Retailing* 44 (Winter 1968–69): 14–20.

Woods, Thomas A. *Knights of the Plow: Oliver H. Kelley and the Origins of the Grange in Republican Ideology.* Ames: Iowa State University Press, 1991.

Worthy, James C. *Shaping an American Institution: Robert E. Wood and Sears, Roebuck.* Urbana: University of Illinois Press, 1984.

Wright, Richardson. *Hawkers and Walkers in Early America: Strolling Peddlers . . . and Others from the Beginning to the Civil War.* New York: Frederick Ungar Publishing Company, 1927.

Writers' Program of the Work Projects Administration in the State of Arkansas. *Arkansas: A Guide to the State.* New York: Hastings House, 1941.

Miscellaneous Items

Butcher, Benjamin C. "The Development of Large-Scale Retail Price-Cutting Institutions in the United States since 1870." Ph.D. diss., University of Illinois, 1965.

Darling, John R. "Retailing in the American Economy, 1948–1962." Ph.D. diss., University of Illinois, 1967.

Ghemawat, Pankaj. "Wal-Mart Stores' Discount Operations." Harvard Business School Case No. 9-387-018. Boston: Harvard Business School Publishing Division, 1986.

Salmon, Walter J. "Wholesale Club Industry." Harvard Business School Case No. 9-586-021. Boston: Harvard Business School Publishing Division, 1990.

Wal-Mart Stores, Inc. Audiovisual program presented at the Wal-Mart Visitors Center, Bentonville, Arkansas.

INDEX

THE AUTHORS

Economic and business historian **Sandra S. Vance** was educated at Belhaven College, Louisiana State University, and Mississippi State University, where she studied under D. Clayton James. Her publications include articles on various aspects of retailing history in business history and other scholarly journals, including the *Journal of Southern History*, and an encyclopedia article in the *American National Biography*. She has in progress an examination of the evolution of discount merchandising in the United States from the post–World War II era to the present day. Dr. Vance teaches at Hinds Community College in Raymond, Mississippi, where she was named "Teacher of the Year" by the school chapter of Phi Theta Kappa in 1984.

Roy V. Scott, a native of Greenfield, Illinois, was educated at Iowa State University and the University of Illinois, where he studied under the late Fred A. Shannon. He has been a William L. Giles Distinguished Professor of History at Mississippi State University since 1974. Among his books are *Railroad Development Programs in the Twentieth Century* (1985) and, with Ralph W. Hidy and others, *The Great Northern Railway: A History* (1988). He has also written or edited five books in agricultural history, the most recent being *Eugene Beverly Ferris and Agricultural Science in the Lower South* (1991), and has in progress studies of farming and farm life in the Middle West since 1900 and of the decay in higher education in recent decades. He has served as president of the Agricultural History Society and of the Mississippi Historical Society and has been the recipient of E. E. Edwards and American Association of State and Local History awards and of grants by the Business History Foundation and the American Philosophical Society.